Robert Stuart MacArthur

Bible Difficulties and Their Alleviative Interpretation

Old Testament

Robert Stuart MacArthur

Bible Difficulties and Their Alleviative Interpretation
Old Testament

ISBN/EAN: 9783337099855

Printed in Europe, USA, Canada, Australia, Japan

Cover: Foto ©Lupo / pixelio.de

More available books at **www.hansebooks.com**

Famous Women of Sacred Story;

the Old and New Testament. **Two Volumes;** Each a Series of Sixteen Popular Lectures, faithful delineations and pen pictures of the most noted characters in History. The good and evil traits in these famous women are made to read a salutatory lesson to their sisters of the present day, emphasizing reverent faith in the Bible, rather than the new versions of "woman's rights." By Rev. M. B. Wharton, D.D. Beautifully illustrated. 318 and 340 pages. Each, **$1.50.**

Historical and Patriotic Addresses,

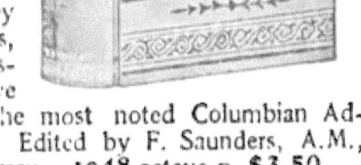

Centennial and Quadrennial, comprising upwards of one hundred select orations and poems, delivered in every State of the Union on the one hundredth anniversary of American Independence, by Hon. Wm. M. Evarts, Rev. Dr. Storrs, H. W. Beecher, Charles F. Adams, Robert C. Winthrop, Horatio Seymour, Geo. Wm. Curtis, Chauncey M. Depew, and others, —issued under the auspices of the respective authors. Including the most noted Columbian Addresses of 1892-93. Edited by F. Saunders, A.M., Librarian of Astor Library. 1048 octavo p, **$3.50.**

E. B TREAT & CO., 211-213 W. 23d St., New York

BIBLE DIFFICULTIES

Old Testament

BIBLE DIFFICULTIES

AND THEIR

Alleviative Interpretation

BY

ROBERT STUART MacARTHUR

Pastor of Calvary Baptist Church, New York

Old Testament

NEW YORK
E. B. TREAT & COMPANY
241-243 WEST 23D STREET
1899

COPYRIGHT, 1898
BY E. B. TREAT & COMPANY
NEW YORK

PREFACE.

During the past few months, the substance of the chapters comprising this volume was delivered in addresses on consecutive Sunday evenings in the regular course of the author's ministry in the Calvary Baptist Church. He has long felt that most of the difficulties generally supposed to be in the Bible are not really in the Bible; but are in the human interpretation of the Bible, rather than in the divine revelation itself. It is vastly important to separate between erroneous biblical exposition and the actual truth of divine revelation.

The newer scholarship, it will readily be admitted, has disturbed the faith of some Bible students; but it is absolutely certain that it has given the Bible a fresh interest and an increased value. It is not necessary to accept all the conclusions of the so-called Higher Critics; indeed, these conclusions are often at variance with one another, and more careful criticism will entirely refute some of the positions taken. But we can readily see that the later criticism has done much to disabuse the minds of some readers of their traditional interpretations and unauthoritative preconceptions of Holy Scripture; and, as a result, the Bible was never so new and so attractive a library as it is at this hour. It never was so carefully studied as now; and it never has been to the church or to the race the blessing which it will be in the near future. The aim of these discourses is to separate between false interpretation and genuine revelation. Miracles which God performs we unquestioningly receive; miracles which men imagine we are free to accept or reject.

This volume contains a selection rather than a collection of difficulties in the Old-Testament Scriptures. Questions asked by members of the author's congregation, and by correspondents in different parts of the country, partly guided him in his selection of the difficulties discussed. Doubtless, many passages of Scripture which are serious difficulties to the minds of some readers have been omitted; but it was not possible to include all within the limits of a volume of convenient size. Still it is believed that the most serious difficulties are here discussed. The author regrets that these discussions do not more fully combine the results of the latest and most reverent scholarship with the spirit of sincere love to the Holy Book and its divine Author. Of his failures in all respects he is distinctly and deeply conscious; nevertheless, he hopes that as these discussions have proved helpful to many hearers, and also to his own spiritual faith and life, they may be blessed in the wider circle to which, through this volume, they are now introduced. This is his sincere desire and earnest prayer as this volume goes forth.

CALVARY STUDY, NEW YORK CITY,
    October, 1898.

CONTENTS:

Chapter		Page
I.	Was there Really Light Before the Sun?	13
II.	Was the World Made in Six Solar Days?	25
III.	Where and What was the Garden of Eden?	39
IV.	What were the Sin and Sentence in Eden?	53
V.	What was Cain's Mark, and Who was his Wife?	69
VI.	Who were the Sons of God and the Daughters of Men?	87
VII.	Does God Repent and the Spirit Withdraw?	107
VIII.	Was the Noachian Flood Universal or Local?	125
IX.	What was the Purpose of the Tower of Babel?	145
X.	Was Lot Wise in Pitching his Tent toward Sodom?	163
XI.	Who was Melchizedek, the Mysterious King-Priest?	179
XII.	Was the Destruction of Sodom Natural or Supernatural?	197
XIII.	Did God Mean that Abraham Should Really Offer Isaac?	217
XIV.	Did Rebekah and Jacob Cheat Isaac and Rob Esau?	235
XV.	Who was the Wrestler with Jacob at Jabbok?	253
XVI.	Did God or Pharaoh Harden Pharaoh's Heart?	269

Chapter		Page
XVII.	Was the Passage of the Red Sea Supernatural?	287
XVIII.	What were the Symbols called the Urim and Thummim?	305
XIX.	Did Balaam's Ass Literally Speak with Man's Voice?	327
XX.	Did the Sun and Moon Stand Still at Joshua's Command?	345
XXI.	Did Jephthah Really Sacrifice his Daughter?	359
XXII.	Did Samuel Appear when Summoned by the Witch of Endor?	373
XXIII.	Did Two She-bears Destroy Forty-two Children?	389
XXIV.	Was the Destruction of the Canaanites Vindicable?	405
XXV.	Are the Imprecatory Psalms Justifiable or even Explicable?	417
XXVI.	Are the Prophet Jonah and the Great Fish Historical?	435

I.

WAS THERE REALLY LIGHT BEFORE THE SUN?

I.

WAS THERE REALLY LIGHT BEFORE THE SUN?

Truly sublime are the opening words of Genesis. No other historical writing approaches its first verse in grandeur and majesty. It implies the existence, the eternity, the freedom, the omnipotence, the intelligence, and the goodness of God. The first sentence denies atheism, for it assumes God. It denies materialism, for it asserts Creation. It denies pantheism, for it declares the personality of God. The word *bara*, translated "created," is one of three words, the others being *yatsar* and *asah*, used in this section, and *bara* always has God for its subject, whatever its object may be. *Yatsar*, formed, and *asah*, made, both refer to construction out of pre-existing materials, and both are predicable of God and man. The verb *bara*, in its simple form, occurs forty-eight times, according to Dr. Murphy, and always in one sense. The word "Elohim," translated God, is found in the Hebrew Scriptures fifty-seven times in the singular, and about three thousand times in the plural, according to the same authority. In the plural it may mean the "Eternal Powers," but it is correctly translated God. Later references will be made to the significance of its plural form, conjoined with verbs and adjectives in the singular, being thus somewhat of an anomaly in language, and giving a suggestion of the doctrine of the unity of the Godhead, which was later fully revealed.

In the preceding verses the inspired writer described the condition of the world while in its chaotic state. Now he enters on the details of that stupendous process by which the whole was reduced to order, and the heavens and the earth were made to appear in their beauty and glory. The great secret of the entire process is the being and the power of God. Remove God from this lofty history, this noble poem, this sublime anthem, this glorious oratorio of primeval wisdom and goodness, and you have nothing left behind but darkness, mystery, and chaos. Insert God in the history, and all becomes perfectly reasonable, and partially explicable. Every thoughtful man must admit that there is far less mystery and difficulty with, than without, God. Eliminate God, and you eliminate reason as well as faith. Atheism has no explanation to give of Creation; it leaves the whole subject involved in impenetrable darkness and hopeless mystery. Admit God, and the hymn of Creation has beauty, majesty, and glory. Thus it comes to pass that "God said" is the keynote to this sublime song. This word of God removes all ideas of blind force and senseless matter. Thus it is that God's presence and power in the first majestic words of Genesis answer a thousand questions of the human mind and heart. Past all the works of Creation we must go to the person of God as the divine Author.

God Not Eliminated.

Behind the visible universe stands God. Men talk of the laws of nature. What do they mean? What is a law? A law is only a name which we give to the manner in which we have observed some force to act. If the force be physical, we have a physical law; if moral, we have a moral law. A law is not a force, but a form; not a motor, but a motion; not a power, but a process. Law implies a lawgiver, evolution an evolver, order an ordainer. There stands God. We have often permitted ourselves to be confused as to the true definition of law. We have allowed ourselves to think of law as if it were endowed with power and possessed of personality. Even if evolution were fully established, it would not eliminate God. Nothing can be evolved that has not first been involved. There stands God. Back of all processes is God as the almighty power. But how are we to understand the words "and God said"? Did God literally utter His voice in that primeval solitude? Did His voice echo through that chaotic abyss? This we cannot suppose. We have here an example of the application to God of terms which usually are applied to human beings. In this way the Bible often speaks of

God's face, ear, hand, and voice. In harmony with this usage the Bible speaks of God as repenting and as performing other acts characteristic of man. This usage is what the theologians call an example of anthropomorphism. If God is to communicate with men He must adopt methods which men can understand, and if men are to speak of God, they must use the only language which it is possible for them to employ. "God's speaking is His willing, and His willing is His doing." This is the first time that the phrase "God said" is used in this narrative, but it is used in all ten times in the account of the creation. It is also a characteristic form of expression in the Old Testament. We have it in such forms as "God spake, saying," "Thus saith the Lord of hosts," and such other expressions as "the word of the Lord came, saying."

On reading the first chapter of Genesis we are reminded of the first chapter of John's Gospel, "In the beginning was the Word." Observe the similarity between these two great opening chapters. What is the irresistible conclusion? The "God-said" of the Old Testament is the God-word of the New Testament. The Jehovah of the Old Testament is the Jesus of the New Testament. In John we further read that Jesus made all things which were made. At this point also the two records harmonize. In Genesis we have the majestic words, "Let there be light, and there was light"; or, more literally, "Light be, and light was." The sublimity of these words in the original cannot be fully reproduced in English. It appears more completely in the Greek of the Seventy and in the Latin Vulgate. Longinus, the famous Platonic philosopher and finished rhetorician, born at Athens or in Syria, about 213 A.D., a student in Alexandria and finally a teacher in Athens, the man whose knowledge was so great and varied and his critical taste so acute that he was called a "living library" and a "walking museum," refers to these words as an illustration of his theme when writing of the Sublime. The Eternal Word speaks, and light is. Finely has Dr. George Dana Boardman said: "Man's words are but sounds, God's words are deeds. He but speaks, and lo! light, sky, ocean, mountain, tree, animal, man, star, universe. He spake, and it was; He commanded, and it stood fast."

Light before the Sun.

But just here a difficulty arises. Whenever the mind of the Infinite comes into contact with the finite, an insoluble problem emerges. The finite can apprehend, but cannot comprehend the Infinite. Now we know God, not as He is, but as we are. Now at best we see through a glass darkly. Could there have been light before the sun's creation? Can there be any alleviative explanation? Assuredly there can. We are told that the sun is the primary source of light, and, in a measure, the statement is true. We are now, let it be borne in mind, in the first day of Creation, but when we reach the fourth day we are told that God made the sun. We immediately ask, "How, then, could there have been light on the first day?" At this point many are embarrassed and some are staggered. I well remember how I once was puzzled because of this apparent contradiction in the inspired narrative. Sceptics quickly seized upon these statements as if they were the result of crass ignorance on the part of the writer of the Creation records. As early as the days of Celsus, who lived in the second century after Christ, and wrote about 150 A.D., this objection to the Mosiac record of the Creation was urged. But in wonderful ways have the authoritative conclusions of science come forward as witnesses to the truth of this sacred story.

Let us look at some of the explanations which have been offered. Some say that the sun was created at the first a perfectly luminous body, but that the vapors arising from the condition of the world at the time shut out his light, and that when God said, "Let there be light," He simply dispersed these mists and vapors and thus caused the light of the sun to be seen. They thus make the light only a manifestation of what was previously in existence, and not the creation of something which until then had no existence. But they have still to account for the creation of the sun, or at least for the narrative touching that point in the history of the fourth day. This they do by supposing that there we have not the account of the sun's creation, but only the record of the command that the sun was appointed to rule by day. Augustine thought that this was simply spiritual light; and Calvin recognized the distinction between this light and that mentioned in connection with the creation of the sun, but he had no very clear explanation to give. But the narrative tells us not simply that light began to be visible, but it asserts that light began to be; and it seems certain that the majestic language here attributed to Elohim is too lofty and sublime to be applied to so comparatively unimportant an event as the scattering of the mists and clouds. Here comparatively late discoveries, or at least applications, of scientific knowledge come forward to solve the problem. We know that light was once supposed to be a distinct element or substance; but now it is believed to be simply a mode or condition of matter. Thus it is now known that the light-giving qualities of many bodies are due to their condition of incandescence. It is certainly known that light is not entirely dependent on the sun. No one who is at all familiar with the subject now doubts that there is a kind and degree of light apart from the sun; and it is certain that this chemical or cosmical light possesses some qualities conducive to the growth of vegetation. It is beyond any question true that "any solid body can be rendered incandescent by being heated up to between 700° and 800° Fahrenheit," and liquids also which are capable of being heated up to the required degree emit light. We know also that fire-flies, certain kinds of wood, and still other substances in their normal condition, throw out light. We know, indeed, that there are many theories as to the phenomenon of light, but much connected with it is still wrapped in mystery. It travels much faster than sound. When a cannon is fired at a distance we first see the flash and then later hear the sound. Light travels 186,000 miles a second, or more than a million times faster than sound. It therefore takes the light of the sun eight minutes to travel from the sun to the earth. Light travels farther as well as faster than sound; in proof of this statement is the familiar fact that we often see lightning so far off that we cannot hear the thunder which accompanies it at the point of its origin. But much as we know of it, it still has its mysteries. The Pythagorean and Newtonian theory was that light was transmitted to the eye by the emission of small particles of luminous matter. This is called the emission corpuscular theory. The earlier theory made light an attenuated, imponderable substance; the undulatory theory makes light to be propagated by the vibrations of matter called ether. These theories were long rivals, but the undulatory theory has completely triumphed over the other.

Professor Dana affirms that the wave lengths in the vibration of molecular force have been ascertained. He also reminds us that the laws of heat and of electrical and chemical action are so involved with those of light that all these conditions are convertible and one in molecular origin.

The nebular hypothesis of La Place, who stood second to none but Newton in the great science of mathematical astronomy, asserts that the condensation of the originally void, dark, gaseous chaos would be accompanied by intense molecular or chemcial activity, and so would assuredly emit light. Infidelity called Moses a blunderer and the Bible a fraud for affirming that there was light before the sun; and now all the scientists declare that this very result must have occurred. Moses was no scientist; he lived in an age when nothing was known of molecular activity. He never heard of Newton or La Place; he could not have understood the nebular hypothesis if he had heard of it. How came he to anticipate the conclusions of modern science? God taught him; he was inspired of the Almighty. Let infidelity be dumb; let it hide its empty head. God taught Moses, and Moses teaches the scientists of the nineteenth century. In medicine, as in astronomy, Moses is abreast of the science of to-day. Regarding all sanitary laws, the medical profession of to-day is only struggling up to the point reached by Moses ages ago. Who taught Moses? The Almighty. How came the cosmogony of Moses to be right, according to the latest dicta of science, while the cosmogonies of all heathen nations excite the laughter of all scientific men to-day? There stands God. It is high time for a shallow atheism to be entirely silent, or to speak with great modesty. Let all believers in divine revelation rejoice in God's Word, the glorious old Bible, which God is magnifying in the halls of scientific learning, in the homes of devout believers, and in the churches of Jesus Christ throughout the world!

II.
WAS THE WORLD MADE IN SIX DAYS?

II.

WAS THE WORLD MADE IN SIX DAYS?

In Genesis, the first chapter and the fifth verse, our attention is called to the first day in the history of Creation. In the same verse we are told that God called the light day, and the darkness night. We need not be surprised that God gave names to the things which He had created. The names given to things by us express the impression which they have made upon our minds; but the names given by God express the nature of the things to which they are given. It seems certain that God, in naming the day and the night, had reference to their phenomena rather than to their duration. The names were not for the benefit of men when first given, as there were no human beings then to make use of the names which God gave; but these names were rather a declaration of the qualities or nature of the things to which they were applied. It is still true that, in a real sense, "words are things." We may be absolutely certain that there was a significance in the words employed by God, which made it fitting that they should be applied to the things which He made. We cannot, for a moment, suppose that the name given to one object could with equal propriety have been given to another. But it must be admitted that there is still much uncertainty as to the etymology of the words which God employed. The Hebrew word translated day is *yom*, and the word translated night is *layela*. These names, let it be borne in mind, were descriptions of nature rather than measures of time.

Some scholars suggest that *yom* expresses "the tumult, stir, and business of the day." Those who give it this meaning probably connect it with the word *yam*, which depicts the boiling or foaming of the sea. They make *layela* refer to "the yelling or howling of wild beasts at night," and so connect it with the Latin *ululare*. But probably Gesenius and others are more nearly correct in deriving the word *yom* from a root meaning "to be warm, to glow with heat." This derivation makes it analogous to the Arabic, *yahina*, to glow with anger. It has been well said that in a sultry climate, like that of the East, this would be a suitable description of the day to distinguish it from the night. Gesenius and other Hebrew scholars associate the word for night with the rare Hebrew root *lul*, meaning to roll up; and the idea suggested is that night rolls up or wraps all things in the curtains of obscurity and darkness. We may be quite sure that there was entire appropriateness in the terms applied by God to the day and the night. God has a reason, doubtless, for every name He gives and for every act He performs; and whether or not we fully understand the etymology of these words, we may be sure that they point out the distinguishing peculiarities of the objects to which they are applied. A similar remark will apply to the names given to the heavens and the earth, to the sea and to the dry land, and to all the other objects named in the account of Creation.

We read in the latter part of this fifth verse, "And the evening and the morning were the first day." The more literal translation is, "And evening was, and morning was, day one." Because the darkness preceded the light, the evening is probably mentioned first; and it is likely that for this reason the Jews began their day of twenty-four hours from the evening. There has always been some difference of opinion as to the exact meaning of the language here used. Some have affirmed that we have here an ordinary solar day of twenty-four hours. This, it is claimed, is the natural meaning of the language here employed; and the words of the fourth commandment are quoted to show that here we have simply an ordinary astronomical day. But some who so affirm reckon the day from daybreak to daybreak, while others reckon it from sunset to sunset.

Meaning of "One."

Let us look carefully into the Scriptural use of the two words "day one." Let us entirely free our minds from any real or supposed necessity, as the result of modern scientific discovery in geology or any other science, to understand the word "day" as meaning a period of indefinite duration. Let us, without prejudice one way or the other, get the heart meaning and the Scriptural usage of these two words translated in our version "first day" and more literally "day one." The two words in Hebrew are *yom*, day, and *ahad*, one. The numeral "*one*" is several times used in Scripture when clearly it means *certain, peculiar, special, unique*. It is in these passages used in the sense of the Latin *quidam*. Thus we have the word in Daniel viii. 3: "Then I lifted up mine eyes, and saw, and, behold, there stood before the river a ram which had two horns, and the two horns were high, but one was higher than the other, and the higher came up last." The word *ahad* is certainly used here to describe a ram of a peculiar character; that is, one having two horns of unequal height, and so a certain, a peculiar, a unique ram. So in Ezekiel vii. 5, it is used of an evil, an only evil; that is, an evil of an unwonted character, an evil of a peculiar nature. In Solomon's Song vi. 9, we have the words: "My dove, my undefiled is but one, she is the only one of her mother." It is quite certain that in this passage also the word "one" expresses the idea of something peculiar, something especially distinguished, something quite out of the ordinary character of things and persons of the same general class. It would be easy to give still other references illustrative of the same meaning of the word. Now, apply this Scripture use of the word *one* to the case in hand, and the meaning, will be, "And evening was, and morning was, a peculiar or unique day." Thus we see that the evening and the morning here mentioned were, according to this explanation, a certain, a peculiar, a unique, and not an ordinary day. This so-called day, as we shall later more fully see, constituted an epoch, an era, a period of time of indefinite duration.

Scientific and Other Considerations.

We shall soon take up the Scripture use of the word day; but there are a few antecedent considerations which ought to receive our passing attention. Geology has long declared that the earth required vast epochs to bring it into its present condition; but it is not proposed to burden this article with geological technicalities, or any other form of wearisome scientific terminology. It may, however, be safely affirmed that science probably shows that the order of creative development was that of the Mosaic record, first plants, then fish and fowl, and finally animals and man. If we were to go carefully into the testimony of rocks and were to consider that testimony as admissible, it would certainly be strongly in favor of an era of indefinite duration rather than a day of twenty-four hours, an era perhaps of thousands, possibly of millions, of years. Indeed, without any special scientific knowledge it can readily be seen that the works of the different days of Creation could not be put into the compass of days of twenty-four hours each, except by continuous miracles of the most stupendous character. That God could do this, no one who rightly believes in His omniscience and omnipotence can for a moment doubt; but that God did this is open to doubt so strong as to be virtually a denial. Such enormous haste as the hypothesis of days of twenty-four hours would necessitate is not in harmony with God's methods, as we see them in Creation or providence. Take, for example, the work of the sixth day. On that day the animals were created; Adam was made; the animals were collected together and named as they passed in review before Adam; on that day he was cast into a deep sleep by God, and a rib was taken from his side, was fashioned into a woman, and she was presented to Adam. If these were days of twenty-four hours each, then all that is recorded in the first five verses of the first chapter of Genesis took place in twenty-four hours. Who can believe it? No one doubts that God *could* have done this, but it is difficult to believe that God *did* all this in that time. If these were days of twenty-four hours each, then the world could not have been more than one hundred and forty-four hours older than man; and if he were created in the early part of the sixth day, the world was not even that much older than man. Is this conceivable? It is so only, as already remarked, by supposing continuous miracles of the most stupendous character; but in the economy of God, so far as we can learn His ways, He has always kept the miraculous displays of His power within economical limits. The length of the seventh day determines the length of the other six; but most commentators consider that God's Sabbatic day extends from Creation to the present hour. Must not then the other six days be days of indefinite duration? If the six days mentioned in Exodus xx. 11 are days of twenty-four hours each, so must the seventh day be one of twenty-four hours; but God is represented as having rested on that day from His creative labors. If that day is still continued, and so is one of indefinite duration, are we not justified in affirming that the other six were also periods of undefined length?

Attention has often been called to the fact that many heathen cosmogonies give indirect confirmation to the view here presented. Egyptian, Persian, Indian, and Etruscan legends are named by different writers on this subject, and while not of authority in themselves, they may be quoted as showing that this idea was widely diffused. Many Christians can remember how a generation ago their simple Christian faith was rudely shocked by scientific affirmations that the world was not made in six days of twenty-four hours each. The writer well remembers that in his boyhood his faith was greatly disturbed, and for a time almost wrecked, by statements of men older and wiser than himself, men who read widely in the scientific literature of the times, and who affirmed that the statements of the Bible were disproved by the absolutely conclusive demonstrations of science. He was not able to refute these statements; he thought the Bible taught that the world was made in six days, of twenty-four hours each. He thought he must hold on to the twenty-four-hour theory or reject the Bible. Thank God! we now see that neither science nor Scripture teaches that the world was made in six days of twenty-four hours each! To believe the Bible is one thing, but to believe all the interpretations which some men choose to give the Bible is quite another thing.

Scripture Use of the Word "Day."

Now, let us look at the Scripture use of the word "day." Perhaps the highest Hebrew authority favors the etymology which refers the word to a root meaning "to be warm, to be hot, to glow with heat," as already suggested. If this origin of the word be correct, it might refer to the glowing or heated periods through which the world passed in its successive developments. But the purpose at this point is simply to refer to the Scriptural use of the word; thus Scripture will interpret Scripture. Nothing is more certain than that the word *yom*, day, is repeatedly used in the Scripture when reference is made to epochs, eons, periods of indefinite length. We have the first instance in this immediate connection in the record of Creation itself; the word is found in Genesis ii. 4. There we read: "These are the generations of the heavens and of the earth, when they were created, in the day (*beyom*) that the Lord God made the earth and the heavens." Here the word "day" is clearly not a solar day; it is most certainly used to cover the entire period of Creation. This is the first time the word occurs after the history of the day of the creative week, and it will be admitted by all that it is here applied to the entire period. It would seem as if there were a providential purpose to show us at this point that the word "day" in the account of Creation meant an epoch, and not a period of twenty-four hours. It is strange that many of the readers of the Bible seem to have overlooked this verse, when they have insisted that the six days of Creation were days of twenty-four hours each. It is astonishing that traditional interpretations often close the eyes of even scholarly commentators to the plain reading of God's Word. The Hebrew Scriptures generally clearly show that the word "day" often denotes a period of past or future time without limit. In Isaiah xxx. 8, we read, "Now go . . . and note it in a book, that it may be for the time to come for ever and ever." The phrase "time to come," as seen in the margin of our Bibles, literally means, "the latter day." Nothing could be clearer than that the word "day" here refers to an indefinite period. In Job xviii. 20 we read, "They that come after him shall be astonied at his *day*." Here the word "day" stands for the whole period of a man's life. In Isaiah ii. 11 we have ". . . the Lord alone shall be exalted in that day," and in the next verse we have a reference to "the day of the Lord of hosts." The word day here clearly means the time when God would punish His people for their sins; it probably refers to the captivity in Babylon. This is a time when Jehovah will inflict vengeance on the people; a time is coming when God's righteous anger would be revealed. In Jeremiah xlvi. 10 we have the words, "the day of the Lord God of hosts, a day of vengeance." In Ezekiel xxx. 3 we read: "For the day is near, even the day of the Lord is near, a cloudy day, it shall be the time of the heathen." In Zephaniah i. 7 we read, "For the day of the Lord is at hand." In Joel ii. 31 we have the words: "The sun shall be turned into darkness, and the moon into blood, before the great and the terrible day of the Lord come." In all these passages a period of trial on the part of the people, and of righteous judgment on the part of God is announced. In Judges xviii. 1 the word days is used for a period of time in history, and in Ecclesiastes xii. 3 we have the expression, "In the day when the keepers of the house shall tremble," where the word day is used for old age. We use the word often with that meaning now. We still speak of "his day," "my day," "your day," referring to periods of time and to sections of one's age.

There is one very striking passage to which attention should be called. In Zechariah xiv. 6, 7 reference is made probably to the time of our Lord's coming, and to the entire Gospel dispensation; the words are: "And it shall come to pass in that day, that the light shall not be clear, nor dark, but it shall be one day which shall be known to the Lord, not day nor night." The day to which reference is here made is certainly a day unique in the world's history. It is one of God's days, not one of man's days. It is such a day as distinguishes it from all of man's civil or solar days. It is a special time, a unique period, known as the day of the Lord. Reference might be made also to Psalm xc. 4; xcv. 8; Isaiah xlix. 8; 2 Corinthians vi. 2; John ix. 4; 1 Thessalonians v. 2; 2 Peter iii. 10; Hebrews xiii. 8; and in 2 Peter iii. 8 we have the words: "But, beloved, be not ignorant of this one thing, that one day is with the Lord as a thousand years, and a thousand years as one day." Unfortunately, many of the Lord's children have seemed to be ignorant of this very one thing.

Prof. Tayler Lewis is authority for the general statement that Scripture clearly shows that there are days or eras which God supernaturally divided by His own power in the creation of the world, and that there are other days concerning which God said, "Let the sun divide them." These latter are the natural, the solar days, measured off by the returning course of nature. Thus we have in the Bible two kinds of days; the one kind is directly God-made, the other is indirectly sun-made. Nothing is more certain than that the Bible does not teach that the days of Creation were days of twenty-four hours. We ought not to let any affirmation to that effect disturb our faith. We ought to be calm, truthful, and joyous in the Lord and in the word of His truth. Some of the scaffolds which men have erected around the temple of revelation are falling. Let them fall! Their disappearance will permit the divine temple to be the more clearly seen in its perfect symmetry, spotless beauty, and divine majesty. Away with false interpretations, away with all forms of superstition, away with all kinds of infidelity! With glorious old Isaiah, writing under the inspiration of the Almighty, we shall say, "The grass withereth, the flower fadeth, but the word of our God shall stand forever."

III.

WHERE AND WHAT WAS THE GARDEN OF EDEN?

III.

WHERE AND WHAT WAS THE GARDEN OF EDEN?

The Scriptural account of the Garden of Eden is found in the second chapter of Genesis, beginning with the eighth verse and going to the end of the seventeenth. The question as to the location and character of the Garden of Eden has always been one of fascinating interest. The writer of the Book of Genesis, in harmony with the well-known character of Hebrew composition, having carried his subject to a convenient resting-place, often reverts to a point already passed over. So, in giving an account of the Garden of Eden, he goes back to a time antecedent to man's appearance on the earth. It is evident, from this account, that the garden was fully prepared some time—how long, of course, we do not know—before the intended occupant was prepared to possess it. A wonderful name is Eden! It is music on the tongue as it is pronounced, and its sound thrills the heart. It awakens the most delicious memories, and it suggests the most glorious prophecies. The word translated garden properly means an enclosure, from a word meaning to fence or to protect. In the Septuagint it is usually rendered Paradise, but this is a word neither of Greek nor Hebrew origin. It is found in Xenophon's "Cyropædia" and other of his writings, about B.C. 400. The Greek translation of the Bible took this word as the translation of the garden which the Creator prepared for innocent man. The word has been generally supposed to be Persian, from which language Xenophon derived it. In that language it represents a park, a pleasure garden, a woodland enclosure, protected by a wall, abundantly watered, and abounding with fruit-trees, flowers, and other objects of beauty. The word finally came to be applied to any delightful region, and was in this sense introduced into the later Hebrew in the form of *pardees*. In our version it is sometimes rendered forest and sometimes orchard and garden. Probably the derivation should be carried farther back than the Persian.

The word is certainly found in the Armenian tongue, one of the oldest languages of one of the oldest people in the world. In this language it is compounded of two words, meaning edible grains or herbs. The Armenians frequently use the word as applied to a garden adjoining a dwelling; but it is almost certain that the origin of the word goes back to the Sanscrit, *paradeesha*, standing for a region of surpassing beauty. The word became finally a metaphor to express the idea of exquisite delight, and so it was used not only for the abode of our first parents in their innocence and bliss, but as a figurative name for Heaven, the home of the blessed. In this sense it is several times used in the New Testament. The word Eden is therefore one of the most venerable and beloved names in geography. The Greek word *hedone* is nearly identical in sense as well as in sound. It ought to be constantly borne in mind that Eden was a tract of country, of which part, and as we may well believe the most beautiful part, was the Paradise, park, or *gan*, garden of all delight. We ought not to suppose that Eden is identical with the Garden of Eden. They are to be constantly distinguished if we are to have an intelligent conception of the Biblical narrative.

The Allegorical Interpretation.

In almost all ages of the church there have been writers who interpreted the Biblical narrative of Eden as a mere allegory. The same remark will apply to their interpretation of the whole story of the Creation and Fall of Man. Many of these allegorical interpretations are beautiful in themselves, and are suggestive of important truths, although they are not adequate interpretations of the Biblical story. In harmony with this method of exposition, Philo made Paradise the governing faculties of the soul. The four rivers described in the Book of Genesis he made four virtues: Prudence, temperance, courage, and justice. Origen, under the general influence of this method, makes Paradise, Heaven; the trees, angels; and the rivers, wisdom. Other mystical interpreters have given different significations to the various features of the Biblical narrative, but have still retained the chief features of this allegorical method. A few more heroic interpreters have cut the Gordian knot by declaring that the entire story is the spurious interpolation of a comparatively late age. Luther believed that the garden remained under the guardianship of angels until the time of the flood, and that so great was the convulsion of nature incident to the flood that all traces of Eden were obliterated. But the narrative in Genesis seems clearly to imply that at the time of the historian the countries and rivers described were still in existence. That impression grows constantly upon the mind of the careful reader of the Biblical story; he strongly feels that the description of the garden is vividly present to the mind of the writer, and that the garden was capable of being visited by him and his readers.

Traditional Edens.

Almost all nations have had the idea of a terrestrial Paradise. The conception of Eden, as in some sense the Garden of God, retains its hold not only on the minds of Hebrew prophets and poets, but in the hearts of poets, historians, and philosophers among all the nations with whose records we have become familiar. Arabian legends tell us of a garden on the summit of a great and glorious mountain inaccessible to men. Hindu traditions have their Garden of Eden on the top of a mountain shaped like the seed-cup of the sacred lotus. In this blessed abode of divinity is the holy grove of Indra; there also is the Jambu tree, whose fruit fed the waters of the Jambu River, waters which impart immortal life, beauty, and glory to all who drink thereof. The Chinese have their enchanted garden in one of the high ranges of the Houanlun Mountains. The Medo-Persians had theirs also. The Greeks had their Hesperides, suggestive of innocence, beauty, and immortality. All these traditions are but echoes of the Hebrew story. They bear eloquent testimony to the reality of the Biblical narrative. It is difficult, if not impossible, to account for the universality of this belief, except on the hypothesis of the historicity of the thing so widely believed.

The Location of Eden.

Where were the tract of Eden and the Garden of Paradise in Eden? Is it possible for us to answer these questions with any degree of certainty? In making this search, a starting-point is found in the second chapter of Genesis. This is an artless, child-like, and altogether charming description. In this respect it is in harmony with all the narratives of the primitive Hebrew Scriptures. Some would interpret the expression, "Eastward in Eden," in the eighth verse of the second chapter of Genesis, to mean eastward of the place of the writer. We may ask, Where was that writer's standing-point? Perhaps in Palestine. In all ages and lands the religion of the rising sun is poetically supposed to be of surpassing beauty. As a matter of fact, the cradle of the race did lie eastward to the land of Israel. But perhaps the phrase, " Eastward in Eden," means in the eastern part of the tract of Eden; this seems to be the most natural interpretation of the phrase. We also have the description of the river which watered the garden, and its division into four distinct streams, to guide us in our discussion. It is well known that few questions are so difficult of a satisfactory solution as the location of Eden. Its discussion has ever temptingly invited, and has often utterly baffled, the investigation of scholars. Europe, Asia, and Africa have been carefully examined to find this garden of beauty.

It has been said that from "China to the Canary Isles, from the Mountains of the Moon to the coasts of the Baltic, no locality which in the slightest degree corresponded to the description of the first home of the human race has been left unexamined." Eden has been sought for all the way from Siberia to the South Sea Islands. Hasse gratified his national pride by placing it on the shore of the Baltic. Rudbeck, who was a Swede, located Eden in Scandinavia. The Greeks placed the Garden of Hesperides in the extreme west, and others would have it, as we have seen, in some of the ranges of the glorious Himalayan

Mountains, near the region which traditionally, and perhaps correctly, is called the cradle of the race and the birthplace of mythical gods and historical men. Some have given up the quest as utterly hopeless. They put the solution of this problem in the same category with that of perpetual motion, the quadrature of the circle, and the interpretation of unfulfilled prophecy. Two points, however, are absolutely clear in this whole discussion. We must find a river which is divided as one current, or, as a river system, into four streams, two of which are the Tigris and the Euphrates. The identification of these two rivers with the Hiddekel and the Phrat, has never been disputed. But what rivers shall stand for the Pison and the Gihon? It may be said that investigators here usually divide themselves into two great classes—those who place the Garden of Eden below the junction of the Tigris and the Euphrates, and those who seek it in the high tablelands of Armenia. All other interpretations may be readily eliminated from our problem. Those theories which make the Ganges, the Indus, or the Nile the rivers described in the narrative may at once be set aside. The men who suggested these theories, as a rule, deny the historical reality of the Biblical description. They reduce the inspired narrative to the level of a myth or saga.

Let us again bear in mind that Eden was not a garden, but the region or territory in which the garden lay, and that there is no good reason to suppose that the deluge greatly changed the face of the country. As already suggested, the writer was evidently describing a territory which in his day was, in his judgment, capable of identification. Let us also remember that the Hebrew word *Nahar* stands not for an individual river, but for the river system of the country to which it is applied; and let us further bear in mind that the general situation is clearly fixed by the rivers Tigris and Euphrates. We are now prepared to affirm with these facts in mind that Eden was in the highlands of Armenia. To the illustration of this statement a few facts clearly contribute; let us look closely at these facts. A careful examination of the highlands of Armenia, west of Mount Ararat, and about five thousand feet above the sea, will show that it corresponds, in a remarkable and fascinating degree, to the description of Eden given in the Book of Genesis. It is well known that, within a circuit of a few miles in diameter in this general region, four great rivers take their rise; and it is equally well known that those four rivers have many branches. These rivers are the Euphrates, which is at least sixteen hundred miles long; the Tigris, which, there is good reason to believe, is the Hiddekel—a word which really signifies "the rapid Tigris"—of Genesis, and which is 1,146 miles long before its junction with the Euphrates at Kurnah, where they form the Shat-el-Arab, which flows on about one hundred and twenty miles to the Persian Gulf. Midway between these two main sources of the Euphrates rises the Araxes, which flows northeast for a thousand miles and then pours its waters into the Caspian Sea. At no great distance from the Euphrates is the Halys, or Phasis, which runs a winding course northwesterly for seven hundred miles to the Black Sea. Two of these rivers are unquestionably among those named in Genesis, and the Phasis, or Halys, is supposed to be the Pison of Genesis, and the Araxes, the Gihon. A little study of comparative philology helps us at all these points, since both Gihon and Araxes mean practically the same thing; both names admirably describe the dart-like swiftness of the river. All travellers who have carefully examined this region testify that it is to this day one of wonderful fertility and of surpassing beauty. It is almost certain that in this region, occupying the highest portion toward the east, was the Eden of the Book of Genesis.

Fruitful Lessons.

The story of man's occupancy of the Garden of Eden, previous to his fall, is full of lessons of the greatest interest and importance. Attention has often been called to the fact that Eden was a place of work. Even in his spotless innocence Adam was commanded to dress the garden and to keep it. Work is God's benediction and not His malediction. Christ taught us that work was

His own normal condition as well as that of His Father. Horticulture was the first of all arts, and the first of all laborers was a sinless man. Indolence and barbarism are ever close neighbors. The man or the nation that refuses to obey God's law of subduing the earth must perish. A lazy man must greatly try the patience of the Infinite God. The Apostle Paul becomes righteously indignant at the Thessalonian idlers, declaring that if they will not work neither shall they eat. The cure of pauperism is found in the opportunity and the disposition for hard and remunerative work. No law of political economy is more universal and irresistible than this law. There is absolutely no hope for the American Indian except he be taught to work. Few men die of overwork. It has been well said that it is friction and not revolution that destroys machinery. Work is the inseparable condition of human happiness and progress.

Eden was the birthplace of language. Dr. Boardman has charmingly illustrated this truth in his "Creative Week." Speech is the most wonderful faculty in man. It allies him to angels and to God. It proves his heirship to immortality and divinity. The origin of language is one of the most subtle and fascinating of problems. Perhaps speech came as a direct gift from Heaven. It is a wonderfully interesting thought that man's first recorded act was the giving of names to God's creatures in Eden. The study of words is really the study that touches life and thought at their deepest points. It practically includes all other kinds of study. "Words are things," as the fiery Mirabeau said when addressing the stormy French Assembly. Our Lord has taught us that we are to be judged by our words. The gift of language is both sublime and awful. The tongue may be almost angelic or it may be altogether Satanic. The tale-bearer or scandal-monger is the child of Hades.

Every man has his Eden. There is a time of childlike innocence in every life. Innocence is not necessarily virtue. Virtue implies the test of temptation and the victory over temptation. In Eden man had his period of probation, involving both permission and probation. Adam must be taught the distinction between right and wrong. He must learn that he was a finite creature, and that God alone was infinite. The prohibition thus given to Adam was necessary to teach him whether or not he was obedient. All human life is a prohibition; there is a forbidden something in every man's life. Every man has his Eden; every man is in some sense his own Adam. As often as any man chooses the evil rather than the good, the lower rather than the higher self, and Satan rather than God, he has repeated Adam's fall. It is useless to chase Adam up and down the ages; it is greatly wise to make sure that we stand when our test comes. Thank God! the second Adam stood, although the first Adam fell. Our true golden age is in the future.

There is a diviner tree of life, more crystalline water, a sublimer and diviner Paradise than that of Eden. The rainbow of promise spans the firmament of Revelation, and the glory of Paradise lost is ineffably transcended by the glory of Paradise regained.

IV.

WHAT WERE THE SIN AND SENTENCE IN EDEN?

IV.

WHAT WERE THE SIN AND SENTENCE IN EDEN?

The account of the temptation, transgression, and sentence in Eden is found in the third chapter of Genesis. We are safe in saying that no words can overestimate the happiness of Adam and Eve during the period of their innocence. Made in the image of God, unassailed by temptation, pure in thought, word, and act, and holding communion with God as a man does with his dearest friend, theirs was celestial joy amid terrestrial environments. But a sad experience awaited them; their joy was to end in sorrow, their innocence in transgression, and their Eden in Aven. Their history is forever after associated with that of a malignant spirit, and they are to become sinful, wretched, degraded, and despicable.

We do not know how long was their period of joy and felicity; many writers have given us various speculations on that point, but the Bible gives us no information. Somehow, in reading the story, one cannot help feeling that the period was short, although on that point no affirmation can be made. We now enter on the story of the introduction of sin and all its woes. This chapter gives us the tragic scene which brought Eden to an end. The story is the saddest which was ever told. The sin of our first parents changed Paradise into pandemonium and Edenic bliss into Hadean woe.

The Temptation.

Our attention is directed in the study of this chapter to the instrument in the temptation of Adam and Eve; this instrument or agent is introduced to us as "the serpent." It should, however, be borne in mind that the English word serpent comes to us from the Latin word *serpo*, to creep, and when we turn to the Hebrew word, *nahash*, we see that it has no suggestion whatever of the motion of the serpent. The Hebrew word translated serpent is one of extreme difficulty. It would have been vastly better had it been simply accurately transliterated, rather than incur the liability of being incorrectly translated. Gesenius, in his Hebrew and English lexicon, informs us that the word is unused in Kal, is onomatopoetic, and that it means to hiss, to whisper, and is used especially of the whisperings of soothsayers. In Piel he makes it mean to practise enchantment, to use sorcery, and also to augur, to forbode, to divine. He gives us a second root, probably signifying, as he says, to shine, and from that he gives us the word meaning brass. The question arises as to whether the latter word which he gives is really a second root.

Prof. Tayler Lewis, in his comments on the passage in Dr. Lange's Commentary, quotes from Gesenius, and then adds: "It (this word) is far more likely, however, to have had for its primary sense that from which comes the secondary meaning of brass, or rather of bronze—*shining* metal. This gives, as the primary, the idea of splendor, *glistening*. The name may have been given to the serpent from its glossy, shining appearance, or more likely from the bright glistening of the eye. This would bring it into analogy with the Greek *drakōn*, from *derko, derkomai*—sharp, piercing sight. There is the same derivation from the eye in the Greek *ophis*, or from the general shining appearance, as a striking and beautiful, though terrible object. . . . The Latin *serpens* is simply a generic name—*reptile*." If the word has really for its primary sense the secondary meaning of brass or of bronze, then it is used in Scripture in a variety of meanings.

In certain of its uses and connections it will mean to examine fully, to discover by trial, or to practise divination. The name, therefore, applies more appropriately to an intelligent being than to a reptile. Following the Septuagint, most modern translators have rendered the original word by serpent; but even a casual study of the Scripture use of the word, especially if Professor Lewis is correct in his suggestion regarding its primary and secondary senses, shows us that it has many significations. It is translated divinations and enchantments; it is also rendered brass, brazen, chains, fetters, and in several places it is translated steel, 2 Samuel xxii. 35, Job xx. 24, Psalm xviii. 34. It is also rendered in Ezekiel, xvi. 36, filthiness. In Job xxvi. 13 we have the Hebrew words *nahash bariach*, rendered "crooked serpent"; but many commentators affirm that the reference is to some form of sea animal, perhaps the sea-horse. The fact is that the word — if its primary sense was, as Professor Lewis suggests, that from which comes the secondary meaning of brass or bronze — is so broad and varied in its meaning that it is not possible always to be sure of its right translation. The Septuagint translation, as already suggested, renders the Hebrew word *nahash* by the Greek word *ophis*, a serpent. But there is no certainty that this translation was chosen because it was its fixed meaning, but rather because it was difficult to determine its fixed meaning, and this word, on the whole, seemed to the translators the most appropriate. Indeed, they do not seem to have carefully studied the original; and we have seen that they have not rendered the word uniformly, but variously. The New-Testament writers almost always quoted from the Septuagint version, and they seldom changed a word in their quotations. They, therefore, carried over this word *ophis* into their writings; and thus we come, as already intimated, to have the English word serpent as the translation of the Hebrew word *nahash*, coming through the Greek word *ophis*.

A diligent study of the narrative in Genesis shows that the *nahash* stood at the head of all inferior animals. He walked erect; he was endued with the power of speech; he could reason, allure, and persuade. Adam had named the animals, perhaps, according to their distinguishing characteristics; but the power of speech on the part of the *nahash* does not seem to have surprised Eve at the time of her temptation nor Adam later. They seem to have been familiar with the possession of this power on the part of the *nahash*. It has sometimes been said that certain species of serpents have rudimentary feet; but no one will affirm that any serpent ever had the gifts of speech possessed by the *nahash*. Serpents have no organs of speech. God could, of course, have given this power to a serpent in Eden; but there is no hint that any special bestowment was made in this case, as in the case of Balaam's ass, whether that narrative be subjective or objective.

The question arises as to what this agent was, and who was the principal behind the agent. Is this narrative history or allegory? It is easier to admit the historicity of the narrative than to explain it on any other hypothesis; but even if we admit that it was allegory, its profound truths and lessons would still remain. The presence of some skilful principal back of the active agent is apparent at every stage. That principal was Satan, as many passages of Scripture clearly teach. But what was this creature, here called the *nahash?* Did a slimy, loathsome snake tempt our first mother? It is almost impossible so to believe; and the Scriptures do not so affirm. No mere reptile—except by the presence of continued miracle—could do the things attributed to this *nahash.* It is far more natural to believe that we have here some apostate spirit, erect in attitude, attractive in form, resplendent in appearance, and eloquent in speech. The sentence later pronounced on this creature clearly shows that with the sentence came humiliation, manifested in a degrading form of motion and method of securing food. If a serpent had tempted Eve; there would be no significance in the sentence inflicted. Our Lord clearly teaches us in John viii. 44 that the devil was a murderer and the father of lies from the beginning; and the Apostle Paul, in writing to the Corinthians, compared the seduction of Eve to that of the Corinthians; but the Corinthians were in no danger of being deceived by a brute animal, hence Eve must have been beguiled by something more than a reptile. We are distinctly told that Satan can be transformed into an angel of light; and there seems to have been no other time when such a transformation was so important to his Satanic purposes as in the Garden of Eden. One can scarcely help feeling that he was so transformed there. He may have assumed the form of some glorious and winged creature, such as in Scripture was known as a seraph; some creature with angelic attractions in dress, appearance, and eloquence. It is certain that the sentence pronounced changed the shape and properties of this creature; it was then that it was commanded to go on its belly and eat dust. Before this curse was pronounced this being may have been one of the most intelligent, gentle, and beautiful of creatures. His mode of attack was wonderfully skilful. He took advantage of Eve when she was alone, and thus without the counsel and succor of her husband. He does not contradict the word of God; he merely asks questions. He insinuates doubt; he implies that it cannot be possible that God would lay upon Eve an arbitrary command. At the outset the woman answers well; but it would have been better if she had not parleyed with the arch-traitor. Satan denies nothing, affirms nothing; but he questions everything. Finally he becomes bold and blasphemous. He suggests that God is jealous of His honors and fears to have His creatures become wise as gods. His language is so artful that while he means one thing, Eve understands him to mean another. We never can explain how the first thought of sin can arise in the minds of innocent beings. This is the first time that a lie was even suggested to Eve. The origin of evil is a metaphysical problem which the Bible does not attempt to explain. It is the bottomless abyss of rationalistic thinking and of theological teaching. It baffles speculative philosophy as truly as Scriptural theology. To explain sin from our point of view is to excuse sin. The Bible clearly shows that God is not the author of sin, and that it was man's volition which brought his pristine innocence to an end. The finest metaphysical analysis of the progress of sin is given us by the Apostle James i. 13-15; here we have the natural history of sin, and no human reasoning has ever approached the skill of this analysis.

The Transgression.

Eve's curiosity was excited. She had listened with interest; she had gazed with longing. Desire brought forth sin, and sin when finished brought forth death. The sophistry of the *nahash* was too much for her unsophisticated nature. He seemed so wise, so noble, so good; and the promised result was so entrancing! The frail mother of the race in that evil hour disobeyed God, partook of the fruit, and gave it to her husband; with fatal facility her husband ate, and, as Milton says, "brought death into the world, and all our woes."

We know not what the fruit was of which they partook. Many Greek traditions make it the fig; some of the rabbis suggest that it was the vine or the olive; but the Latin fathers and Milton suggest that it was the apple. He sings of it as "that crude apple which perverted Eve." We probably have in this later supposition an unconscious testimony to the value of the apple as, all things considered, the best fruit the world has produced. Were Adam and Eve forced to eat? Certainly not. It was their own voluntary act. Satan could tempt them to sin, but he could not sin for them. He can incite men to sin, but he cannot compel men to sin. They lifted the floodgate admitting the stream of evil to flow into the world, and they did it of their own deliberate choice. God is not the author of sin. But why did God permit such a result? Could God have prevented it? Yes, by making man a machine. If man be man, he must be free; if not free, he is not man. Freedom is the inalienable attribute of manhood; but if free, he may use his freedom for evil rather than for good. That is the solemn, awful, and yet glorious responsibility of manhood. God could not—it is said reverently—have prevented man's sin without doing violence to the nature of man as a free agent, of man as man. God gave him every persuasive to obedience, and every dissuasive from disobedience. Milton, to quote him once more, expresses a true thought regarding man in his actual strength and inherent freedom, "Sufficient to have stood, but free to fall." Had God by physical force interposed to prevent this act of disobedience, there would have been no virtue in obedience. Involuntary obedience is no obedience. If there be not freedom, there is neither virtue nor vice. The introduction of sin is the problem of the ages. We can, however, see some signal benefits arising from these sad catastrophes. If the first Adam had not sinned, the second Adam had not redeemed; where sin abounded, grace superabounded. The loss of the terrestrial Paradise made possible a celestial Paradise. The fall gives incomparable glory to the manifestation of God's wisdom, mercy, and love. Redeemed sinners will sing songs in Heaven, to which unfallen angels will ever be strangers. Eternity will be the witness of God's refulgent glory, ineffable love, and immaculate holiness in the salvation of lost man!

The Sentence Inflicted.

The eyes of Adam and Eve were opened. The commission of sin always lets in a terrible light upon the soul. Our judgment of sin changes the moment we have committed sin. Innocence had previously clothed Adam and Eve as with a robe; now leafy vestments perform that office. Conscious guilt made them cowards, and they escaped into the dark recesses of the garden, as if they could hide from the all-seeing God. God in the cool of the day sought them out. He was already the good Shepherd, going after the wandering sheep. In the ethnic religions we see man toilfully seeking after God; in revealed religion we see God lovingly seeking man. Sin existed in the universe before it blighted the blessedness of Eden, and love was eternal in the heart of God before Adam and Eve were placed in Eden.

Adam's lack of chivalry, born of sin, blames the woman, and the woman blames the serpent, and the inference is that the *nahash* would blame God; but Adam's reply was too witless to deserve God's notice. God does not interrogate the *nahash*. Out of pure malignity he was self-moved in harmony with his inherent Satanism; on him, therefore, first falls the terrible words of doom. Doubtless the curse fell both upon the principal and the agent. It is now that the *nahash* becomes degraded to its present loathsome appearance, though formerly it may have been beautiful and may have moved with wings, with head erect and with beauty and dignity in its form. Doubtless, also, the curse was a typical prophecy of the great victory which Christ was to win over Satan and all his works. Enmity was now put between the seed of the *nahash* and of the woman. From this time forth two kinds of people are seen struggling in the world. Evermore there will be a Cain and an Abel, an Ishmael and an Isaac, an Esau and a Jacob; the one will be after the flesh and the other after the spirit. This enmity underlies the mighty conflict of the ages. Under Christ go forth the hosts of truth and righteousness; under Satan the forces of death and hell. The battle will be waged until Christ becomes King of all nations, and is recognized as Lord blessed for evermore.

Motherhood was henceforth to bring sorrow. Motherhood is the glory of womanhood. In motherhood woman loses herself in another life. In giving another life to the world motherhood becomes like Godhood. If motherhood multiplies a woman's sorrows, it multiplies also her power to bestow blessings. Christianity everywhere puts the crown of glory upon the brow of woman and mother. In bestowing a new life the rapture of life is wondrously and almost divinely experienced.

The very ground was cursed for man's sake, and in more sweat and toil than otherwise would have been necessary was man to eat his bread. Eve's name is now changed from *Isha*, manness, to *Chavah*, life or living—as the mother of all living. From the skins of animals, probably slain for sacrifices, they made clothing for themselves. They are now sent from the garden; and God, probably in holy sarcasm, rebukes Adam's attempt to become like God. He listened to the voice of the tempter, and instead of becoming like God, he has become an outcast. Behold the cherubim and the flaming sword at the gate of Eden! All connected with the cherubim is very obscure. This seems to be the first occasion of the introduction of this mystic symbol, which later was to represent some of the profoundest mysteries of redemption. In this symbol was a glorious element of hope. Promises of Paradise restored marked the sorrowful departure of our first parents from Paradise lost. The gleaming sword from the midst of the cherubim pointed to the cross of Calvary.

Ethnic Traditions.

Many nations have legends of the fall. The Chaldean mythologists make a thirst of knowledge the cause of man's fall. In the Persian legends we have a happy pair, *Meschiah* and *Meschiane*, who were holy in deed and word, and who dwelt in a garden. In the Hindu mythology there is a king of dragons named *Naga;* probably this is a form of the Hebrew *nahash*. The first being created by Brahma, Krishna, triumphs over *Kalinaga* by trampling on his head. Doubtless all the nations absorbed something of the truth fully revealed in the Bible. The Bible story teaches the utter malignity of Satan. Every man has his own Eden. Every man is in some sense his own Adam. Every man must watch and pray that he be not led into temptation. God's mercy runs as a golden thread through the whole story of revelation. Preparation of the incarnation of Christ is seen at Eden's gate. It is the splendor of prophecy, the charm of history, and the glory of psalmody; and it reaches through the Bible and through the history of the race from Eden lost to Eden found.

V.

WHAT WAS CAIN'S MARK, AND WHO WAS HIS WIFE?

V.

WHAT WAS CAIN'S MARK, AND WHO WAS HIS WIFE?

THE fullest account of Cain's life is found in the fourth chapter of Genesis. There was doubtless much significance in the name by which Eve called her first-born son. What is the meaning of his name? To this question many answers have been given. Some writers connect it with the Arabic *kayn*, meaning a smith, or *kayin*, a lance, because of the arts which the Cainites introduced. Others derive it from a word meaning envy; others from a word signifying to beat, with a possible allusion to the murder of Abel. Still others from a word meaning to lament. But the best authorities derive it from the word *kanah*, to create, to acquire, to obtain, making the name mean "possession," or "acquisition." This seems to be the meaning of Eve's words when she said: "I have gotten a man from the Lord." He was, according to the record, the first-born of the human race, and also the first murderer and fratricide. What did Eve mean by her statement regarding his birth? Did she imagine that the son now born was no other than the divine personage promised in the gracious assurance recorded in the fifteenth verse of the preceding chapter? Did she really say, "I have gotten a man (even) Jehovah"? No one will doubt that her words can fairly be so interpreted. She may have really believed that the seed promised which should bruise the serpent's head had now come. Others make her words to mean, "I have gotten a man with the help of Jehovah." Those who so interpret her words are not governed so much by the language of the text as by the opinion that she could not so soon have developed the Messianic idea, that this belief would credit her with too mature a christological conception. But we know that Enoch, in the seventh generation, recognized Jehovah as the coming one; and Eve might have done so thus early. It is certain that the mind of Eve was much occupied with the idea of the coming deliverer. It was natural for a young mother, especially in the wonderful circumstances of this birth, to cherish high hopes of her first-born son. In any case, her words indicate a beautiful faith. In the birth of Cain, her faith laid hold of the word "Jehovah," as seen in the fact that she used the divine name Jehovah, and not the vaguer Elohim, the name she used when holding the colloquy with the wicked *nahash*. Some have supposed that previous to this she had borne daughters, and that the birth of a son was thus emphasized; but the natural impression in reading the narrative is that Cain was the first-born of the human race. What delight must have been experienced when this child was born!

Every mother can recall the marvels of this wondrous experience. But imagine the feelings of the first mother—at least so far as this record informs us—at the birth of the first-born man child. No imagination, however vivid, can fully conceive the reality of this impressive case. Well might Eve think that this child was no other than the promised deliverer. This child was at least, we are safe in saying, the pledge of the deliverer at some time, even if he were not himself that deliverer. In this particular case the young mother was greatly mistaken in her estimate of Cain's worth. It would seem as if the tempter in the garden had more to do with him than Jehovah.

Offerings by Cain and Abel.

To Adam and Eve another son was born. Him they called, perhaps by divine direction in allusion to his untimely end, Abel, meaning vanity, a term which the psalmist applies to the race as a whole. Eve seems more sober now in naming this child than when she named Cain. Life's experiences are more numerous and serious. The historian seven times, with a pathetic iteration, mentions the fact that Abel was Cain's brother. If the name were divinely given, then it was an unconscious and melancholy prophecy of Abel's early death. Abel was a keeper of sheep; Cain was a tiller of the ground. The parents brought up their sons to habits of industry. The duty of **religious** worship had also been taught the two sons. There was already a special time and place for worship. Already the Sabbath seems to have been observed, as indicated by the phrase, "in process of time," or more literally, "at the end of days." To the place where the visible glory of God was displayed, or the Shekinah, the sons brought their offerings. Cain brought of the fruit of the ground, and Abel of the firstlings of his flock. Thus in the dawn of human life we see the offering of sacrifices to God. God must have given some instruction regarding these offerings. Here at the very threshold of history we come on the mystery of the institution of sacrifices. This fact suggests profound questions in life and its relations to God. For Abel and his offering God had respect; but not unto Cain and his offering. There was a difference between the offerings, and also between the offerers. Cain's offering was an acknowledgment of God as a benefactor, he bringing a *minchah*, or thank-offering. But in his offering there was no confession of sin, no plea for pardon, no suggestion of atonement. His offering was such as any self-righteous man could make. Abel seems to have brought a thank-offering and also a victim to be slain for his sins. Here is a suggestion of the sacrifice of Christ, who was a lamb slain from the foundation of the world.

There was also a difference in the spirit of the offerers. In Hebrews xi. 4 we read that "by faith Abel offered unto God a more excellent sacrifice than Cain." This is suggestive language. It teaches that Abel's offering had much more in it than Cain's; it was fuller—*pleiona*—than Cain's. Wickliffe's translation is, a "much more sacrifice." It possessed a principle which Cain's lacked; for Abel already by faith grasped the hope of the coming Messiah. The brothers were here and thus divided. They were types of the two great classes found in all ages; one serves God only from the head, giving Him distant homage as Creator; but the other draws near to God, acknowledging the offerer's personal sinfulness and God's divine and immaculate holiness. Already we have a suggestion of the truth that without the shedding of blood there is no remission of sin.

Cain's Awful Crime.

God's rejection of Cain's offering made him very wroth. He showed fierce anger against his brother. His state of mind was thoroughly Satanic; but God was patient with him, notwithstanding his contumacy. God expostulated with him as to how he also might receive a blessing. For him also there might be a lifting up of the countenance of God. But if repentance was not exercised, sin, like a wild beast in ambush, would crouch at the door ready to spring upon the sinner. Sin did so crouch and so spring, and it finally made Cain its prey. It has been said that the first murder was caused by a religious dispute; and it is certain that many times since disputes about religion are responsible for acts of irreligion. Cain concealed his true sentiments toward Abel and conversed freely with him until he could carry out his murderous design. So acted Joab toward Abner and Amasa; so acted Absalom toward Amnon. Cain was naturally a morose and vengeful man; and so he rose up and slew his brother. We are fully informed as to why he committed this Satanic deed (1 John iii. 12), "because his own works were evil, and his brother's righteous." No crime in the world's history impresses the mind with horror more than the crime of Cain; and treachery adds blackness to the fratricide. Perhaps he did not fully know how small a matter might cause death, as, according to the record, this was the first instance of human mortality. But it is certain that the spirit of murder was in his heart. Solemn to us are the words of our Lord at this point, teaching us that the spirit of hate, ardently cherished, makes any man a murderer in God's sight. Thus by the act of Cain death came into the world, and the first man who became its victim died a martyr for truth and God. How the hearts of Adam and Eve must have bled! Their first-born son is a murderer, and their next born is the victim! We may be sure that over the living sinner they grieved more than over the dead saint. Abel was the first from earth to enter Heaven, and he entered it as the first of the noble army of martyrs. It was marvellous mercy on the part of God that He should enter into a colloquy with Cain, who now added lying to murder. It would be difficult to use words which were more insolent, contemptuous, and mendacious than those of Cain who said to God, when He asked concerning Abel, "I know not; am I my brother's keeper?" His heart was already hardened toward his brother, as it was impious toward God. Terrible is God's curse upon Cain! Abel's voice was silent, but his blood was shed, and that blood with trumpet tongue shall cry from the ground until its voice shall reach the throne of the Almighty, calling down vengeance on the guilty. To Cain the very ground is cursed, so that it could not yield adequate results for the most careful tillage. A fugitive and a vagabond shall he be. Well might he exclaim, "My punishment is greater than I can bear." If we can take as accurate the other rendering, "My iniquity is greater than forgiveness," we may cherish the hope of his repentance. He is driven from the place where the visible symbols of God's presence were manifested, and no more shall he see the divine glory shining forth between the cherubim. From the society of his parents he is driven forth as a vagabond on the earth, which is cursed to a double barrenness wherever he shall set his foot. Remorse shall gnaw his soul. Every stranger he fancies will seek to slay him. Thus the guilty wretch almost excites the pity of angels, and he has altogether won the fellowship of devils.

His Mark.

We do not know where the "land of Nod" was. The name means simply flight, or exile, or vagrancy. Some have fancifully supposed that they found a connection between the original word and India; others have seen a relation between the words Cain and China; but all that we know of its position is that it was "east of Eden." It is utterly vain to attempt the identification of Nod with any definite locality. There he built a city, or fort, or kremlin, and named it after his son Enoch, as his own name would dishonor the place, he built the fort, or keep, for self-protection under the instinct of fear. Perhaps in his effort to build a city he disobeyed God; and possibly, also, in that effort we see how vigorously he strove to overcome the disadvantages under which he suffered as a tiller of the ground, which now, as a part of his curse, had become virtually barren under his hand. As a vagrant, perhaps hating and hated, he lived, with awful memories of sin, and thus with terrible experiences of remorse.

This leads us to ask, What was the mark which, in our common version, it is said that the Lord put upon Cain? This question has given rise to many foolish conjectures. Four out of every five persons whom we meet believe that some brand, mark, or stigma was placed on the brow of Cain. Nothing is further from the truth. The Scripture, properly translated, makes no suggestion of such a brand, and yet this thought has gone into literature, into speeches in our courts, and into much of our common phraseology. It is a thousand pities that the Bible is so often mistranslated, misinterpreted, and misapplied. He is doing a genuine service for God's Word and for the young people of our churches who clearly and wisely separates between God's revelation and man's misinterpretation. From the Septuagint version in which we have the words, "groaning and trembling shalt thou be," some have supposed that he became a pitiable paralytic. One old writer, author of "Bereshith Rabba," says the mark was a circle of the sun rising on him; another that it was Abel's dog which constantly followed him. Some interpreters of the Talmud say that it was the letter *tau* on his forehead, as the first letter of the Hebrew word *teshubeh*, meaning repentance; and one learned rabbi, to surpass all other ridiculous interpretations, affirmed that Cain's mark was a long horn growing out of his forehead. This is all pure tradition, superstition, and nonsense. The wretched fratricide was filled with alarm lest all he met should slay him, and God, as an act of special grace, declared that sevenfold vengeance should be taken on the slayer of Cain. To comfort the wretched outcast, as the Revised Version has it, "the Lord appointed a sign for Cain." This is an excellent translation of the original phrase. He did not put a mark upon Cain; that would have been the most likely way to have brought upon him the dangers which he feared. The Lord simply gave him a sign, or token, as a memorial that he should not be slain. The word translated "mark" is *oth*. In like manner God gave a sign, or token, to Noah, Genesis ix. 13; to Moses, Exodus iii. 12; offered one to Ahaz, Isaiah vii. 11, and to Hezekiah, Isaiah xxxviii. 7, 8. Probably this sign was visible to Cain only, and was not in any way perceptible to others. Just what the sign was we may never be able to determine, but nothing is more certain than that it was not a brand upon himself. One is almost impatient that such misconceptions of Scripture should be found in the thought and literature of our time, as well as through the past centuries. A mistranslation often perpetuates itself in the daily speech even of those who know the true meaning of the passages which they continue to misrepresent.

Cain's Wife.

Who was Cain's wife? This question is one of the standing conundrums on the part of certain irreverent or religiously indifferent men and women. It has also perplexed some of the most thoughtful and devout believers in divine revelation. It is astonishing that so many men are ready to neglect known duty in their desire to find objections to the inspired narrative. When urged to follow Christ they immediately ask unanswerable questions regarding the Bible. It is well to remind such cavillers that it will be quite time enough for them to demand solutions of perplexing problems when they have obeyed God in all known duties. So long as they are disobedient to what they thoroughly know, they have no right to expect light on problems which they may never be able exhaustively to understand. Some one has quaintly said that these critics are determined to choke themselves with bones, while they reject the supply of boneless fish which is sufficient for all their wants.

Every earnest student of the Bible, however, may properly study and, if possible, discover all the truth which it contains. Doubtless, as John Robinson in circumstances of the greatest interest said in substance, God has more light yet to break forth from His word. We do well to study it carefully, and to master all the discoverable truth which it contains. Was Cain's wife his sister? So it has been frequently and emphatically affirmed.

If there were not various centres of Creation, and so a possible pre-Adamite race, there must have been a marriage between some brother and sister in the Adamite family. It is barely possible, however, that this incestuous marriage, as we now judge, was not between Cain and his sister. Adam must already have had daughters of whose birth we have no information. There was now a very considerable population. We know that at the birth of Seth, Adam was one hundred and thirty years old, and in all probability there were many sons and daughters besides those specifically named. There certainly was a population whom Cain feared, lest he might be put to death. We can hardly suppose that he was afraid of his father and mother. It is not at all improbable that there was a very considerable population before Cain's marriage, and his wife may have been from one of these families. It is not impossible, however, that she was literally his sister. We may well believe that if she stood in this relationship she was married to Cain before the death of Abel, for we can hardly believe that after that event she would have been willing to become Cain's wife. The marriage of brothers and sisters may have been considered at that time a necessary condition to the propagation of the race. We may well believe also that in that early day the contrasts between members of the primitive family, as between Cain and Abel, were strongly marked Thus the conditions of marriage would be more normal than between members of the same family in our day. We know also that the laws prohibiting the union of brothers and sisters, which afterward were enacted, were then unknown. It is a remarkable fact also that in very much later times and among what were then the most civilized nations, such alliances were not forbidden, and were not considered incestuous. We know that not only did the Athenian law not forbid such marriages, but it made it compulsory for a brother to marry a sister, if after reaching a certain age she had not found a husband. We know also that Abraham married Sarah, who was his half-sister, and Moses was himself the offspring of a marriage which the laws he promulgated would have prohibited as unholy. The question as to Cain's wife is not really one of much importance. The frequency and persistency with which it is asked is no evidence of its real importance, but rather of the inquisitive, if not perverse, spirit of the questioners. It is fitting, however, that all the light which the Scripture enables us to possess should be thrown upon the subject. When objectors to divine revelation ask this question, supposing that it is in some sense an excuse for their neglect of duty, they deserve very little consideration at our hands. When they will in the spirit of reverence obey all the commands which they fully know, it will be quite time enough for us to give them solutions of the perplexing problems of Scripture. Were God to give them full light on unknown duties, so long as they refuse to walk in the light they now have, God would then be putting a premium on their disobedience and perversity. Those who do God's will fully know that will. This is a law illustrated in the study of every science and art, as truly as in the experience and practice of true religion. Only as we walk in the light which we have, in the study of any physical phenomenon, can we expect to have additional light falling upon unseen paths. We must walk up to the limit of the known, before we can step over into the realm of the unknown, in all the broad spheres of scientific thought, as truly as in the great realms of divine revelation. There is so much worthful knowledge which we can acquire that it is useless to spend time in the effort to acquire knowledge which never can be certain, and which if certain is practically worthless. It is well sometimes frankly to say, "we do not know." Often the profoundest ignorance is the serenest knowledge. Time and energy are too valuable to be wasted in useless pursuits; and further inquiry concerning Cain's wife belongs to this class of useless efforts.

His Fate.

His character seems to have been morose and malicious to a remarkable degree. His descendants are enumerated to the sixth generation. They became numerous and powerful. Lamech instituted polygamy. Jabal adopted a nomadic life. Jubal invented musical instruments, and Tubal-Cain was the first of the great family of smiths. The civilization of this line was marked by violence and godlessness and by song and love. The names of the women bespeak their beauty and attractiveness. Theirs was an unsanctified civilization, while that of Seth was marked by great simplicity and godly sincerity. Cain may have obtained divine forgiveness. His penitence may have been long and sincere. If the translation of Genesis iv. 13 may be, "mine iniquity is greater than that it may be forgiven," there is some hope of his sincere repentance and final salvation. We know that our Lord in dying prayed for His murderers, and we know that Stephen followed the example of his Lord in this regard, and possibly so did Abel. We know that we are all in danger of being murderers in heart, for hatred of our brother, according to Christ's higher law, is murder.

Thank God! that for us and for Cain there is power enough in the cleansing blood of Christ to give us the whiteness of snow! The words of God, in Isaiah i. 18, fall like a benediction upon our hearts, conscious of their many and heinous sins: "Come now, and let us reason together, saith the Lord; though your sins be as scarlet, they shall be white as snow; though they be red like crimson, they shall be as wool."

VI.

WHO WERE THE SONS OF GOD AND THE DAUGHTERS OF MEN?

VI.

WHO WERE THE SONS OF GOD AND THE DAUGHTERS OF MEN?

In Genesis, the sixth chapter and the first and second verses, our attention is called to these two classes, and to their relations with each other. It is quite certain that the patriarchal age was not one of general innocence. So soon as daughters were born, the beauty of womanhood tempted depraved men, and the holiness of married love soon gave place to unhallowed desire. Thus the primeval sanctities of domestic life early degenerated into sinful unions between those who were called "sons of God," and those who are described as daughters of men.

Distinct Classes.

Soon after the sin of Cain mankind was divided into two distinct classes; the one class was represented by Cain, who went out from the presence of God, and the other class was represented by Seth, who still abode where God's glory was specially manifested. The Sethites were of the seed of the woman; the Cainites were of the seed of the serpent. We see that in his exile Cain built a city, a fort, or a keep, the fear of harm and the instinct of self-defence being strong in his mind.

When the Cainites were released from the fear which marred all the happiness of their progenitor, they became numerous and prosperous. Therefore we now first learn of the building of tents, and thus we see that the people must have had some skill in carpentry; they also showed that they had acquired some knowledge of spinning, weaving, and working in iron and brass for agricultural implements and martial weapons. They also manifested considerable skill in what may be called the fine arts. Lamech's fragment of song exhibits the poetical knowledge which the people thus early possessed; for that song, according to authoritative critics, possesses the characteristics of perfect Hebrew poetry.

The birth of Seth Eve distinctly recognized as a compensation for the death of Abel. In a special sense she received him as a gift from God; and she expected that his descendants would be worthy to be called the "sons of God." We shall later see that her hope was realized, for the descendants of Seth were ruled by the spirit of God, and so were truly the sons of God. With the birth of Enos we are told that men began to call upon the name of the Lord. The interpretation of this statement is not free from difficulties. Some suppose that this language means that men and women began profanely to use the name of God. It is barely possible that the words are capable of such a meaning; but it is more natural to see in them a solemn invocation of God in audible and social prayer. This method of approaching God took place, as we have seen, at the birth of Enos, two hundred and thirty-five years after the creation of Adam. Some have supposed that the words mean that God's name was now called upon or applied to certain men. That sense of the expression is not really opposed to the idea that men now began to call upon the name of the Lord. It seems wellnigh certain that we are here taught that a new method of approaching God was introduced. It is an interesting fact that up to this time we never read that man spoke to God, although we often read that God spoke to man. It is difficult correctly to appreciate the primeval simplicity of the thoughts then entertained regarding God. Perhaps a sense of guilt, after the disobedience of Eden, prevented Adam and Eve from addressing God; and perhaps a profound reverence might produce the same result. The lines of human life are now diverging; faith is growing on the one side, and iniquity is increasing on the other. The race is passing beyond its infancy. We are not to suppose that all of the line of Seth were righteous, and all of the line of Cain iniquitous; but believing penitents were chiefly in the line of Seth, and proud defiers chiefly in the line of Cain. The progress of evil showed itself in fratricide, in polygamy, and in many forms of violence.

Statistical and Genealogical.

Dr. Murphy calls the first four chapters of Genesis the primeval Bible of mankind. With the beginning of the fifth chapter we enter upon a document containing a genealogy which is far-reaching in its relations. The fifth chapter contains the history of the line from Adam to Noah, the genealogy ending with the flood.

Dr. Joseph Parker entitles his paragraph on the fifth chapter, "Nobodyism." There are, however, names in this chapter which shine like diamonds amid common stones and semi-precious jewels. Noah was the second head of the line of faith and hope, of which Adam was the first head. Enoch "walked with God." This is a remarkably suggestive statement in the midst of the comparatively dry list of names in this chapter. Enoch's life was far in advance of the highest attainments of his ancestor Seth. Singularly enough we have in this connection the word God for the first time with the definite article—God with whom Enoch walked; but this sacred name often appears afterward with the definite article. He is thus clearly distinguished from all the false gods of all times and peoples. In Abel's offering we had a suggestion of an atonement; in Seth's time we had the devout heart voicing itself in prayer; and now, in Enoch's life, we have a man walking with God; and for three hundred years at least he so walked, and during this period he was not withdrawn from the world, but begat sons and daughters, and discharged the varied duties of his station in life. He was accounted a prophet, and the epistle of Jude shows that he foretold the coming of the Lord. It is said afterward of Noah, as now of Enoch, that he "walked with God," and of no other in the history is this affirmation made. Enoch was translated, as we learn in the epistle to the Hebrews, and did not see death. In his walking with God we have Eden partially restored. We are told that Methuselah lived to be nine hundred and sixty-nine years old. We have no warrant for supposing that at that time a year stood for a month now, or that there was any real difference in the style of recounting time. Perhaps the tree of life gave the proper support to the human constitution, and, perhaps also, bodily vigor was greater in that primeval period than now. There is no good reason for doubting that, by a proper observance of all human laws, human life might be much more prolonged than it is in our time; but such a prolongation would not be an unmixed blessing. It is difficult to conceive of a life spent in the primeval simplicity of the days of Methuselah. We live more in a decade now, with our steamships, railways, telegraphs, telephones, and all the other multiplied activities of the closing days of the nineteenth century, than Methuselah could have lived in a millennium. We can truly say with Bailey in his "Festus":

"We live in deeds, not years; in thoughts, not breaths;
  In feelings, not in figures on a dial.
  We should count time by heart-throbs. He most lives
  Who thinks most, feels the noblest, acts the best."

THE DOWNWARD TREND.

A long period has elapsed since the creation of Adam before we reach Noah, perhaps not less than fifteen hundred years. We are now told, at the opening of the sixth chapter of Genesis, that the race had made great progress in moral evil. We shall soon see that God is preparing to inflict summary vengeance on the guilty, if they will not listen to the voice of His servant Noah, and repent of their evil ways. The divergence between the two lines of human character to which reference has been made has now become very marked, but as the race began rapidly to multiply the representatives of the two classes came into close relation. Corrupt men partook in a remarkable degree of the worst qualities of the fallen Adam. The purpose of the sacred writer is to trace to its fountain-head the stream of corruption which resulted finally in bringing the deluge upon the world of the ungodly. Promiscuous marriages he emphasizes as the chief cause of general degeneracy, and of hastening the judgment of God. One of the old divines has well said that "but for the deluge of sin there had not been a deluge of water." To inequality in the yoke of marriage, the union of believers with infidels, of the pious with the profane, was due this superfluity of wickedness. Inequality in marital relations led to inequality in all the relations of life. Unequal marriages resulted in the birth of impious sons and daughters, rather than of sons and daughters of God.

The Sons of God.

Who are meant by the "sons of Elohim," mentioned in this Scripture? To this question many and contradictory answers have been given; these questions must be fairly considered in their order. Several difficult questions arise at this point. Who were the "daughters of men"? Who were the "*Nephilim*"? What is the meaning of "the Spirit's striving with men"? What of the limitation to one hundred and twenty years? Several of these questions will later receive consideration; but the one immediately before us is concerning the "sons of God."

Some writers have said that they were sons of princes or other men of high rank. We know that in Psalm lxxxii. 6 we have this language when it might have that interpretation. But does the sacred writer here mean simply to say that men of high rank degraded themselves by marrying women of inferior position? This opinion was early held and learnedly advocated by Hebrew and other scholars, and in later times it was carefully elaborated by Schiller. But it is now held by very few commentators of wide reputation, careful scholarship, and sound judgment. It may at once be eliminated from our discussion. A second interpretation is, that the "sons of Elohim" were servants and worshippers of false gods. Those who hold this view make the word Elohim mean not the true God, but idols; they also make the servants or worshippers of these false gods to be the descendants of some pre-Adamite race. This view, therefore, is obliged to assume different centres of creation and various orders of created beings. If it could be proved that there was a pre-Adamite race, new meaning would be given to Romans v. 14: "Nevertheless death reigned from Adam to Moses, even over them that had not sinned after the similitude of Adam's transgression." That view makes the "daughters of men" to be the daughters of the Adamites, as contradistinguished from the sons of the pre-Adamites. It holds that the women thus descended from Adam were true in their spiritual faith and worship, but were now perverted by their marriage with idolatrous men. This opinion has been supported with striking ingenuity. It quite reverses the ordinary explanation of both the classes mentioned in the narrative. The earlier chapters of Genesis, however, confine our attention simply to the Adamites.

A third interpretation is that which understands by the phrase "sons of Elohim," angels. This explanation requires careful consideration; and it is not so easily disposed of as the others, to which attention has been directed. It was held by some Hebrew scholars of the early days and of well-known repute; it was also emphatically taught by many of the Christian fathers, and in our day by the learned Delitzsch, by Kurtz, and by so popular a writer as Canon Farrar. We know also that Byron, in his "Mystery of Cain," has taken advantage of this interpretation for some of his finest dramatic effects; and that Moore in his "Loves of the Angels" has with glowing imagery, poetical fervor, and rhetorical beauty embodied this theory, which may be so presented as to be attractive, but at other times is simply monstrous. It is only fair to those holding this view that the grounds upon which they maintain it should be stated. They affirm that generally in the Old Testament the phrase, "the sons of God," is a name for the angels; and it is frankly admitted by those who oppose the theory that at times the phrase is so used in the Old-Testament Scriptures. But with equal earnestness it is denied that it always has this meaning. It will scarcely be claimed that this is the necessary meaning even in Psalm xxix. 1, or Psalm lxxxix. 6; but that this is its meaning in Job xxxviii. 7, and in Daniel iii. 25, is generally admitted. In these two places the phrase with its context certainly refers to angels. The strongest argument in favor of this interpretation is found in the epistle of Jude, and in 2 Peter ii. 4. Perhaps both these writers refer to the same apostasy. Jude quotes from the book of Enoch, which apparently indorses this view. It seems clear that angels possessed the power of assuming the human form. Without doubt this interpretation gave rise to many of the heathen mythologies regarding the relation of the gods above to men and women on the earth; and the heroes of classical story are generally supposed to have found their origin in fantastic legends of this character; so also probably had the vague myths of the Incubi and Succubi of the Middle Ages. But there is so mythical a character to these stories of the loves of the fallen angels with the daughters of men that it becomes difficult to receive such an interpretation of a passage of Scripture. To this view reference will again be made a little later.

A fourth interpretation is that which understands by the phrase "sons of God" the descendants of Seth, and by the "daughters of men" ungodly women. Who, then, are the "sons of God"? A host of commentators, some ancient, nearly all of the leading reformers, and many scholars of the present day on both sides of the sea, adopt this view. They make the descendants of Seth to marry the descendants of Cain, and to this mingling of the races they refer the corruptions which preceded the flood. These are called the sons of God because they have the spirit or disposition of God. Those mentioned in Job xxxviii. 7, as joining in the symphony of the universe, seem to be an order of creatures existing before the creation of man. As holy beings they might well be called the "sons of God." Those referred to in the Scripture we are especially considering approached God with appropriate offerings. They rightly called upon His name; and, like Enoch, they in some measure daily walked with God. By ancestry they were nominally the "sons of God," and in actual life they were personally the "sons of God." We know that the word son is often used in Scripture to describe a variety of relations. When Seth was born he was recognized as given in the place of Abel, and so, in a special sense, was the son of God. We have already seen that when Enos was born men began to call upon the name of the Lord. They were thus set apart as standing in a special relation to God. They were believers; they walked not after the flesh, but after the Spirit. They were born of the Spirit, were led by the Spirit, and so were the "sons of God." They thus had the lofty qualities of likeness to God. Here was already the essential idea of the church of God. These men were the salt of the earth; and, when they contracted promiscuous marriages with the heathenized races about them, they brought the corruption of the world into the church of God. We cannot, therefore, think that they were angels in the usual sense of that term. We are distinctly informed that the angels neither marry nor give in marriage (Matthew xxii. 30). The teaching of

Scripture seems to be that angels have no distinction of sex, and have not the sexual affections characteristic of men; and, moreover, we cannot conceive of different species, even of earthly creatures, being attracted to one another in these relationships. Much less can we suppose that superhuman spirits would have affectional desires after human creatures. The whole narrative implies that we are in the region of humanity, and not of angelic beings. If these were good angels we can hardly suppose that they would commit the sin here charged, and we cannot suppose that if they were bad angels they would be called the "sons of God." We are not to give this interpretation to the statement in Jude, except it be impossible otherwise to interpret the passage; and it is clear that there is no absolute necessity for so forced an explanation. When we take the phrase "sons of God" to mean the pious Sethites, we have an interpretation which is natural, consistent, and scriptural; and it enables us to avoid the mythical and often suggestively monstrous exposition which makes the "sons as of God" to be angels.

The Daughters of Men.

By the "daughters of men" we need not understand the daughters of the Cainitic race exclusively; it includes the daughters of men generally. They were "the daughters of Adam"; they were the daughters of the profane and impious race of the "old Adam"; they had in them the nature of the fallen Adam. In several passages of the New Testament the word "men" is used as equivalent to fallen, degenerate, and sinful men. These "sons of God" departed from the precepts of their early and godly training; they thus relaxed the strictness of their religious and social relations. They yielded to the fascinations of mere physical beauty, and their sin was that of promiscuous marriage, irrespective of moral and spiritual character.

Their Sinful Choice.

They were governed simply by what was pleasing to the eye, as was Eve when she partook of the forbidden fruit. Thus it came to pass that "they took them wives, of all which they chose." Here we see laxity of choice without discernment of character. It has been well said that they chose wives, "not from the godliness of their lives, but for the goodliness of their looks." Social man now repeated the act of individual man in the first sin; thus socially they apostatized from God as Adam did individually. The sensual triumphed over the spiritual; the nobler elements of the marital relations were debased to the level of mere physical attractions. Thus God's professed people destroyed the last hope of the church of that day by their profligacy. It was folly to suppose that ungodly mothers would be likely to train up godly children. The sin of promiscuous marriages opened the way to the evils which finally overwhelmed the race. Degeneracy of the whole race must now go on apace.

Unequal Yokings.

We have already seen that in the seventh generation Lamech became a polygamist. We have also seen that the Cainitic women possessed the charms of beauty, grace, and other forms of physical attractiveness. Their very names indicate their personal charms; they were Adah (beauty), Zillah (shade), and Naamah (lovely). These names suggest the dominant characteristics of the Cainitic race. Fascinated by the charms of beauty, the "sons of God" cast aside all religious principles. They were ensnared by outward charms rather than by inward character. They did not deliberate upon the consequences of their sensual choices. Young men and women commit similar sins to-day. They are attracted by the charms of beauty, by the graces of mere intellectual culture, and by the fascinations of wealth and station. Many a woman virtually sells body and soul for a title, and some for a home; and many a man sells all that he has for filthy lucre. Such marriages are not marriages in the eyes of God, and perhaps ought not to be so considered in the eyes of men. Many young men and women enter the marriage relation with as little thought as if they were birds of the air. There are marriages which ought for physical reasons to be forbidden by the laws of the State. We pay vastly more attention to laws of pedigree, heredity, and affinity among animals than we do among men and women. One's heart is saddened as he thinks of the reckless manner in which many enter the bonds of holy matrimony. It is sufficiently difficult for a man to climb the rugged heights of fame when his wife keeps equal step by his side; but it is almost impossible for him to climb when he must drag her up by main force. Many men and women become engaged in early youth, the man to pursue courses of liberal education, and the woman to starve in the daily routine of domestic duties. Soon an impassable intellectual chasm will separate them. They grow apart, and broken lives and bleeding hearts are the inevitable result. Tennyson in "Locksley Hall" tells the sad story:

"He will hold thee, when his passion shall have spent its novel force,
Something better than his dog, a little dearer than his horse."

Often the case is reversed, and the other words of Tennyson have their sorrowful application:

"As the husband is, the wife is; thou art mated with a clown,
And the grossness of his nature will have weight to drag thee down."

God help the girls who marry young men to reform them. They are undertaking a tremendous responsibility. God help the girls the breath of whose lovers is tainted with intoxicating drink. There is little before such but fearful anxiety, hopeless sorrow, and indescribable grief. Too often in the marriage relation the bad corrupts the good, and the good does not convert the bad. Wrecked lives, broken homes, and bleeding hearts are the almost inevitable results of such marriages. O Christian men and women, be not unequally yoked with unbelievers. Marry in the Lord. What fellowship can light have with darkness, the church with the world, Christ with Belial?

Glorious is the river Rhone as it leaps from the Rhone glacier, more than five thousand feet above the sea. Turbid are its waters as it enters Lake Geneva; but stand on this bridge and watch it as it issues from the lake, with the clearness of heaven's blue, and with the swiftness of an arrow. Nearly two miles below Geneva, the Arve, milky with powdered granite, pours its waters against the cerulean Rhone. The Rhone resists the proposed union. Side by side they run for many miles, the milky Arve and the azure Rhone. Slowly but surely the muddy waters of the Arve are gaining the ascendancy. Standing upon the bridge at Lyons the mighty river rolls beneath us, a muddy, milky stream, and so pours its waters into the Gulf of Lyons, after its course of six hundred miles has been run. God help us that the heavenly purity of our Christian lives may never become the muddy waters of earth, when the streams of other lives are mingled with ours in our marriage relations. God help our young men and women to live for truth, for honor, for love, for God, for Heaven!

VII.

DOES GOD REPENT AND THE SPIRIT WITHDRAW?

VII.

Does God Repent and the Spirit Withdraw?

This is a startling heading for a chapter or an article, but it is fully justified by the narrative in the sixth chapter of Genesis, beginning with the third verse and ending with the eighth verse. The human race is approaching a fearful crisis. The cup of divine judgment is almost full. The whole race is on probation. Part of it has received God's gracious approbation, but the greater part must suffer His righteous reprobation. We are brought face to face with the terrible fact that man is unworthy to be longer the tenant of the glorious temple erected by God for his occupancy. It is difficult to exaggerate the language of the Scripture, which describes man's sinfulness before God. Man has become flesh rather than spirit; and the temporal and sensual have triumphed over the spiritual and eternal. Man has become renowned for violence rather than honorable for reverence. A deluge of evil will be followed by a deluge of water. The whole race, with the exception of one family, must suffer the infliction of God's righteous judgment.

The Spirit Ceasing to Strive.

The language of the third verse of this chapter is somewhat obscure, but is tremendously solemn. We suppose the spirit here named is the *Ruach Elohim*. Here, as already taught us in the inspired narrative, the plurality of the Godhead is implied. When we read the words, "Jehovah said," we understand that God spoke to Himself or to others in the sacred Trinity. The language is equivalent to saying that God purposed or resolved upon the course of action later described. There is some difference of opinion as to the exact meaning of the word translated "strive." It may mean to keep down, to rule, or to judge; it has in it usually the thought of reproving in some judicial sense. It might, indeed, mean that God's spirit might not longer be humbled by dwelling in man, because he has become flesh. By flesh we are to understand sinful beings, and not simply corporeal creatures. The word *bashar* is here used in its ethical significance, as is the word *sarks*, flesh, in the New Testament. Possibly the idea of the carnal man, as distinguished from the spiritual, so often expressed by the Apostle Paul, has its origin in this verse.

It is a solemn but blessed fact that the Spirit of God does strive with men. Our Lord taught us that one of the offices of the Holy Spirit, when He should come in His fulness, would be to "reprove the world of sin, and of righteousness, and of judgment." We see the Spirit, thus early in the history of the race, engaged in this blessed work. In the negative statement contained in this verse we have shining forth the bright light of God's mercy to sinful man. His Spirit comes to illumine their darkness, to arouse their conscience, and, if possible, to win their affection to truth and to God. We cannot too strongly emphasize this blessed truth. Graciously does the Spirit call to mind former judgments; lovingly does He present persuasive arguments, and repeatedly does He emphasize encouraging promises. During the period of one hundred and twenty years the Spirit did thus intercede for God with the antediluvian world. But the striving of the Spirit implies resistance on the part of men, and that resistance may so increase that the Spirit may finally entirely withdraw. The Spirit's withdrawal forbodes temporal and eternal destruction. There certainly is a point beyond which He will not go in His entreaties with men. In harmony with our freedom and God's divine purpose the Spirit will not exercise force on the wills of men. God will not interfere with the law of freedom which He has established in His control with free moral agents. Involuntary obedience is not obedience. Compulsory love, faith, and hope are a contradiction in terms. The Spirit of God ceases to strive with men when they drive him from their hearts. The whole world is vocal with God's calls of mercy; the very air we breathe is laden with God's gracious ministries. The Spirit pleads, wrestles, and even agonizes with men. Nothing in human thought is more wonderful than God's patience with the disobedient and rebellious. The history of the world is a history of rebellion against God. Think of the sins of that antediluvian world, so aggravated and so heinous! God was patient with men, even though they were ripe for destruction. He could do nothing more then, he can do nothing more now to induce men to repent, without interfering with their moral freedom. The Spirit of God knocks at all the doors of the heart, but the time will come when He will depart and leave men to the terrible fate which they have brought upon themselves. God condemns no soul to eternal death; men bring condemnation upon themselves. They are lost because they wish to be lost; a little reflection will show that this statement is true in its deepest meaning. Every man will go where, in his deepest heart, he wishes to go. God's providence simply registers the judgment which men pass upon themselves. The time will come, if men continue to resist the Spirit, when God must say of each soul, "Cut it down, why cumbereth it the ground?" We all may well pray with the Psalmist, "Take not thy Holy Spirit from me."

We now see that God declares that man's days are to be one hundred and twenty years. It seems clear that the reference here is not to the life of men, but to that of the race, before the coming of God's primitive judgment. The writer goes back to a point of time already passed over, the time before the birth of Shem, Ham, and Japheth; one hundred years intervened between their birth and the flood. It thus seems certain that the reference is to the period of grace allowed the nation, because, while we are not told of men living, after the end of this period, nine hundred years and upward, we know that Noah, Abram, and others, from Shem to Terah, greatly exceeded the limit of one hundred and twenty years. Man is thus seen to be flesh, to be dominantly carnal; the breath which the Almighty breathed into his nostrils is triumphed over by the corporeal nature. His day of grace is therefore limited. By his act in building the ark as well as by his word in preaching the truth, Noah is to exhort, warn, and rebuke. We are told that Noah was a just man, that he was perfect in his generation, and that he walked with God; these are certainly marked qualities of excellence. The evening of opportunity has come to the doomed race. Their cup is rapidly filling, and its terrible contents will soon be poured out.

Who Were the Giants?

We are told in the fourth verse that there " were giants in the earth in those days." These were men of vigorous bodies and of violent wills.

The word translated giants is rather descriptive of cruelty than of great strength. These giants were not the issue of the promiscuous marriages, to which reference is here made, for they existed before that time. They ought not then to be confounded with the children of these mixed marriages, as the latter form a separate class. It is perhaps unfortunate that the original word is translated by our word giants. The Septuagint is responsible for this translation, as it gives us the word *gigantes*, which literally signifies earth-born, but we have translated it giants, and thus conveyed the idea that these were persons of enormous size. The Hebrew word is *nephilim;* this word is derived from *naphal*, meaning to fall. It may refer to apostates, fallen from God and the true faith, and then to violent men, such as tyrants, usurpers, and oppressors, who fell upon their fellow-men. Later in this verse we have the *gibborim;* they were "mighty men, impetuous, heroic men." The whole subject of the *Anakim*, *Nephilim*, *Gibborim*, *Rephaim*, *Emin*, and *Zuzim*, variously translated by our word giants and by similar terms, is obscure to a remarkable degree. Calvin calls these men "the first nobility of the world; honorable robbers, who boasted of their wickedness." Some have doubted whether they were men of large physical stature; but perhaps it is not at all surprising that there were physical giants in that early day. The primitive records of most nations contain stories of gigantic men and women. This is true of Great Britain and most European countries. The possibility of gigantic human creatures is in harmony with the great structures, such as the pyramids and the great gates of ancient cities; and geological investigations reveal to us gigantic ferns, trees, and mosses, and in the animal kingdom we have evidences of the megatherium and other enormous creatures, which may have inhabited the world in the earlier day.

God Vindicated.

Beginning with the fifth verse and going to the end of the eighth verse, we have a striking vindication of God in His terrible acts of judgment. We see here that God did not act in haste, and as the result of a sudden impulse. We are told that He carefully observed the wickedness of His creatures. The description of the sinfulness of man is minute and accurate. The sin of the race was not local and limited, and was not characterized by ordinary corruption. The one hundred and twenty years of grace have passed, and the iniquity of man was widespread and deep-seated. Nothing could surpass the carefulness of the description here given of man's sin. It had reached a fearful climax. It was characterized by brutal outrage and abominable lust. We are told at the outset that men had become flesh; that they no longer discerned their high destiny, but were brutalized and sensualized. We are next impressed with the fact that the wickedness of men was not simply an accident but a state. They were corrupt within and without. Their wickedness,—*ra'ath*, from the root *raa*, to make a loud noise, to rage, hence to be wicked—"was multiplied," and it was continually increasing. Marvellously strong is the statement in the latter part of the fifth verse, regarding the sinfulness of "every imagination (*yetser*, a device) of the thoughts of his heart." We are here taught that the very materials out of which ideas were formed were evil. The embryo of every thought was sinful; the deepest fountain of life was poisoned. The picture is still more fully darkened by the thought that this unmixed evil was without interval of good. It was evil continually, literally, *every day*. This is the most terrific picture of fallen souls to be found in any literature. The more carefully one studies the words of the original, the more awful does the picture become. Instead of having the excellences of a Seth, an Enoch, or a Noah, we have men and women possessed of the darkest features of a diabolical character, which the strongest Hebrew words can describe.

God Repenting.

We are not surprised that we should read in the sixth verse that "it repented Jehovah that he had made man on the earth, and it grieved him at his heart." These are startling words. How are we to understand this language? Can God repent? Do not the Scriptures say that He cannot? In

Numbers xxiii. 19 we read: "God is not a man, that he should lie; neither the son of man, that he should repent. Hath he said and shall he not do it, or hath he spoken and shall he not make it good?" And in 1 Samuel xv. 29 we read: "And also the strength of Israel will not lie nor repent; for he is not a man that he should repent." These are strong words. Can a God of infinite perfection be grieved at His heart? Does not the suggestion even of this possibility detract from the glory of God's perfection? If rightly understood we shall find that this language gives us new, tender, and beautiful conceptions of the mighty and loving God our Saviour. We have here an illustration of what has been called the frankness, even the imprudence, of Scripture. Scripture must be compared with Scripture, in order that we may get its teaching in entirety. The word *yinnahem*, repented, is from *naham*, to pant, to groan, and finally to grieve. It reminds us of the German *reuen* and the English *rue*. Let us remember that when repentance is ascribed to God we must not suppose that it implies a change of purpose in the Almighty. When we attribute this act to God it is expressive of our conception of God rather than of God's essential character. The language is rather the manner of men; it is simply and frankly anthropopathic speech. Thus understood it is perfectly intelligible. We cannot speak of God or to God, or He to us, unless language is adopted which we can understand. As far back, however, as the days of the Seventy an attempt was made to soften this language; but such an attempt is utterly unnecessary to a true understanding of the Scripture. In harmony with the anthropopathic principle, it speaks of God's hands, eyes, ears, and feet. The meaning simply is, that God has power to perform the acts which we perform in the use of these parts of our bodies. Thus the Scripture represents Him as exercising the passions of anger, love, and grief which we discover in ourselves unavoidably. We must reason about God in the use of comparison and analogy. Repentance in God is a change in His attitude toward men, rather than a change in His mind and will. An old divine thus speaks: "Repentance with man is the change of will; repentance with God is the willing of a change." The language used here of God gives us a wonderful picture of the tenderness of His fatherly heart. His heart is grieved even when he permits the blow of justice to fall. It has been well said that "though the divine purpose is immutable, the divine nature is not impassable." God's heart is pitiful as the heart of the tenderest earthly father, and gentle as that of the most loving mother. We are sure that not until men rejected, grieved, and despised His Holy Spirit was the punishment of their sin inflicted. We must not deny to God the attributes of freedom, personality, holiness, and justice. We may be sure that this statement regarding

God, in some way not fully known to us, implies processes analogous to those of the human heart and will. In God are found attributes which to us may seem to be inharmonious and contradictory, but which in Him are in eternal and glorious unison.

Righteous Noah.

The eighth verse teaches us that "Noah found grace in the eyes of Jehovah." The various descriptions of Noah in this connection are peculiarly attractive. They set him before us as a man of a beautifully balanced character. His name means "rest," or "consolation," and probably in giving it his father believed that he was the promised deliverer. The old man's sad heart turns with hope to the birth of his son; but Lamech was deceived in his hope regarding Noah, as Eve was mistaken in the birth of Cain. Nevertheless we feel the charm of Noah's beautiful name. He was the tenth from Adam in the line of Seth. He is the first man whom the Scriptures call "just." We are glad to read that he found grace in the sight of Jehovah. For the first time "grace," which in evangelical theology has so tender and beautiful a meaning, finds expression in a word. God's love, revealing itself in human character in Abel, in Enoch, and in Noah, here reaches a higher elevation.

We now have revealed to us the blessed fountain whence comes true nobility of character and likeness to God. Noah was a preacher of righteousness. This truth must ever be emphasized, and the passage in 1 Peter iii. 18-20 should be studied in the light of this antediluvian history, personal and general. We there learn that the Spirit of Christ, through the instrumentality of the pious patriarch, preached to the disobedient spirits of the old world. This passage occupies a prominent place in modern theological discussions. It has been cited in support of a second probation, and in proof of a purgatory. We ought to bear in mind that the spirits, to whom reference is thus made, are the souls of those men in prison who once heard the Gospel, and enjoyed the opportunity but rejected the duty of repentance. By the Spirit of Christ we may understand either the Holy Spirit or the divine nature of Christ. These men were the sinners destroyed by the flood; their spirits, shades, or *manes*, were popularly supposed to be imprisoned in the caves of the earth. To these spirits Christ, through Noah, preached during their lifetime. The fables of the Greeks that the earthquakes were caused by the efforts of imprisoned giants to shake off the mountains heaped upon them, have their origin in the tradition respecting the fate of these antediluvian rebels, who were shut up in subterranean regions because of their rebellion against God. These antediluvian sinners were those "which some time (once or formerly) were disobedient"; "the long-suffering of God waited in the days of Noah, while the ark was a preparing." If Christ had gone after His death and had preached to these spirits, we should have read, "waited until after Christ's death."

Scholars have given us examples from Demosthenes and other Greek writers, as well as from the Scriptures, to show that the phrase, "he went and preached," is simply a pleonasm for "he preached." We have a suggestive example of this construction in Ephesians ii. 15-17, "having abolished . . . came and preached peace to you which were afar off, and to them that were nigh." It is certain that after His resurrection Christ did not personally go to the Gentiles to preach to them; He went by His apostles. We are familiar with the Latin phrase, *Qui facit per alium, facit per se.* Paul in writing to the Ephesians represents Christ as doing that which He did do through His apostles. In like manner Peter represents Christ as doing that which He did through Noah. Peter spoke of the antediluvians who at the time he wrote were spirits in prison; that is certainly the fair meaning of his words. This is the only passage in the New Testament on which the Roman doctrine of purgatory is supposed to rest; it is the passage also on which some base their belief in a second probation. It is also one authority for the clause in the so-called Apostles' Creed relating to the descent into hell; but we know that this creed was repeated for hundreds of years before this clause was introduced. No one knows by whom or when it was inserted. In its present form, this creed cannot be traced to a period earlier than about the middle of the eighth century. This scripture is certainly a foundation of sand for both these groundless theories. The argument from this passage, promising a second probation to those who die in ignorance of Christ, is wholly irrelevant. These spirits in prison did not die in ignorance of God's word and will; for they had frequent and solemn warnings. Divine patience waited until divine mercy was exhausted. Even if it be granted that Christ did in person preach in hades, there is no evidence that any spirits there confined repented or were liberated therefrom. This passage suggests hopelessness rather than hopefulness, even granting, what is not taught in Scripture, that Christ did teach in person in the region of lost souls. We know that but one voice came from that dark region, as taught us by our Lord, and it was a voice of hopeless misery and of sinful unbelief; that voice gives us the only example in the Bible of a prayer offered to a saint, and that prayer came from hell and was never answered. Romanists certainly have not much encouragement to pray to saints.

Solemn are the echoes coming to us from the antediluvian world. Does God's Spirit strive with any to-day? Grieve not the Holy Spirit. Quench not the heavenly flame. Resist not the loving voice. Joyously yield to the gracious promptings of the divine Spirit. Let the prayer of every heart be, with the deepest tenderness and solicitude, that of the Psalmist in his sincere repentance, "Cast me not away from thy presence, and take not thy Holy Spirit from me."

VIII.
WAS THE NOACHIAN FLOOD UNIVERSAL OR LOCAL?

VIII.

WAS THE NOACHIAN FLOOD UNIVERSAL OR LOCAL?

The account of the ark, the deluge, the assuaging of the waters, and God's covenant with Noah is found in the book of Genesis, sixth, seventh, and eighth chapters. We have already seen that the cup of God's righteous judgment was full. The deluge of sin is now about to bring a deluge of water; but it is to be a lustral wave that shall sweep over the corrupt earth. We are familiar with the covenant given to Noah to prepare an ark and to enter therein with his family.

The Ark.

It is difficult to know the exact meaning of the Hebrew word *tebath*, translated ark. The word is found only here and in Exodus ii. 3, where it is applied to the basket in which the mother of Moses laid her babe. A different word is used, *aron*, for the ark of the covenant (Exodus xxv. 10). The ark which Noah was commanded to make was to consist of gopher or cypress wood, if we mean any particular species of tree; this wood, because of its lightness and durability, the Phœnicians used for building their vessels, the Athenians their coffins, and the Egyptians their mummy-cases. These trees were such as contained pitch, turpentine, and similar resinous materials. We know that the ark was divided into a number of small compartments placed in three tiers, and we also know that light was admitted through openings called windows; but great obscurity attaches to the word *tzohar*, translated window. It is likely that it was a series of light and air holes of lattice-work. A different word is used for the window, *halon*, which Noah is said to have opened at the end of forty days. The word *tzohar* implies that the window was in some way connected with the transmission of light, as it comes from a root meaning shining. It was probably a collective term for skylights, in which there may have been revolving lattices, or some transparent substance with which we are not familiar. The door of the ark must have been of considerable size to admit the various animals, and it must also have been above the highest point which the water would reach; perhaps the word translated door is also to be used in a collective sense, implying a number of openings in the different stories of the ark.

We are told that the ark was 300 cubits long, 50 cubits wide, and 30 cubits high. What was the length of a cubit? The cubit later in Jewish history came to be six hand-breadths, or about twenty-one inches; this was known as the sacred cubit, although there was a common cubit of eighteen inches. Taking the longer of these measures as correct, the ark would be 525 feet long, 87 feet wide, and 52 feet and 6 inches high. The *Great Eastern* is 680 feet long, 691 on deck, 83 feet wide, and 58 feet deep. The ark was intended only to float, to have ample storage, and to keep reasonably steady on the waters. It was a great oblong floating house, a building in the form of a parallelogram. It was without sails or rudder; it was not a boat in any modern sense. It has been estimated that it would carry at least 20,000 men with ample provision for six months, besides eighteen pieces of cannon. It was not, of course, intended to move rapidly through the waters. We are told that Peter Jansen, a Dutch Mennonite merchant, constructed in the year 1609, at Hoorn, a vessel on the same model as the ark. His vessel was 120 feet long, 20 feet broad, and 12 feet deep. It is also said to have been well adapted to freightage, but not appropriate for a long voyage. This great vessel failed to accomplish any practical purpose, as it was soon broken to pieces by the waves. The ark of Noah was a colossal oblong chest, smeared with bitumen, and, although well suited for the purpose for which it was constructed, it would not have been of practical service outside of that purpose. It is also known that several vessels called *fleuten*, or floats, were built in Denmark after the proportions of the ark.

The Animals in the Ark.

Did Noah literally take into the ark a pair of the animals of the whole world? The answer to this question depends upon the question, "Was the flood universal or local?" Could all the animals of the world, by sevens or by pairs, with food sufficient for a year, have been stored away in the ark? This question has been often asked, and detailed mathematical answers have been frequently given. Hugh Miller, in his "Testimony of the Rocks," takes up the question in a practical way. He quotes Sir Walter Raleigh's calculations on the subject, but it must be borne in mind that Sir Walter proposed space for less than one hundred distinct species of creatures. His calculations are remarkably interesting, as he arranges the animals in one story, the birds in another, and the provisions in another, with ample space for Noah and his family. There were still earlier classifications of animals and birds, making the number of species larger than that given by Sir Walter Raleigh; but the knowledge which we now possess of the animal kingdom throws all these calculations into utter confusion. Buffon made the distinct species of animals and birds double what Sir Walter reckoned; and now, so astonishing is the progress made, we should have to make the number of species many times greater than that which Buffon gives. A great world is open to us which was entirely unknown even a few generations ago. Vast discoveries are made in every department of inquiry. These facts incidentally show, what later will be proved from other considerations, that the flood was only local and not general, only partial and not universal. To believe that the flood was universal is to believe in continuous miracles of the most stupendous character, and miracles as needless for the moral purpose for which the flood came as they would have been gigantic in themselves. All who believe in an infinite God believe that He could have performed all these miracles. The only question is, Did He perform them? From all that we know of God's methods we are abundantly warranted in saying that He is invariably economical in the displays of His power, and that He thus always keeps the miraculous element at a minimum.

Then we have, if we believe in a universal flood, to get the animals from the ends of the earth. This could not be done, except again by continuous miracles of an enormous nature. Once it was held that all the animals which now are found in all parts of the globe originally proceeded from some common centre, such as the ark might easily have occupied; but no reputable zoologist, no reasonably intelligent man, reasonably well acquainted with the numbers and distribution of species, will venture now to express such an opinion. Attention has often been called by writers on this subject to the fact that South

America has animals totally distinct from those of Europe, Asia, or Africa, and Australia has a whole class of marsupials utterly unknown in other parts of the world. New Zealand has birds so ill-provided with wings that they can only run on the ground. It is also affirmed by competent authorities that this remarkable distribution of species existed long before the period of the deluge.

False Views of God.

It is astonishing that some interpreters of the Bible think that they honor God and the Bible by taxing our credulity to the utmost, when the fact is that by so doing they dishonor both God and the Bible. They put God, to some degree at least, into the category of heathen deities, delighting in vast displays of power, without necessity, without reason, and without wisdom; and they do something toward reducing the Bible to a level with the senseless legends of barbaric gods and mythological deities. We ought to thank God for the larger element of sanctified common sense which now enters into the interpretations of the oracles of God. This element honors alike God and the Bible. Only by continuous miracles could the animals be brought into the ark. How could the sloth and the armadillo have been brought across continents and seas from their home in South America? How the kangaroo from the forests and prairies of Australia? How the polar bear from the icebergs of polar regions? How were the carnivorous animals supplied with food during the year's abode in the ark? Were these animals miraculously supplied with food? Were their teeth and digestive organs so changed that they could live on vegetables? To care for a year for even the limited number of animals which have their home in Noah's vicinity, it has well been said, must have been a task not easy of accomplishment. To care for all the animals which would have been collected together, if the flood were universal, would have been absolutely impossible, except by daily miracles of the most enormous character.

But was not Noah told to take two of every living thing of all flesh into the ark? Most assuredly. But how would he understand such a command? Would it suggest to him armadillos from South America, kangaroos from Australia, polar bears from the North Pole? Surely not. He would understand it—how could he understand it otherwise?—to mean two of every kind known to him. Surely he was not a zoological professor. Would any one with sense, except for a few misunderstood expressions in the narrative, ever suppose that Noah or Moses had such a conception of the meaning of God's words as a belief in a universal deluge supposes? Noah and Moses could hardly have been nineteenth-century zoologists. How could they, after the subsidence of the flood, have been carried back to the distant countries whence they came? Who could have transported them? By what ships or railways did they come and go? How have all vestiges of their journey back and forth been concealed? It is quite too bad that certain classes of biblical students have thought that they honored the Bible by making it as difficult as possible of belief. Thank God, wiser methods of investigation and interpretation now prevail. We can still believe in God and in the Bible without taking farewell of sound reason, clear judgment, and common sense.

The Bible Narrative.

Does the Bible teach that the flood was universal? That is the chief, really the only, question. If it does I accept its statements, even though to me they are inexplicable. But the Bible does not so affirm. Fairly interpreted, it makes no such statement. Explaining Scripture by Scripture, we shall see that its strongest expressions are capable of being interpreted in harmony with the idea of a local flood. True, it speaks of the destruction of "all flesh" and of "all in whose nostrils was the breath of life"; but how did the writer understand such language? Was he referring to North or South America, to Australia, to China, to Japan? Did he not mean all in his own locality? Did he not mean all the world which he knew? How could he have meant anything else? Was he not using such language as is used constantly in the Bible, when clearly only a limited locality is intended? Let the Bible interpret the Bible. Let us read it when it says, "*All countries* came into Egypt to buy corn." What countries, America, Europe, Australia? Clearly the countries with which the writer was familiar. Hear another passage, this time from the New Testament: "A decree went out from Cæsar Augustus that *all the world* should be taxed." What world? Are we to take such passages in an absolutely literal sense? Such an interpretation would be nonsense. It was all the world with which those concerned were familiar. The words of Obadiah in 1 Kings xviii. 10, "There is *no nation or kingdom* whither my lord hath not sent to seek thee," no one ever dreams of interpreting literally. One of the strongest expressions in the narrative of the deluge is, "All the high hills which were under the whole heaven." But this is no stronger than another Scripture which says, "This day will I begin to put the dread of thee and the fear of thee upon the nations that *are under the whole heaven.*" Even the terms of the blessing promised Noah after the flood, though it regards Noah as the head of a new human family and the representative of a new race, can all be interpreted by supposing that the flood, in the mind of the writer, was universal only in the sense that it extended to the whole world as then known.

There is no reason for supposing that the ark rested on one of the peaks now called Ararat; for Ararat was a country, and not simply a mountain; and a range like that of the Zagros would answer all the purposes of the narrative. The local tradition, which finds parts of the ark on the top of the mountain, is, of course, of no authority whatever.

Some great and sudden subsidence of the land accompanied by an in-rush of the waters of the Persian Gulf, or some other body of water, together with the rain for one hundred and ninety days, would comply with all the conditions of the breaking up of the great deep and the opening of the windows of heaven. In the year 1819 a severe earthquake shock caused a great depression in a part of the salt marsh called the "Runn of Kutch," in India, and many lives were lost and a vast inland sea was soon formed. No reference in the sacred narrative is made to any land, or to any world, except that portion of the earth's surface known to the writer. That territory, and an unknown margin adjoining it, were covered with water. The Scripture says nothing of distant portions of Asia, Europe, America, Africa, or Australia; and when the Scripture is silent we ought not to speak. We ought not to be wise above that which is written. The writer speaks constantly as an eye-witness; and within his horizon all the hills were covered.

We are at this time removed from Adam by ten generations, including Noah's. A careful estimate of population would give us from three to four millions in the time of Noah; and every indication suggests that the population was confined to a limited territory. Dr. Murphy expresses the opinion that an area equal to that of the British Isles would be amply sufficient for the entire population of men, women, and children. It is easy to locate a territory of this size where the subsidence would be a comparatively easy matter, even as judged by recent inundations in different parts of the earth. The earth which was submerged is the earth which was corrupt before God; it was the earth which was filled with violence. It was this earth, and not any other, which was destroyed by the flood. It is easy to see how a people of four millions could be living in the great basin of the Euphrates and Tigris, and how an area in the vicinity of the Indian Ocean, the Persian Gulf, the Caspian, the Black, the Mediterranean, and the Red seas could readily be submerged, in full harmony with the teaching of the Scriptures, while the rest of the universe would not be affected. It must ever be borne in mind that the description is by a man and from his point of view, and not from the point of view of the all-seeing God. It is absolutely certain that the Bible does not affirm that the whole globe was covered with water. If the Bible did so affirm, I should believe it without any hesitancy whatever; but we have no right to read into God's word our unwarranted thought; we ought to get out of God's word simply His authoritative teaching.

Additional Difficulties.

The astronomical difficulties in the way of a universal flood are insuperable. If the flood were universal, the water must have risen several miles above the sea-level. Such an increase of water would have affected the equatorial diameter of the earth and its orbit around the sun, and would have increased the sun's attraction on the planets; and thus disorder would have been produced throughout the remotest regions of space. After the waters had been assuaged enormous changes would have been necessary again in order that the former relations of the heavenly bodies might be reëstablished. God would have had practically to create the world anew. Can we conceive that this enormous series of miracles could have occurred simply for the punishment of a comparatively small number of people inhabiting a limited portion of the earth's surface? God does not waste power in this way. The geological objections are scarcely less great than the astronomical. The zoological difficulty, as we have already suggested, is perhaps greater than either the geological or the astronomical. Had there been a general deluge, apart from continuous miracles, there would have been a general destruction of marine life. The changing depths of water would have destroyed the coral reefs of the Pacific. Yet Noah does not seem to have taken any kind of marine animals into the ark. A general deluge would have entirely changed the climate of the whole world; it would have destroyed all kinds of fresh-water fish, and such a submergence of the land in sea-water would have brought destruction upon all terrestrial plants. We have no reason to suppose that Noah took any stock of such plants into the ark. It was once supposed—and the old books may yet so affirm—that geological discoveries confirmed the opinion that the deluge was universal. The existence of shells and corals upon the high mountains was supposed to be evidence of the universality of the deluge. Voltaire once found it difficult to answer the arguments of those who cited the existence of fossil shells on high mountains, and his arguments to explain away these supposed evidences are as childish as the evidences themselves were imaginary. Greater knowledge removes the difficulties inseparable from the belief in a universal deluge, and enables us readily to accept the statements of God's word. All these considerations, therefore, lead us to believe that the flood was local. The moral purpose for which it occurred is fully subserved by a limited, rather than by a general, deluge. Accepting this view, nearly all difficulties vanish. With charming simplicity, as well as marvellous sublimity, the Bible narrates the story. Its narrative is free from the heart-rending scenes which the painters have so often depicted. The two ideas constantly dwelt upon in the Bible are the blotting out of the sinful race in the submergence of the polluted earth, as far as the eye could see, and the absolute safety of Noah and his family in the ark. The sending out of the dove, and its final return with the fresh olive leaf, is one of the most charming of pictures. In Psalm xxix. 10, the poet sings of the majesty of God, and gives a sublime conception when he says, "Jehovah sat as king at the flood." The prophet Isaiah introduces God as referring to the flood to emphasize the truth of His promise. The New Testament gives its full sanction to the historicity of the narrative. Our Lord clearly declares that the state of the world at His second coming will be like what it was in the days of Noah. The Apostle Peter draws from the flood lessons as to the longsuffering of God and the separation of the church from the world. He also makes it an instance of the righteous judgment of God, who spared not the old world when it was corrupted by sin. Most beautiful is the closing scene after the judgment had been inflicted. Noah then built his altar, the first altar of which we read in the Bible, and then Jehovah smelled an "odor of satisfaction" and promised that never again would he, for man's sake, curse the ground nor smite any living thing. Then the rainbow received its new meaning, and the special promises were given regarding seedtime and harvest, cold and heat, day and night. This is a peaceful, beautiful, and divine picture of the cleansed earth, spanned by the rainbow in the clouds after the fearful deluge had passed.

Traditions of the Deluge.

The literatures of many nations abound in legends of the flood, and between these and the Bible narrative marked resemblances are found. In various forms these traditions describe the preservation of one righteous man with his family. The Chaldæan traditions are nearest to the Hebrew records. The god Belus foretold a vast rain flood. The structure of a great ship is described; a raven is sent out, and the ark itself is said to have been preserved on the high mountains. There are many other notices of the flood, such as those in the Phœnician mythology and in the Phrygian story of King Annakos. There is also a cycle of traditions in Eastern Asia, such as the Persian, Indian, and Chinese. These traditions, though varying in so many respects, all point to the truth of the Bible narrative. There is also the cycle of tradition found among the American nations, such as those of Mexico, those of the Hawaiian Islands, and those of many Indian tribes. There are also legends of the flood preserved by the Fiji Islanders, by the Scandinavian Eddas, and also the account in the Koran; but the most interesting of all these myths are those of the Greek legends. They had two such myths—that of Ogyges and that of Deucalion and Pyrrha. This latter is the best known of the ethnic traditions. It teaches us that the world had sunk into iniquity, and that mankind was doomed to destruction. The ocean and the clouds combined to drown the sinful race. The pious Deucalion, with his wife Pyrrha, floated in a chest, which bore them safely to the peaks of Parnassus. He, like Noah, sent out a dove, which returned the first time, but not the second. God gives in all these traditions confirmation of the truth of His holy Word.

Lessons.

This solemn and sublime event teaches us important lessons. We see that God is able to execute judgment against the greatest sinners. Though sinners join hand-in-hand they shall not escape God's righteous justice. Sinning angels cannot escape. God burned up the filthy Sodomites and drowned the sinful antediluvians. All the resoures of nature are at God's command. He wields the thunderbolt; and through heaven's open windows He poured the flood, and the volcano and the hurricane are obedient to His will.

God gives ample warning to sinners and abundant opportunity for repentance. For one hundred and twenty years Noah was a preacher of righteousness. His acts in building the ark, as well as his words in preaching the Gospel, were warnings to impenitent sinners. Doubtless he was often the subject of sneers and jeers. The people may have considered him a good old man, but with strange fancies and amusing forebodings. They doubtless thought him lacking in sense, and perhaps wrong in his head; but he still kept on preaching. God's infinite holiness patiently waited. Wonderful was the long-suffering of God in the days of Noah. Well might the Apostle Peter dwell upon God's matchless patience; but the blow eventually fell. This terrible judgment manifested God's holiness, even as it was seen in Eden or on Sinai.

There is safety for all true believers. God said to Noah, "Come thou and all thy house into the ark," and then God graciously closed the door and Noah was safe. The world without perished. God can save all His children, whatever destruction may befall others. Sodom was destroyed, but Lot was saved. Jericho was destroyed, but Rahab was saved. Without, to-day, the flood of evil prevails. Christ is the true ark of safety. Come into Him, and you shall outride the storms of life, and land at last on the shining hills of glory, in the enjoyment of a new heaven and a new earth, wherein dwelleth righteousness.

IX.

WHAT WAS THE PURPOSE OF THE TOWER OF BABEL?

IX.

WHAT WAS THE PURPOSE OF THE TOWER OF BABEL?

The account of the Tower of Babel is found in the eleventh chapter of Genesis and the first nine verses. Reference is made several times in the preceding chapter to the division of the race into various settlements; the narrative now before us explains the divisions of the race and the diversities of the languages there assumed. This division and diversity resulted from the project of building the temple and tower of Babel, and of God's displeasure with the purpose of the people. In harmony with the method often employed by inspired writers, the dispersion of the people is first mentioned, and then the cause of that dispersion is fully described.

It is quite certain that the early fathers of the human family, after the deluge, wandered about for some time without any fixed place of abode; but it was also quite certain that they could not always live a nomadic life. Gregariousness is an inseparable instinct of humanity; this tendency of human nature is shown to-day in the desire for city life. It thus comes to pass that the population of our great cities is increasing at the expense of rural populations. This tendency is seen in all the countries of the globe. British and continental cities are growing almost as rapidly as are the most enterprising cities in America. In harmony with this ancient and universal instinct the descendants of Noah finally made a permanent residence in the land of Shinar. Shinar was the ancient name of Babylonia or Chaldæa, as the tract of land in later times came to be known. This was a great alluvial district through which the Tigris and Euphrates flowed before reaching the sea. This country was marked by the absence of stone for building material, but it was famous for the excellence of the bricks there made, and for the slime that was used for mortar. It was known also for its textile fabrics; the "goodly Babylonish garment" of Joshua vii. 21, which proved a snare to Achan, was a "garment of Shinar." This country is probably to be identified with the Sumer or the Shumer of the cuneiform inscriptions, and so a name denoting the southern portion of the "land of the Chaldæans." The name usually includes the whole rich and populous alluvial plain to which reference has been made, reaching from the Persian Gulf to a point north of the modern Bagdad, a little more than two hundred miles.

"One Lip."

Up to the time mentioned in the Scripture under consideration the people had remained together, speaking one language. We are told that they were, to render the words literally, "of one lip and of words one"; that is, they employed one kind or stock of words. They also developed one kind of civilization. As the lip is the principal organ in the utterance of words, the word *saphah*, lip, is here employed, although a frequent Scripture term for language is *leshon*, tongue. The confusion of the lip is probably a change in the pronunciation of words, and this change will account for the babel, or confusion, which took place at this time. The people finding a home in the rich plain of Shinar, the derivation suggesting its name as the land of "the two rivers," they determined to build a city and tower of great height. All ancient authorities and modern travellers affirm that building material was easy to find in this valley. The people, therefore, proceeded to burn bricks, "burning them to a burning," that is, burning them thoroughly, and to use slime or bitumen for mortar. Bricks were often dried simply by the sun, but these heroic builders wished to secure the most durable material, and so they thoroughly burned the bricks. The Scripture narrative teaches us that God interposed and frustrated all their plans, and this interposition was brought about by the introduction of hopeless confusion into their lanugage. They were thus unable longer to understand one another. They therefore "left off to build the city," and soon were scattered abroad on the face of the earth. This remarkable circumstance gave rise to the word babel, perhaps meaning confusion. This name the Greeks corrupted into Babylon, and although originally applied only to the Tower of Babel, it was afterward extended to the city of Babylon, which grew up about the tower; and finally it was extended to the whole province of Babylonia. We thus see that God did not intend that men should always remain in a limited locality and should speak only one language. Perhaps the account here given will not explain fully the origin of languages; but it is at least suggestive of elements which entered into that origin, and into the conceptions of the times of the writer regarding the diversity of speech. Some would derive the word Babel from *Bab-ilu*, meaning "the gate of the god." This is in substance the story as found on the inspired page. It is narrated in a dramatic manner and with rare poetic beauty.

Ethnic Traditions.

The Chaldæan traditions state that the first men became proud of their great strength and raised a tower reaching toward heaven in the place where Babylon afterward stood. They state also that the gods, assisted by fierce winds, hurled the building down upon the heads of the builders, and that out of the material thus collected the city of Babylon was built. These traditions harmonize with the Bible narrative in saying that before this event all the people spoke one language, but after it they differed widely in their tongues. Greek traditions are in substantial harmony with those of Chaldæa. Plato makes the uniformity extend to animals as well as to men in the golden age. Perhaps the advance of linguistic science will yet enable us to understand the language of animals, as these traditions affirm concerning the early period of human history. Plato also echoes other parts of the Bible story in saying that men in their unholy ambition aspired to immortality, and that they were punished by Jupiter, who utterly confounded their language. Attention has also been called to the fact that in the account of the wars of the Titans against the gods, we clearly see traces of the traditionary resemblances to the narrative in the Bible concerning Babel. Other traditions associate these events with Nimrod, a "bold, bad man," who strove to alienate the minds of the people from God, and to build a tower too high for the waters ever to reach its top. This he did, the traditions affirm, in order to take revenge for the punishment of the deluge. But this explanation for the cause of the erection of Babel is very unsatisfactory. We know that the people could not have feared another deluge, for God had given an express promise to the contrary; and if another deluge should come, they must have known that no tower they could build would protect them, as the waters went over the highest hills in the parts submerged.

Several writers on this subject remind us that it was long believed that the native Babylonian records contained references to the tower of Babel and the confusion of speech; and, it is stated, that recently such a record has been discovered. Mr. George Smith brought a number of clay tablets from Babylonia and deposited them in the British Museum, and among them is one, unfortunately badly mutilated, but still sufficiently legible to show that it probably contained the Babylonian account of this whole deeply interesting history. Herodotus, in simple and graphic language, describes the building of the walls of Babylon in expressions which remind us of the Biblical narrative of the building of the tower of Babel. In both narratives there is a reference to the excellent building materials which the Babylonian soil furnishes in such abundance. Bitumen pits are still found from which bitumen bubbles up, and which can be readily manufactured into cement for use in buildings at the present day. It is known that in some parts of southern California there is soil containing materials not unlike those found in the alluvial plain of Babylon. The tablets found in the British Museum state that the tower was erected under the supervision of a semi-divine being called Etanna. In Central America there are traditions similar to the story of the tower of Babel. Xelhua, one of the seven giants rescued from the deluge, so the tradition affirms, attempted to storm heaven and oppose all the gods, and so he built the great pyramid of Cholula. But in this case also the gods interposed, destroyed the tower with fire, and utterly confounded the language of the builders. In northern India traces of similar legends are found; and even among certain African tribes Dr. Livingstone met with traditions possessing features similar to the narrative in the Bible. There are also Australian legends regarding the origin of the diversity of speech kindred to those already named. All these traditions point to an original historic incident; they tend to confirm our faith in the Bible narrative. They are all eloquent as to the original unity of the race and the reality of the divine purpose in its dispersion.

Reasons for Building the Tower.

It is clearly shown in the sacred narrative that the design of the builders was threefold. They wished to make a name; this is distinctly stated in Genesis xi. 4. A tower is simply another name for a citadel, or place of defence. This reason for the building of the tower sets aside a great many foolish conjectures as to its design. The primary object was to transmit an illustrious name for grand designs and heroic enterprises. The project had reference to some warlike movements which would enable the people to defend themselves against insurrections, and probably to enforce an unholy despotism. Nimrod was probably the leader, and he was one of the first who is recorded to have attempted the exercise of despotic power over his fellow-men. A second reason was an ambition to erect a structure which in itself should challenge attention and evoke admiration. A third reason is that the people might not be scattered abroad. The Bible gives no intimation whatever that the tower was built for the purpose of escaping another flood. The great height of the tower would make it a rallying point in the level plains where it was located. In these wide and level plains this was an object of great practical importance, as there are few objects to guide the traveller in his journeys, the plains being virtually a vast sea of land. In the simple fact that the people did not wish to be scattered abroad they were opposing God's purpose as several times declared. It is quite certain that some unworthy motives and ungodly ambitions were blended with the desire of the people to remain together. There is much in this desire which elicits our commendation, but we must see that the conduct of the people evinced pride, arrogance, and disobedience against God. They were forcing a conspiracy to establish a universal temporal monarchy. God intended that the people should spread themselves abroad, and they attempted to defeat the purpose of God in this regard. They resolved to establish a civilization of their own; they planned to build society, not upon faith in an unseen God, but on lofty brick walls and sky-kissing towers. Thy were believers in a merely material civilization. Their work was an offspring of an unholy ambition. Philo narrates a tradition that each man wrote his name on a brick which was to be placed in the structure. The same tendency is seen to-day. Men strive to shut out God from personal, family, and national life. They talk simply of law, of culture, and of civilization, ignoring God and spiritual and eternal things. God will in some form confound their plans as surely as He did those of the builders on the plains of Shinar. God can overrule and frustrate the ambitious dreams of the Nimrods, the Nebuchadnezzars, the Alexanders, the Cæsars, and the Napoleons of all centuries, countries, and civilizations.

The Original Language.

We do not know what the original language was which was confounded at Babel. For a long time it was claimed that it was the Hebrew, but that idea has now been largely abandoned. Learned men have not yet reached any satisfactory conclusion regarding the original tongue.

Some suppose that it is entirely lost. It may have been the Hebrew or the Aramaic. We know that the Aramaic was long dominant in the valley of the Euphrates, and that it is closely allied to the Hebrew; these two facts make a strong plea in favor of the Aramaic, or Chaldee, as the very language of Noah, or at least as belonging to the same family of languages as that which he spoke. Enthusiastic Highland Scotchmen are firmly convinced that the language of Adam and Noah was none other than the Gaelic, and some of the arguments which they use in the attempt to establish this point are, to say the least, most suggestive and striking. This, however, is a point regarding which scholarship has not yet reached any definite conclusion. The science of comparative philology has in recent years made tremendous progress. It has enabled us to determine the relations between the Saxon and the Norman, and between the conquering Aryans in India and the many conquered tribes in that great peninsula, and it may yet enable us to determine with some degree of certainty the language which was spoken before the confusion of tongues and the dispersion of the peoples occurred. God will eventually use the scholarship of the world for the glory of the Bible, the salvation of men, and the honor of Jesus Christ.

The Modern Representative of Babel.

This historic tower is mentioned only once in Scripture, in the passage now under review. Was it ever completed? All the indications confirm us in believing that it was not; perhaps it never advanced much beyond its foundations. The Jewish tradition is that fire fell from Heaven and split the tower into fragments. It is believed, however, that the "Tower of Belus" occupies the site of the original tower of Babel. Classical writers, in describing Babylon, uniformly refer to a tower-like building which they call "The Temple or Tomb of Belus." This structure is described by Herodotus, and is probably represented by the modern "Birs-Nimrud"; some writers in this connection speak of what was called "The Temple of the Seven Lights of the Earth," dedicated to Nebo at Borsippa, a suburb of Babylon. This structure was completed in the reign of Nebuchadnezzar. When he conquered Jerusalem he put its captured treasures in the temple of Bel at Babylon. When the Jews were carried captive into Babylonia they saw in many of the great buildings reminders of the tower mentioned in their Scriptures. Christian travellers were accustomed to call any great mass of ruins "The Tower of Babel." There was long a consensus of opinion among the learned that Birs-Nimrud, or Tower of Nimrod, was the tower of Babel; and it is now pretty generally agreed that it at least is a good representative of an ancient Babylonian temple-tower. Dr. William Hayes Ward, of New York, as the head of the Wolfe expedition, had it photographed by Mr. J. H. Haynes, and Dr. Ward has fully described this historic ruin. He is disposed to regard the story in Genesis as an interesting illustration of folklore; but his description and illustrations tend to confirm the truth of the story. The building is an oblique pyramid. Its first basement stage is an exact square 272 feet each way, 26 feet high; the second is 230 feet each way, and the third 188 feet. It thus decreases in width as it increases in height. It has been recently conjectured that the upper portions of this tower were used as an observatory for astronomical observations. It is well known that the Babylonians were earnest students of astronomy, and the elevation of this tower, the clear atmosphere, and the broad plains were all conducive to the careful study of this ennobling science. It has also been suggested that the upper portions of this tower were used by the priests as sleeping-places in the summer-time, as they gave greater coolness and greater freedom from insects than the lower stories furnished. All travellers agree that this mass of ruins is deeply impressive as it rises out of the desert plain. Parts of it show the effect of great heat, as they are vitrified. It is a fire-blasted pile and is rent and fragmentary. Its dreary aspect has led to its being called "Nebuchadnezzar's Prison." The entire neighborhood indicates that here there was some signal overthrow in former times. Perhaps the vitrification is a justification of the tradition that the tower was blasted by the lightnings of Heaven. The pyramidal temples of other countries make belief in this great tower of Belus less difficult. All who have visited Tanjore, in India, are familiar with a tower which will at least suggest that of Babel—the Tower at Tanjore. It is built entirely of stone, and on its top is a chapel or temple whose design is in harmony with that of other sacred structures in India. The gate of these pagodas always fronts the east; they are generally on the banks of great rivers, and are usually surrounded by courts. The great Mexican pyramid is not much unlike that of Tanjore. These pyramids show the tendency of former days in different parts of the world and among various peoples.

God's Purpose in the Dispersion of Races.

It was the purpose of God that the three primitive families should migrate. From the central regions, where they developed their first civilizations, they went out by successive colonizations, and soon they established distant communities. Marvellously interesting is it to trace God's hand in the boundaries and characteristics of various nations. The Hamitic, the Semitic, and the Japhetic had each its work to do, and its triumphs to achieve. The sons of Japheth were men of resistless will and tireless muscle. Westward and northward they pushed, and finally they became the authors of Greek literature, of Roman government, of modern Europe, and of marvellous America. This commingling of races is God's plan for saving man physically. No unmixed race can long hold its own. The native Hawaiians must speedily die or unite with some other races. The modern Frenchman has in his veins the blood of the Celt, the Frank, and the Norman, and he is better than either one alone. In the veins of the modern Briton are the commingling streams of the blood of many nations; and the modern Briton is marching to the ends of the earth, carrying with him law, liberty, civilization, and Christianity. The American of the future will be an amalgam of many nations; and he ought to be the noblest product of civilization and Christianity which the world has yet seen. America deserves the best from all the nations of the earth. The worst nations of southern Europe should no longer be permitted to dump their refuse populations on our American shores.

Lessons.

There is great danger that we may still manifest the spirit of the builders of Babel. Men are still under the power of unholy ambitions and material civilizations. God should be the guide of every life. God should be the senior partner of every business. It is daring impiety which leaves God out of our plans for life.

The church of Jesus Christ had its natal day on the day of Pentecost, and Pentecost is the counterpart of Babel. Pentecost made it possible for the messengers of the cross to go to the ends of the earth with the message of the Gospel of salvation. Babel made men in some sense aliens; Pentecost aims to make all men brothers. In the Fatherhood of God we have the true brotherhood of man. The church calls us to labor as builders of the true city of God. Its living stones are cemented together by the unity of the faith. The city we are building has enduring foundations, and its top will finally reach to Heaven. In Heaven there is one language, one life, one love. God hasten the blessed consummation when the kingdoms of this world shall become the kingdom of our Lord and His Christ!

X.

WAS LOT WISE IN PITCHING HIS TENT TOWARD SODOM?

X.

WAS LOT WISE IN PITCHING HIS TENT TOWARD SODOM?

In Genesis, the thirteenth chapter and a part of the twelfth verse, we read concerning Lot that he "pitched his tent toward Sodom." Did he act wisely in so doing? The story suggested by these words is full of interest and instruction. It opens with associative glimpses into family life of the ancient time.

We here see how in private life there are opportunities of displaying a rare heroism and a fine chivalry. We shall observe in studying this narrative that common events may reveal selfishness or generosity of character, and may be made an occasion for developing the noblest qualities of manhood and the broadest principles of godliness. This ancient story shows us how true religion beautifies and glorifies domestic life, and how the lowliest duties may manifest the loftiest qualities in human action.

Lot's Name and Family.

His name means a covering or a veil. He was the son of Haran, and so the nephew of Abram. His grandfather was Terah. About two thousand years before Christ he removed with his grandfather to Haran in Mesopotamia. There Terah died aged two hundred and five years. About a year later, in company with Abraham, Lot came into the land of Canaan. In consequence of a famine, he went with Abram and Sarai into Egypt; soon after he returned to the southern part of Canaan, and then went to the region of Bethel and Ai, where Abram built his first altar and called upon the name of Jehovah. We shall get a true conception of Lot's character and history by a series of pictures representing both, at which we may now look.

First Picture.

We have before us Lot making a selfish choice of the best pastures. This is a most instructive picture. In the background are seen the herdsmen of Lot engaged in strife with the herdsmen of Abram. Still farther in the background are seen the Canaanite and the Perizzite who still dwelled in the land; and in the foreground are seen the noble Abram and the selfish Lot. The presence of the heathen in the land ought to have warned the herdsmen of the danger of their family quarrels. But the spirit of rivalry and jealousy broke forth, notwithstanding the danger to which it subjected both Abram and Lot. They went down into Egypt poor, and they now return rich. The Hebrew words translated "very rich" literally mean *exceedingly heavy*. The term rich is, of course, a relative one, and judged by British or American standards a wealthy Arab sheik would be considered poor. The wealth of these emirs consisted mostly in flocks of sheep and goats, and in camels. Their increased flocks made herbage in the vicinity of Bethel too scanty for their accommodation. Behold the two men standing on one of the round swelling hills near Bethel! So far as we can discover, there is no strife between them; it is limited to their herdsmen. But Abram was sagacious enough to foresee that these jarring jealousies would increase more and more, and might finally cause an estrangement between him and his nephew. These two men stand looking out over the empty land in the direction of Sodom. The land before them is beautiful to the eye; it is well watered—literally it was "all a-watering"—showing the fertilizing effect which irrigation by various streams produced.

The language of the Scripture at this point is very striking. The land is as beautiful as the wonderfully green Egypt which they had just left, and beautiful even as the garden of Jehovah, whose superhuman charms still lingered in the thought of the time. Abram gave Lot his choice. Through the clear air of Palestine the distant valley could clearly be seen. It has been well remarked that we are here reminded of the choice of Hercules, as described in Grecian legend, and of the turning back of the prophet from Damascus as represented in the fables of Islam. Abram here treats Lot as if they were really brethren, instead of uncle and nephew. The prospect was fascinating in the extreme, and Lot could not resist its attractions. He chose all the plain of Jordan; he journeyed east, he pitched his tent toward Sodom, and he separated from his noble uncle. The conduct of Abram was eminently considerate; it was generous almost to a fault. Not only was he the senior and superior of the two, but he was especially called of God to lordship in the land. The conduct of Lot was selfish and covetous to a remarkable degree. His finer feelings were deadened, and he assumed enormous risk in going toward Sodom, because of its well-known character for the practice of abominable evils.

This picture makes a powerful appeal to the imagination. We shall later see that Lot paid an enormous price for his rich pastures. We ought always to remember, when we yield to the gratification of the moment, that there is a to-morrow with which we must reckon. The people of Sodom were not only wicked, but desperately wicked; they were high-handed and heaven-daring sinners. Yet Lot chose their neighborhood for the sake of its temporal advantage. It may be that the word translated *toward* means *at*, or in the vicinity of, Sodom; but it is not quite in Sodom. Choices reveal character. A man is really what his choice declares his inner life to be. The man who prefers pebbles to diamonds manifests insanity. The man who chooses a temporary earthly good and rejects eternal and spiritual things is morally insane. So Lot chose. He removed his tent from place to place, but gradually he approaches Sodom. Perhaps he intended to keep at some distance from this perilous place; but still he goes imperceptibly onward. He nears this sink of corruption. He treads the borders of forbidden ground.

So men trifle to-day with evil; so they parley with the devil. They lie on the bank of the narrow stream dividing right from wrong. They do not intend to cross that stream; but they love to look upon the blooming flowers and to breathe the pleasant odors of the forbidden land. Things inevitably follow their tendencies. If these men do not quickly change their course both they and Lot will be in Sodom. "Let him that thinketh he standeth take heed lest he fall."

Second Picture.

We next find Lot, together with the inhabitants of Sodom, made a prisoner by Chedorlaomer. Let us quickly get the salient features of this picture. Chedorlaomer came from beyond the Euphrates; he was king of Elam, in Persia. He was the leader of the several allied kings, who invaded Canaan. He had already brought a number of small states under tribute, and among these were the five cities in the region of the Dead Sea. These states were impatient under their burden of tribute, and finally they withheld its payment. This led to the invasion of the country, and to the ravaging visitation of the whole country south and east of the Jordan. Soon the kings of the plains were defeated and carried away as slaves, as was the custom of the times. Lot was included in this unfortunate number of slaves. He had cast in his lot with these people, and he must share with them in their evil fortune. This is part of the price which he is paying for his good pastures. Behold him now borne off, a slave in the power of his cruel captors!

Nobly does the character of generous Abram appear in this crisis in the life of Lot. Abram heard of his misfortune and hastened to his rescue. The brave uncle immediately armed three hundred and eighteen of his retainers—a fact that shows he was a sheik of wealth and power—and joined by three friendly Amoritish chiefs, he pursued the returning invaders. Near the fountains of the Jordan he overtook them as they fled in haste. Some of his allies attacked the enemies by night on the one side, and some on the other; and soon they were thrown into utter confusion and fled in hopeless dismay. On, on over the hills went the brave Abram and his heroic men in hot pursuit until they reached the neighborhood of Damascus. They then returned victorious, carrying back the men and the property seized by the invaders. Doubtless Lot's sad plight influenced Abram to undertake this exploit; but in delivering Lot he conferred signal benefits on many tribes and peoples; and, as a result, his courage and wisdom were greatly honored throughout the land. It was while on his return from this successful expedition that he was met by Melchizedek, king of Salem, and priest of the most high God.

Abram might have kept, according to the usages of war, then and there, and in many parts of the Orient still, the recovered goods; and the king of Sodom, who met the victors in the valley near Salem, freely admitted this right. But Abram, with a truly noble spirit toward men and a loyal devotion toward God, refused the goods, saying: "I have lifted up mine hand unto Jehovah, the most high God, and I will not take from a thread to a sandal-thong, lest thou shouldst say, I have made Abram rich." These are stirring words; they thrill our hearts to this hour. These heroic achievements and generous sentiments gave Abram much deserved celebrity in Canaan. The people owed their deliverance to Abram, and even Lot, for his uncle's sake, must have received some respect and gratitude. But the Sodomites were so besotted, corrupt, and bestial as to have few sentiments of gratitude or generosity above the level of their degraded instincts and sensualized desires.

Third Picture.

We now find Lot actually living in Sodom. He is now married, and probably he found his wife in Sodom. That was a bad place in which to find a wife. Better never be married than marry in Sodom! Were there no other women whom he could have chosen? Had his own tastes already become degraded? Nothing more surely suggests a man's measure, intellectual and spiritual, than the wife he chooses. Marriage should be the outcome of the deepest choice and the noblest ambition; it should be the wisest act of life, and the fullest proof of divine guidance. Think of marrying a woman in Sodom! This name through all the ages has been the symbol of all that is vilest in human relations. Abram's nephew married to a woman of Sodom! Soon there are in his household sons and daughters marriageable and married. One would have thought that he would have had more sense, a nobler ambition, and a truer piety than so to marry. He is now a well-known resident of the town; he is a leader in its affairs. All these sad results have come from pitching his tent toward Sodom. His family later showed the degrading influences of the social atmosphere in which they lived. Lot is paying a terribly high price for his good pastures. Men make a fearful mistake when for the sake of business prosperity they knowingly form partnerships with bad men, and willingly subject themselves to moral dangers in their choice of a residence. No man has a right to assume these terrible risks. God help us to avoid even the appearance of evil!

Fourth Picture.

Behold Lot a judge in Sodom. This is the rabbinical tradition, and there are hints in Scripture looking in this direction. In Genesis xix. 1 we read of Lot as sitting in the gate of Sodom. He had thus thoroughly identified himself with the city and its people. In ancient times and cities the gates were the chief places of resort. There social intercourse took place, there pleasant recreations were enjoyed, there the markets were held, there public affairs were discussed, and there courts of justice held their sessions. All these things brought great concourses of people to the gate. Modern Arabs and other Oriental people still flock to the gates of the towns and cities; there the news of the day is heard, and all forms of social life are enjoyed. The Jewish commentators, as already suggested, understand the reference to Lot's sitting at the gate as implying that he exercised the authority of a magistrate. The elders of the cities in those early days readily became the acknowledged judges in civil affairs. Lot was now a comparatively old man; he was a resident of long standing in Sodom. He was acknowledged to be a leader in business and in social life; his business interests and his social relations are in Sodom. Mrs. Lot, it is fair to assume, was also a recognized social leader in the best or worst circles of society in Sodom. The young ladies of the family were possibly the belles of the town. It is an awful thing for a man to begin by pitching his tent toward Sodom; there are ten chances to one that he will end by landing in Sodom. It is an unspeakably foolish thing to put one's head into the lion's mouth. One day the lion will close his mouth, and there will be a headless man at the menagerie or circus. Often the best way to overcome temptation is to avoid temptation. It is mockery of God to pray, "Lead us not into temptation," and then recklessly run into temptation. God help us to avoid pitching our tent toward Sodom!

Fifth Picture.

Behold Lot thoroughly humiliated while entertaining heavenly visitors. He still preserves in the midst of the licentious corruptions of Sodom some of the nobler qualities of a generous hospitality. Behold him inviting those heavenly visitors to turn in and tarry all night in his house. We see the water brought for the dusty feet of the tired travellers; we see bread offered them for their hunger; we witness all the rites of a chivalrous hospitality, even as these mysterious wayfarers had enjoyed the hospitality of Abram that very morning on the heights of Hebron. The author of the Epistle to the Hebrews does not fail to mention with commendation this charming trait. The Apostle Peter tells us that Lot's righteous soul was vexed, wearied, burdened, from day to day by the filthy conversation and unlawful deeds of his fellow-townsmen. God did indeed keep him from the grosser contaminations of his neighbors; for the Lord knoweth how to deliver the godly out of temptation. Lot was in some sense a just man in the midst of a mob of lawless, sensual, and utterly abominable neighbors.

But a greater trial than ever before is now in store for him. We have seen him extending the hospitality of his tent to his heavenly visitants. They are the avenging angels sent to destroy guilty Sodom. The news of their arrival is noised about the town; the brutal men of Sodom surround the house of Lot and make a demand for the strangers. Their purpose has made the name of Sodom a synonym for infamy throughout all the ages. The demand is resisted; the house is attacked; and then the angels, thus having a fearful illustration of the wickedness which they came to punish, struck the worse than beastly men with blindness. The Hebrew word translated blindness is *bassanverim;* this word literally means with "dazzled blindnesses." We have the original word only here and in 2 Kings vi. 18, where a similar effect was produced on the Syrian army in answer to Elisha's prayer. In both cases a confused vision, such as is caused by vertigo of the brain, resulted. Still these satanic Sodomites madly persisted in their abominable purpose. Think of bringing up a family in such a social atmosphere! Truly Lot was paying a high price for his good pastures. Truly the Sodomites were ripe for the judgment which was about to fall upon them from God. Little did they think that vengeance was so near. Men are still fascinated by evil; they are still blind to the coming of God's judgments. Lot is now told that Sodom will be destroyed, and he is urged to flee with his family from the doomed place.

Sixth Picture.

Behold Lot in the midst of all the horrors attending the destruction of Sodom. This is a fearful picture; it is impossible to paint its colors too vividly. The angels promised deliverance to Lot's daughters who had married in Sodom, but they scorned the offer of mercy. Hastened by the angels, Lot, his wife, and two unmarried daughters, start for a place of safety. His wife lingered, looked lovingly backward, and was soon covered with an incrustation from the saline storm. See him and his daughters hastening to Zoar! This was the smallest of the cities of the plain; and to afford him a place of relief it had been spared. In a cavern in the mountains he and they abode for some time. Well had it been for him if he had remained with Abram. All his property is gone, several of his family are gone, his wife is gone, and soon his honor and that of his daughters will go. Terrible is the price which Lot paid for his good pastures!

Seventh Picture.

One wishes to draw a veil over this picture and forever to hide the later scenes of Lot's life. Only the barest outlines of this picture can be given. Already the taint of Sodom is manifested in Lot's daughters. They are dishonored, and he is unconsciously degraded. Thus sprang the Moabites and the Ammonites. Many attempts at excusing this transaction have been made; but apology for it is impossible. Charity covers it with a mantle.

Lot's preservation is alluded to by our Lord, and his character is honored in certain respects by the Apostle Peter. The Mohammedan traditions affirm that he went to Sodom as a preacher of righteousness. They still point out his grave east of Hebron. The names of Lot and Sodom are still associated with the sins which are said to be still the most common in Eastern cities.

Lessons.

We see the terrible depravity of which human nature is capable. The phrase "total depravity" is not found in the Bible, but it sometimes seems as if the thing itself is found in certain circles of human life. It is often a slander on animals to call some men brutes. God alone can fully see the terrible depths of sin to which human souls may fall. There is constant need that we watch and pray that we do not ourselves fall. Sinners are often most reckless when their hour of doom is nearest. The men of Sodom showed their great wickedness in the presence of God's avenging angels. Men little know now how near the cloud of wrath may be whose thunderbolts the prayers of some saints are warding off from their hearts.

We see that God can preserve His saints from the worst forms of contaminations even in fearfully sinful environments; but men ought not needlessly to expose themselves to danger. What right has a reformed man to go into saloons? The tinkle of glasses and the odors of liquors may set his appetite aflame as with the fires of hell. It is a most dangerous thing for some persons to go "slumming." A noble physician will not hesitate to go to a home whose atmosphere is laden with malaria. A true minister, in like manner, will go where the germs of moral malaria fill the air; but even he ought to be very sure that it is God who calls for the visit, and that God calls him, and not some one else, to make the visit. Let us all remember, not only Lot's wife, but Lot's selfish choice and fearful fate. God help us to avoid the very appearance of evil, and to turn our face and direct our steps evermore toward truth, purity, Christ, and Heaven!

XI.
WHO WAS MELCHIZEDEK, THE MYSTERIOUS KING-PRIEST?

XI.

WHO WAS MELCHIZEDEK, THE MYSTERIOUS KING-PRIEST?

The first account of this remarkable personage is found in Genesis xiv. 18–20. Around but few characters of history, sacred or profane, is there so great a cloud of mystery as around this king-priest; and regarding no man whose history is recorded in the Bible has fancy played so large a part. This result is due in great measure to the sudden manner in which he first appears on, and departs from, the page of Bible history. His personality falls upon the sacred narrative as a ray of light from the noonday sky; this old king-priest, like the flash of a meteor, crosses the path of the conquering patriarch. Thus he emerges from the gloom of historic darkness, and he almost immediately disappears into the darkness whence he had emerged, and then into an historic seclusion wellnigh inscrutable. Yet during his brief appearance, he was treated by Abram with so much respect that the mystery of his personality is greatly deepened. Nearly a thousand years pass, and he once more appears upon the historic pages, in the words of the Psalmist; then for a thousand years more there is complete silence concerning him, and his name finally appears, surrounded with deeper apparent mystery, in the fifth, sixth, and seventh chapters of the Epistle to the Hebrews. We there learn that his parentage was unknown, his genealogy unrecorded, and the beginning and ending of his priestly office unchronicled. It is not surprising that in this ancient and enigmatical personage many saw a divinely appointed type of Jesus Christ as the great High-Priest and eternal King. For hundreds, perhaps thousands, of years this unique being has been the subject of earnest discussion. It is almost unpardonable temerity to undertake to answer the question asked in the title of this discourse. We may, however, devoutly study the passages of Scripture in which his name occurs; and we may firmly hold the conclusion forced upon us, when these Scriptures are interpreted without prejudice, and with all the lucidity which the Holy Spirit may give as the reward of their reverent study.

His Name and Office.

Profoundly suggestive is the name of Melchizedek, "King of Righteousness." The name indicates that the Canaanitish language was probably Semitic. This title seems to be personal, rather than official, like the words Pharaoh and Augustus. He is also called "King of Salem"—

the king of peace. Regarding the location of Salem we shall have occasion later to speak; the name, however, is beautifully suggestive in connection with this mysterious king-priest. We are also told that he was "the priest of the most high God." It is a deeply interesting fact that the word *cohen*, priest, occurs here for the first time in the Bible, and it is observable that it is found in connection with the worship of an ancient people outside the chosen people of God. There will always be doubt regarding the etymological meaning of the word. Usually the priesthood of the patriarchs was simply that of the head of the family; but here we have a priest performing solemn priestly acts not limited by the family relation. The appearance of this title indicates the existence of a constituted worship not belonging to what was afterward known as the Mosaic cultus. Perhaps, indeed, the Mosaic ritual was a fuller development of a system of worship which existed from the beginning. Significant also is the name here given to God, "the Most High God"—literally, *El Elion*. This name for the supreme Deity occurs only here; the word *El* signifies the strong One, and is usually applied to God in connection with some qualifying attribute. It recognizes God as the exalted and the supreme One. Probably under this name Melchizedek worshipped the true God.

Various Opinions.

In all periods, alike of Jewish and Christian history, the personality of Melchizedek has been invested with peculiar awe. Some Jewish traditions declare that he was a survivor of the deluge, and was possibly the patriarch Shem. If he were this patriarch, his great age, his wide experience, his relation to Noah, and his approval by God would all tend to advance his dignity, and to make his authority wellnigh supreme. He could readily be conceived of as virtually the undisputed lord of the whole land, and as entitled to convey the possessions under his control to Abram, who received his benediction. Jerome devotes much space to the discussion of the person, position, and territorial dominion of Melchizedek, and he states that it was the prevailing opinion in his day, among the Jews, that Melchizedek was the patriarch Shem. Some authorities ascribe this opinion also to the Samaritans who, although opposed bitterly to the Jews in many things, agreed with them in making Melchizedek none other than Shem. The article on Melchizedek in Smith's Bible Dictionary states that this opinion was embraced by Luther, Melanchthon, Broughton, Selden, Lightfoot, Jackson, and many others. This writer further reminds us, that Origen and others believed that Melchizedek was an angel; it is thus easy for us to see how great reverence would be paid by Jews and Christians alike to such a character as Melchizedek. But a careful examination of the passages of Scripture in which his name appears will show that there is no good reason for believing that he was either the patriarch Shem or an angel from Heaven. Others have thought that he was the incarnation of some power, virtue, or influence of God; but this idea was sharply opposed by other Christian teachers honored for great learning and devout piety. The bold conjecture has been made that he was the Holy Ghost. Still others have affirmed that he was the Son of God appearing in human form. The great Ambrose seems to have adopted this view, and it has found favor among many modern teachers. A former member of the Calvary Church, and a very learned man in many languages, philosophies, and religions, tenaciously held this view. It was always interesting and instructive to hear his reasoning on this subject, and to observe the reverent enthusiasm with which he traced the stately steppings of the Christ in that mysterious land and ancient history. Akin to this Christian idea is that of some Jews that Melchizedek was the Messiah. We all believe that Christ appeared occasionally in temporary incarnations before he became the Son of Man in Bethlehem's manger. That he appeared to Abraham, to Jacob, to Moses, to Joshua, and to Gideon, there can be but little doubt. If we refuse to believe that Melchizedek was a true man, nothing could be more natural than to suppose that he was the Christ. The language of the writer of the Epistle to the Hebrews, some have thought, favors that idea. Melchizedek is there spoken of as without father or mother, and without beginning of life or end of days. We shall, a little later, see that there is a much simpler, more natural, and more literal interpretation of that language, which frees it from giving its authority to the idea that Melchizedek was the Messiah. There have been still other opinions as to his identity, such as that he was a descendant of Ham, or Japhet, or Enoch; but it is needless to multiply these unwarranted and unscriptural guesses, and some of them are not only unscriptural but contrascriptural.

The Teaching of Scripture.

Many of our difficulties in interpreting Scripture are not really in the Scripture itself, but in men's unwarranted additions to Scripture. It is often far harder to understand some human comments on the Scriptures than it is to comprehend the teachings which these comments were intended to elucidate. It is often much more difficult to interpret some so-called Christian creeds than it is to understand the Scripture on which they are supposed to be based. He was not an ignorant man who said, while reading Bunyan's "Pilgrim's Progress," that he got on very well with the large print, but he often found it impossible to understand the notes at the bottom of the page.

We often need to read Scripture afresh; to read it as if the Bible were a book just issued from the press; to read it with the interest which attaches to Dr. Nansen's recent volumes, or to the life of Lord Tennyson. If we were in this way to read the passages bearing on baptism, there would be no further controversy in the churches on that subject. The Bible cannot make its teachings clearer, both as to the subject and the act of baptism. If Christ and the apostles had intended to teach that believers are the only subjects of baptism and immersion is the act in baptism, they would have used the very language which they have employed. The Greek is the most accurate and philosophical of all languages. It has a word meaning to sprinkle and one meaning to pour, but neither is ever employed regarding baptism, but always the word meaning to immerse. But many men read the commands regarding baptism, not to get out God's thought, but to put in their own wish; such reading of the Bible is not *exegesis* of the divine thought, but is *eisegesis* of the human desire. Too many read the Bible through spectacles of tradition and prejudice. No book suffers in this way as does the Word of God. A similar remark will apply to the teaching of the Bible regarding Melchizedek, and many other persons and subjects. Many of the difficulties in interpreting the Bible are of human manufacture; and so many of the objections made by agnostic critics are not really against divine revelation, but against human misinterpretation.

Let us study the Scripture references to this mysterious king. The first one is Genesis xiv. 18-20. Abram is returning from his pursuit of Chedorlaomer and the kings who were with him, and who had taken Lot and others as captives. Abram had now become bold and heroic. When in Egypt he was distrustful and pusillanimous; but now the spirit of family loyalty and divine obedience is strong in his soul. He won a glorious victory. He brought back Lot and the goods which had been taken, as well as the people. This expedition excited great attention, and won general admiration among the Canaanites, and the victorious band was hailed with joy as it returned in peace. Abram surprised all by the brilliant military genius which he displayed. We were prepared to see in him gentleness, benevolence, and magnanimity; but we scarcely expected to see him the leader of heroic exploits, such as we are accustomed to associate with the names of Miltiades, Cæsar, Cromwell, Napoleon, and many brave Britons and Americans of recent days. The king of Sodom went out to meet Abram, and he is filled with admiration over the success of this dashing expedition. Abram is now in the valley of Shaveh, or the level valley, which is the king's dale. This name it may have received because it was used for military exercises and kingly sports; perhaps it was also a place of great beauty, and it may have been associated in all subsequent times with the historic events here narrated. There Abram is met by Melchizedek, king of Salem. He is a much more illustrious personage than the king of Sodom. He is commendable for his personal excellence, his peace-loving disposition, and his religious spirit. He refreshed Abram with bread and wine. He thus expressed his gratitude to Abram, who had won for the land freedom, peace, and prosperity. It is simply ridiculous to find here any direct reference to the Lord's supper. What could this ancient king have known of that ordinance? The bread and wine may have been not only for the refreshment of Abram and his followers, but also as a symbol of the divine blessing. They thus recognized God as the true author of the military successes which had been achieved. Melchizedek combined in himself the offices of priest and king, as was not uncommon in patriarchal times; he was, as he has been called in this discourse, a "king-priest." Balaam was a prophet and Melchizedek a priest among heathen people. God thus, in marvellous ways, caused His light to shine among the benighted nations. The title given to Melchizedek is never given to Abram, and because he was thus honored above Abram, the "father of the faithful," and the "friend of God," many Jewish and other commentators have considered that he must have been a supramundane being, and that his priesthood must have been something quite other than the patriarchal priesthood. The fact also that Abram paid him tithes, tenths, emphasizes this opinion. These were the usual offerings to God, and were a recognition of the divine priesthood of Melchizedek. His priestly benediction on Abram tended also to confirm this opinion. No other priestly act is recorded of Melchizedek, but still others he may have frequently discharged. His hospitality was simply in harmony with the customs of that ancient time and country.

In Psalm cx. 4 we have the words "Thou art a priest forever after the order of Melchizedek"; and in the seventh chapter of Hebrews we have a full reference to Melchizedek, and an argument founded on the facts there stated. But none of these references justify us in supposing that he was Shem; for Moses has continually spoken of Shem under his own proper name, and why should he now speak of him under another name?

The writer of the Epistle to the Hebrews tells us of Melchizedek that he was "without father, without mother, without descent, having neither beginning of days nor end of life." He could not, therefore, have been Shem, for his genealogy is clearly given in Scripture and is traced to Adam. Both the name of Melchizedek and that of the city where he reigned were most appropriate to one who was priest and king, and the predecessor of the Messiah. There would be very little difficulty in the account in Genesis, were it not for the reference to Melchizedek in Hebrews, and the questions which that passage has aroused. The question has often been asked, Where was Salem? Jerome makes Salem to be identical with a town near Scythopolis or Bethshan, which in his day was called Salem, and in which were extensive ruins which were called those of Melchizedek's palace. But it is now more common to make Salem Jerusalem. It was probably called Salem at that time; it is so called as late as the time of the psalmist. In Psalm lxxvi. 1, 2 we read: "In Judah is God known; his name is great in Israel. In Salem also is his tabernacle and his dwelling-place in Zion." Later it was called Jebus, because it was possessed by the Jebusites, and later still Jerusalem.

The valley of Shaveh is the valley east of Jerusalem, through which the Kidron flows. Josephus asserts the identity of the two places, and he also asserts that the king's dale is in this immediate vicinity. We thus locate the place where Melchizedek met Abram, and we have an historical setting for Melchizedek himself.

Not the Messiah.

That he could not have been the Messiah is clearly seen from the language of the Epistle to the Hebrews. If he were the Christ, it could not be said with propriety that he "was made like the Son of God," for that would be saying that he was made like unto himself. Neither could it be said that Christ was constituted a priest "after the order of Melchizedek"; for that would be affirming that he was a type of Himself. A natural interpretation of this passage shows conclusively that he was not the Messiah. The statement that he was without father, without mother, and without descent, etc., has really in it no serious difficulty of interpretation. We know that in the estimation of the Jews it was very important that the line of the priesthood should be carefully kept; that all their genealogies should be accurately preserved, and that the direct descent of their priests from Aaron should be capable of conclusive demonstration. But the writer affirms that in the case of Melchizedek there was no such genealogical table; that there was no record of the name of his father or mother; that he suddenly appeared, then mysteriously disappeared, and that thus he stood alone. He once crossed the track of Abram, as we have seen, at a most interesting time in the patriarch's life. He is then lost to the sacred writings for a thousand years; then, in a few words, he appears for a moment in the ancient psalm as a type of the coming Lord. He came again out of the shadows in the Epistle to the Hebrews, and then retired into eternal silence. The writer of the Epistle is discussing the priesthood of Christ; and, as a priest, he, like Melchizedek, stood alone; his name is not in the line of priests; he pertained to another rather than to a priestly tribe; his ancestors are not mentioned as priests, and as a priest he had no descendants.

Thus, like Melchizedek, he had a lonely conspicuity; as a priest he was absolutely unique, except for the likeness to Melchizedek. The genealogy of Christ as a man can be traced, but not as a priest; and it is His priesthood which is the subject of discussion. Melchizedek may have had a very honorable ancestry, but it is not recorded, for the names of his ancestors nowhere appear in the records of the priestly office. In like manner his descendants were utterly unknown; so far as the genealogical records go, he was without descent. Under the Mosaic dispensation the law determined all things pertaining to the priestly office; and in the time of Moses the Levites were required to serve from the age of thirty to fifty; after passing fifty they were relieved from the more arduous duties of their office. Later they began their service at the age of twenty. But the writer of this Epistle tells us that regarding Melchizedek nothing of this kind occurred. No one knew when he entered on his office, and no one knew when he retired from it. So far as the records go—which were kept so carefully in all other cases—Melchizedek was without beginning of days or end of life. There is no difficulty at any of these points; we have really put the difficulties into the record, instead of finding them already there. After having disappeared for a thousand years, since the time of the psalmist, a reference to Melchizedek appears to teach the Hebrew Christians that it was the purpose of God to abolish the Levitical priesthood. Christ's priesthood is above that of Aaron and all priests. Melchizedek was a priest not by inheritance, but by divine appointment; so was Christ. Thus Christ was a priest not after the order of Aaron, but after the order of Melchizedek. This statement suggests the harmony between the priesthood of both as brought out in the 110th Psalm. The points of resemblance between the priesthood of Christ and Melchizedek are very striking. Neither was of the Levitical order; both were superior to Abram; both were kings and priests; both were kings of peace and of righteousness; and, so far as priestly records are concerned, neither had beginning of life nor end of days. Abram recognized in Melchizedek one higher in official standing as a minister of religion than himself. Abram gave Melchizedek the " top of the heap," as the Greek word rendered spoils in Hebrews vii. 4 literally means. After a battle the Greeks were accustomed to collect the spoils into a heap, and before they distributed them to themselves, they took off a portion from the top and gave it to the gods. So Abram honored Melchizedek; so in all things Christ ought to have the preëminence.

Josephus has probably given us the correct view of Melchizedek; he makes him a Canaanitish prince, a man of noble character and godly life. He seems to have been a man raised up by God in an unlikely environment. He was a man whose genealogy was veiled in mystery, so that in this particular, as in other respects, he is a type of Christ. All God's true children are kings and priests unto God. The lowliest son of God in our day is vastly higher in the kingdom of heaven than was even Melchizedek. We are heirs of God, and joint heirs with Jesus Christ. We are a preserved people for a reserved inheritance. In some sense, the very angels are our ministering servants. Let us rejoice in our high honors, and loyally perform our lowliest duties.

When we return weary from some fierce conflict, there will be some servant of our divine King to minister refreshment in the hour of need. Like Abram we shall eat and be strengthened. Although Melchizedek could have had no thought of the Lord's Supper, we can in that ordinance rejoice that Christ gives Himself to us as the Bread of Life. To us, as weary pilgrims and as tired soldiers, He comes forth to cheer us in the path of duty. The weary march and the heavy fighting fit us for His divine companionship in the sacred ordinance. Fierce temptations assail us, the blood of the battle stains us; but the hour of refreshment assuredly will come.

Let us strive to be God's servants for the refreshment of our fellow-servants. Beautiful was Melchizedek as a type of Christ in his priestly and regal service. Moses did not claim to be either priest or king. David would not intrude into the priestly office. But we are both priests and kings.

Melchizedek in his quiet, pure, and mysterious life may never have realized the great honor which was put upon him when in refreshing Abram he became a type of Christ. He gave to God the honor of Abram's victory. Let us give God similar honor. Let us render similar service to our fellow-pilgrims, and let us ever lay our crowns, here and hereafter, at the pierced feet of him who was the Lord of both Abram and Melchizedek.

XII.

WAS THE DESTRUCTION OF SODOM NATURAL OR SUPERNATURAL?

XII.

WAS THE DESTRUCTION OF SODOM NATURAL OR SUPERNATURAL?

The destruction of Sodom and the other cities of the Jordanic circle, as given in Genesis xix. 23-28, is one of the most solemn events recorded in Scripture. The physical features of this terrible disaster are deeply impressive, and the moral lessons are profoundly instructive. It is quite certain that Sodom was a place of considerable importance. Like the other four cities of the plain, it had a king of its own, and it clearly was the chief town of the Pentapolis. Its name has gone throughout the world as the synonym of degrading vice. These Jordanic cities are first named in Genesis x. 19 as belonging to the Canaanites. They are next mentioned in Genesis xiii. 10-13 in connection with the choice made by Lot, when he and Abram stood together between Bethel and Ai. Before them, and distinctly in view, was at least a part of the "circle of Jordan." Then it was conspicuous for the abundance of its streams, the greenness of its grass, and the attractiveness of all its features. It is spoken of at that time as a "garden of Jehovah." The "ciccar of Jordan" is frequently mentioned as the technical expression used to describe these towns.

Meaning of Sodom.

It is difficult to be absolutely certain as to the meaning of the name Sodom. Some writers affirm that it means "burning"; but others equally learned make it mean "vineyard"; and still others connect it with a word meaning to enclose or to fortify. Probably the word burning better than any other expresses the meaning, although it is possible that the name has this meaning from the subsequent catastrophe. It may, however, be true that fire had already passed over this valley previous to the great destruction now under consideration. In the account which we have of the battle of the kings, we are told in Genesis xiv. 10 that "the vale of Siddim was full of slime-pits." This expression denotes places where petroleum, which became by evaporation bitumen, oozed out of the ground, or places which had been excavated in securing bitumen to be employed as cement in the construction of the houses erected here. In Deuteronomy the place is spoken of as never again to be inhabited; and in several Scriptures it is referred to as a place where no man was abiding, a land turned to ashes, as overthrown and burned, and as cities in ashes at the time of the writers. The fate of the cities is referred to in the New Testament as a solemn warning to those who should live ungodly. Our Lord makes the punishment of those who reject His gospel, and who refuse to listen to His disciples, as worse than that of the people of these doomed cities. Josephus speaks of the five cities whose ashes appear even in the fruit of the valleys which these cities once occupied.

Location of These Cities.

Once it was very common to suppose that the site of these cities is the basin now occupied by the Dead Sea. This supposition makes the Dead Sea to have been caused by the fearful catastrophe which destroyed the cities. The idea was that the Jordan ran through the entire length of the Ghor or valley from the base of Mount Hermon to the Gulf of Akaba. This theory was long maintained with great tenacity, and the evidence in its support seemed to be reasonably strong. It is now, however, abandoned by the most careful students of the locality and of the Scripture narrative. The subject, it is admitted, is surrounded by considerable difficulty; but although Burckhardt discovered the valley of the Arabah between the Dead Sea and the Red Sea, and so gave probability to the idea that the Jordan once flowed through this valley to the Red Sea, until the convulsion which overthrew the cities, the theory is now seen to be untenable. It is admitted that it is an attractive theory; but almost midway between the two seas there is a watershed seven hundred and eighty-seven feet above the ocean level, and north of it streams flow into the Dead Sea, and streams to the south flow into the Gulf of Akaba. It is also affirmed, as the result of careful measurements, that the Gulf of Akaba is thirty-five feet higher than the Mediterranean Sea; it is, therefore, more than thirteen hundred feet above the Dead Sea and the Jordan valley. Dean Stanley has well said that a convulsion which would have depressed the valley of the Jordan so far below the Mediterranean would have shattered Palestine to its centre. Perhaps the whole valley, from the base of Hermon to the Red Sea, was once an arm of the Indian Ocean or adjoining seas. When changes came, which caused the sea somewhat to subside, the three lakes now found in this valley were left with the Jordan as their connecting river.

It is still difficult, notwithstanding all the discoveries that have been made, to locate with certainty these cities of the plain. Josephus speaks indefinitely of Sodom, but he refers to Zoar in such terms as to suggest that it was at the south end of the sea. Eusebius uses language of the same general purport. This was the opinion of most travellers during the Middle Ages, and is still that of the majority of modern visitors and topographers. Dr. Edward Robinson is very clear and emphatic in his affirmations to that effect. We know that the southern end of the sea is quite distinct from all other parts as to its depth; the northern part of the lake being thirteen hundred feet deep, and the southern being only thirteen feet deep, indicating that this latter part is of recent formation. The name Usdum, given to the ridge of salt at the southwest corner, seems to locate Sodom. The name Amrah, given to a valley among the mountains in this general neighborhood, it is easily seen is a modification of the word Gomorrha. Mr. Tristram, however, for a time gave it as his opinion that the cities were at the northern and not at the southern end of the sea; but later he modified this view, and adopted the traditional opinion in its stead. Dr. Selah Merrill, whose long residence in Palestine, and whose careful study of all its features, give his opinions weight, locates the cities at the northern end, and Sir J. W. Dawson adopts the opinion of Dr. Merrill in this regard. With the utmost modesty, and yet with considerable certainty, the traditional view is presented in these lectures. It is not plain, as was once the current opinion, that these five cities were submerged in the lake. It was once affirmed that the walls, columns, and capitals of great buildings were discerned below the water; but that opinion is now virtually abandoned by all whose authority is of any weight. It is not even certain that the destruction was caused by an overflow of water; the probability is that the overflow of water was a comparatively unimportant element in the catastrophe. It is affirmed by those who favor the northern end of the lake that Abram and Lot could not see Sodom as they stood between Bethel and Ai, except the cities were located at the northern end of the lake. But it should be borne in mind that if they saw a part of the circle, that fact would meet all the requirements of the history. Neither is the account of the invasion of the five kings conclusive evidence that the cities were at the northern end of the lake; nor yet is it convincing as to that location when reference is made to Abram's view of the evidences of destruction as he witnessed them from some point near Hebron. The Scripture reference to Zoar gives great weight to the traditional view that the cities were at the southern end of the lake. No one can carefully note the differences between the depths of the lower part of the lake and its other portions, to which reference has been made, without feeling that some terrible catastrophe produced the portion of the lake below the Tongue, or El-Lisan.

The Dead Sea.

In studying this sea we must entirely divest our minds of all the superstitions which are attached to it by all mediaeval and by some modern travellers.

The idea that no bird could fly across the surface without immediately perishing, and that the touch of its water was fatal to health, and even to life, is an utterly groundless and even ridiculous superstition. Ignorant monks are largely responsible for these foolish and false notions. There is not in them a single element of truth. Whether seen in sunshine or storm, the Dead Sea is an impressive and beautiful sheet of water. Its waters are pellucid to a remarkable degree, and they are also free from the pollution common to many of our inland lakes. The neighborhood of this sea before the destruction of Sodom was a favorite resort for invalids and pleasure-seekers, and it would not be at all surprising if it should once more become an attractive place for travellers, and, at certain seasons of the year, for invalids. Great hotels may yet be erected on its shores, and lines of railways may carry travellers to its vicinity. Nothing can surpass the brilliant colors seen in its direction and over the mountains of Moab as one looks out over both from the Mount of Olives. The brilliant tints in Holman Hunt's "Scapegoat" are not an exaggeration of the glowing colors over sea and mountains under the rays of the setting sun. No one who has enjoyed that sight will ever forget the glory of the burnished mountains and the resplendent sea. The enormous evaporation explains in part these atmospheric effects, which transform sea, mountains, and sky into a fairyland of wondrous splendor and glory.

Its Names.

The Dead Sea is a name entirely unknown to Bible writers. They call it the Salt Sea, the Sea of the Plain, the East Sea, and once simply The

Sea. The Greeks and the Romans called it the Asphaltic Lake. The absence of living creatures in its waters, and the supposed deadly influence of its neighborhood, led to its being called the Dead Sea. The Arabs call it Bahr Lut, or the Sea of Lot. Until after the fearful catastrophe, with which its name is associated, no notions of horror attach to its name. The valley of the Dead Sea and of the Jordan is between fifteen and sixteen miles from Jerusalem. The Mediterranean Sea is twenty-six hundred feet below Jerusalem, but this descent is spread over about thirty-five miles; recent and skilful measurements show that the Dead Sea is thirteen hundred feet below the Mediterranean, and almost four thousand feet below Jerusalem, although the distance is less than half that to the Mediterranean. Sir J. W. Dawson informs us that the descent from Jerusalem to the Jordan is about the rate of one foot in twenty feet. The differences in climate are correspondingly great. One may leave a temperate climate at Jerusalem, go fifteen miles, and find a tropical climate at the Jordan; one may leave, as was true in January, 1884, snow-drifts five feet deep at the Jaffa Gate at Jerusalem, go fifteen miles to Jericho, and find there a warm and even a sultry atmosphere. The marked diversities in climate and soil in Palestine must have had a great influence on the habits and character of the people. The Dead Sea occupies the lowest part of the crevasse, about two hundred and fifty miles long, reaching from the foot of Mount Hermon to the Gulf of Akaba. The Dead Sea is forty-six miles long, and is over ten miles wide at its greatest breadth. Its area is three hundred square miles. It receives numerous perennial streams and winter torrents on the east and south, besides the full stream of the Jordan, which pours into it, it is estimated, six million tons of water daily; and this entire amount is carried off by the great evaporation. It is not difficult to see how the hot and dry atmosphere is capable of absorbing this enormous quantity of water. The sea has no outlet, visible or invisible. In the nature of the case, it cannot have an outlet, except there be, as was once supposed, a great pit at its bottom, leading to the centre of the earth. It is the most depressed sheet of water on the globe. Lake Urmia in Persia, seven miles from the town of Urmia, is said to be more salt than the Dead Sea, and Lake Elton, which is on the steppes east of the Volga, and which supplies a great part of the salt of Russia, is also, perhaps, more salt, although it is difficult to get authoritative figures. The great Salt Lake of Utah has marked features in common with the Dead Sea; and this physical likeness confirmed the early Mormons in the belief that this salt sea and its river Jordan were indeed parts of a second land of promise. The American salt sea is daily losing its saltness, and what the final result will be it is difficult to determine. The fish, which are carried down by the Jordan to the Dead Sea, die almost immediately, and even fish accustomed to the Mediterranean die soon in the Dead Sea. The Jordan pushes its brown waters for a considerable distance into the sea, but it soon loses its vitality and becomes sluggish. In the afternoon a deep haze rises and hangs over the sea and the vicinity, and it may be well likened to "the smoke going up forever and ever."

The huge barrier of fossil salt, which is at the south end, accounts in part for the saltness of the sea, and the great evaporation of fresh water completes the result in that direction. The waters are usually placid, and are quite inodorous, blue, limpid, and beautiful. The degree of saltness depends naturally upon the nearness of fresh-water streams pouring into the sea. The waters have a heavy and oily aspect. A gallon of distilled water weighs ten pounds; a gallon of Dead Sea water twelve and a quarter pounds. A large part of this extra weight is chloride of sodium, or common salt; chloride of magnesium causes the bitter taste, and chloride of calcium gives it its oily feeling. So dense is the water that floating is easy, but sinking is difficult; swimming is also difficult, as the feet constantly rise to the surface. One rolls about in the water like a cork tub, and one can almost sit in it as he would in a rocking-chair. Horses experience strange sensations in it, as their feet constantly rise above the water. Irritation of the skin often results from bathing, especially if there are abrasions of the skin, as there are sure to be in a country where insects so abound. In 1848 Lieutenant Lynch, of the United States navy, spent three weeks in a survey of the Dead Sea. It is said that, while coming in metallic boats into the sea from the Jordan, he met a gale, and the heavy waves struck the boat as if they were the sledge-hammers of Titans. Ducks occasionally may be seen floating on the water, utterly contradicting the mediæval theory regarding the water and its immediate atmosphere. Bare mountain ranges flank the sea, rising from fifteen hundred to two thousand feet.

Great quantities of bitumen, sulphur, and musca are found on the shores; from the latter souvenirs are made and offered for sale in Bethlehem and Jerusalem; this substance takes on a fine polish, and will burn like cannel coal, but emits an almost intolerable odor. The low promontory called "El-Lisan," the Tongue, pushes westward and northward into the sea from the eastern shore; it is ten miles long and from five to six miles wide. The greatest depth of the sea is thirteen hundred feet, but south of the Tongue the circular bay, as already remarked, is only about thirteen feet deep. The depth of the sea varies considerably according to the season. It is certainly a remarkable sheet of water. Lake Sir-I-Kol is fifteen thousand six hundred feet above the level of the sea; this is the most elevated sheet of water on the globe, and it is well called by the natives, *Bam-i-duniah*, meaning "the roof of the world." The river Oxus rises in this lake. As it is the most elevated body of water, so the Dead Sea is the most depressed. Beautiful as it is in many respects, it is still a steaming caldron, and so great is the evaporation that it can never be filled to overflowing. The most impressive thought in Norway, as one watches the splendor of the midnight sun, is that of deep and almost holy awe, in the midst of the profound silence and the golden sunshine of the midnight hour. In like manner, a sense of death-like silence, of deepest awe, and of the consciousness of a holy presence impresses the mind and heart as one stands by the shores of this mysterious sea.

PHYSICAL CAUSES OF THE CATASTROPHE.

To the discussion of this thought all previous remarks have tended. Here we are to see the meeting of the natural and the supernatural. If we find adequate physical causes for the fearful cataclysm, let no one say that we on that account deny the supernatural element in the destruction of Sodom. God can avail Himself of His resources stored up in the heart of the earth as truly as of His resources in the region vaguely called the heavens. They are inadequate, and often inaccurate, interpreters of the Scriptures who refuse to see the presence of God in the physical as well as in the spiritual forces employed. These interpreters are often unfair to those who see God as truly on earth as in heaven. The men who say that if we give due place to physical phenomena we are disloyal to the Scripture and its divine author; who say that if Jonah goes the Bible goes, the church goes, and Jesus goes, are guilty of extreme folly, alike in their interpretations of and deductions from Holy Scripture. We firmly believe in the historicity of the story of Jonah, but if it could be proved that the story were not historic, neither the Bible nor Jesus would go. We firmly believe that the divine character and mission of Jesus Christ do not depend for their reality upon any man's interpretation of the story of Jonah. Men who make statements of this kind play directly into the hands of unbelievers; such men do all in their power to give away much of their case. Unbelievers will attack the outposts of these men, and perhaps carry some insignificant place of defence, and then, in harmony with the admission of these interpreters, unbelievers will claim that they have captured the citadel.

We may believe that the Bible does not say, when fairly interpreted, that the sun and moon stood still at the command of Joshua; indeed, we may be unable to discover that Joshua really ever gave such a command. Do we therefore deny the supernatural? Are we therefore infidel toward the Bible and disloyal toward God? Who has the right so to assert? In adopting such an interpretation we may be simply showing our loyalty to the exact teaching of the Bible and our devotion to its divine author. Personally we may believe that ravens fed Elijah at the brook Cherith; but if another interprets the word *orebim*, translated ravens in our common version, to mean, as it may mean, with slight vowel changes which no sensible man considers to be authoritative, "Arabians," or "merchants," or "the people of Orbi," a neighboring town, what right have we to charge him with denying the Bible? He may be only the more strict in his adherence to the Bible. Some men think that if we deny or doubt their interpretation of certain difficult passages we are disbelievers of the Bible and no better than publicans and sinners. Their word they deem to be virtually God's word. Who made these men masters in Israel? Whence gained they such wisdom? The more unscholarly they are the more authoritative do they become. Spiritual insight into the Bible is one thing; it is the chief thing in studying certain passages. But other parts can be understood only by accurate scholarship as the result of prolonged and devout study of history, philology, archeology, and related sciences. Certain peripatetic evangelists are largely responsible for these unscholarly interpretations, illogical deductions, and unscriptural affirmations. However good their intentions may be, the practical result of their methods is to weaken the authority of Scripture, and to dishonor its divine Author.

In discovering the attendant physical phenomena in the destruction of Sodom we recognize God as the God of heaven and earth, and recognize this fearful catastrophe as perfectly natural, so far as regards the means employed, and as entirely supernatural so far as regards their employment at that time, for that purpose, and in the severe degree which secured the result. We are told in Genesis xiv. 10, as we have already seen, that slime-pits abounded in this vicinity. What are slime-pits? Simply petroleum wells. Wherever bitumen abounds eruptions are liable to occur. Petroleum exudes from the rocks, both on the sides and on the bottom, of the Dead Sea; it is then hardened by evaporation, and asphaltum is formed. We know that this plain was liable to earthquakes and volcanic eruptions from the earliest times of which we have any record. We know that the Dead Sea sends up great masses of asphaltum, especially when earthquakes occur, as in 1834 and in 1837. Sir J. W. Dawson is as loyal, humble, and devout as a believer as he is learned, accurate, and fearless as a scientist; and he shows that this valley was subject to conditions which frequently obtain in the oil regions of our own country and Canada. He shows that a few years ago, in the oil district of Petrolia in Canada, a borehole struck a reservoir of gas which rushed up with tremendous force, carrying with it a great quantity of petroleum. This gas at once took fire, rising in a tall column of flame, and burning petroleum spread over the ground, setting fire to many tanks in the vicinity. A village was burned, and several lives were lost; a whirlwind was caused, which carried dense smoke into the air, and soon burning bitumen fell in showers. This is almost an exact description of what happened in Sodom when it is said that God rained upon it brimstone and fire, that is, burning brimstone, out of heaven. The description of the destruction of Petrolia is in many features a description of the destruction of Sodom. Nothing is more certain than that science supports the Bible. Prof. G. F. Wright, of Oberlin College, a man who stands high in the ranks of scientists, shows clearly in his volume, "Scientific Aspects of Christian Evidences," that the whole region about the Dead Sea has the appearance now of being an abandoned "oil district," and that all the conditions for the catastrophe described in the Bible were present in the inflammable accumulations of oil and gas reservoirs.

We have only to suppose that at the time of the destruction quantities of gas and petroleum existed below the plain; then their escape through a fissure would produce the results described. These combustible materials might be ignited by lightning falling upon them, or by a convulsion in the earth. Rising into the heavens, they would then fall like fiery rain upon the earth. There would be an eruption of saline water forming a brine thick with mud. Lot's wife, no doubt, was overtaken and suffocated by this saline storm, and her body was so encrusted as to become not a pillar, but, as the original has it, a mound of salt. The exhaustion of these subterranean reservoirs would cause a subsidence of the earth, and all the facts described in the Scripture would follow in the most natural way. We do God and the Bible great injustice when we shut out the natural phenomena from their appropriate share in this supernatural event. God is as much the God of the earth beneath as of the heaven above. Every unprejudiced geologist must see that the narrative in Genesis is in perfect harmony with the geological features of the district. Nothing but the occurrence of the events could have given rise to the narrative, and from a scientific point of view the account is wonderfully harmonious with all the facts which scientific investigation has discovered in the neighborhood. In giving appropriate place to these physical phenomena we not only do not detract from the miraculous character of the catastrophe, but we give it the greater prominence, because we see that in the soil itself God had stored up all the forces for its production. There is nothing in the Bible narrative suggestive of the wild myths which have often been associated with this overthrow; but all the statements are in the fullest accordance with the physical possibilities of that historic valley.

LESSONS.

We see here how God can punish sinners with physical forces associated with their own sin. We see also the danger of looking back. Looking back leads to going back, and going back is perdition. Obedience would have saved Lot's wife; disobedience wrought her utter bodily destruction. It is possible to be nearly saved and yet be wholly lost. Anxiety for salvation is not salvation. Conviction is not conversion.

Sin may abound amid the most charming environments. Early civilizations gathered about beautiful locations. Civilization without spiritual religion is weakness and danger. God has hidden fountains of judgment about every man's path. Destruction may come in every walk of life.

Even the righteous with difficulty are saved. Angels had to lay hold of Lot and hasten him from Sodom. Lot was saved as by fire, but his whole nature was contaminated by his evil surroundings. Stay not in the plain. Look not backward to Sodom, but forward and upward to Jesus.

XIII.

DID GOD MEAN THAT ABRAHAM SHOULD REALLY OFFER ISAAC?

XIII.

DID GOD MEAN THAT ABRAHAM SHOULD REALLY OFFER ISAAC?

The account of the trial, triumph, and reward of Abraham's faith is found in the twenty-second chapter of Genesis. Abram has now become Abraham, and Sarai has become Sarah, and this change in the names indicates a new relation to God, and suggests a new development of their character. We have passed through several stages of great interest in the remarkable life of the "friend of God." We have seen him leaving country and kin at God's call; and we have seen him in the land of strangers because of the stress of famine. We have seen him returning to his own country, and being separated from Lot, who selfishly sought richer pastures for his numerous flocks. We have seen Abraham winning superb victories over plundering kings and marauding hordes. We have seen him in the midst of grievous doubts about his posterity; and we have seen him surrendering his paternal affection in relation to the son of his bond-maid. We have seen him rejoicing in the possession of a son, whose mother was Sarah, and whose birth was in fulfilment of glorious promises from God.

But we are now to see him passing through the most difficult experience of his heroic career. It is always fascinatingly interesting to see illustrious characters in trying situations, conquering great difficulties, and rising superior over subtle temptations under the inspiration of great moral principles. Abraham seemed at this time to have been approaching the serene evening of his troubled life; the early morning was over, the ruffled noon had passed, and a calm and triumphant evening seemed to have come. But just then the severest trial he had ever known came upon him like a thunderbolt out of a clear sky. The most appalling ordeal now summons him to a new test of faith. The intensity of the strain which he must suffer baffles all description; it even exhausts all our power of thought. The terrible blow must be struck with his own hand. God's precept seems to be antagonistic to God's promise. Never did so terrible trial come to a child of God, and never did a child of God win a more glorious triumph.

The Severe Trial of Abraham's Faith.

All the circumstances of this trial combine to make it extremely severe. To be the means of putting a human being to death as a holocaust was a terrible thought. Perhaps Abraham was not unfamiliar with human sacrifices as offered by the Canaanites and the early Chaldeans; but the peculiar nature of his trial must have severely tested his faith in God as a holy Being. Could God give a command to any man to destroy his own child? Was not Isaac the child of special promise and hope? Did not the future salvation, temporal and spiritual, of millions rest upon his life? Could God give a command which should involve such fearful consequences? The thought of offering any one in sacrifice is terrible; but when the victim is his own son, and such a son as Isaac, the command is ineffably severe. The language of the command must have lacerated the heart of Abraham to its very core. Isaac is called "thy son," "thine only son, Isaac, whom thou lovest." The terms of this command must have gone like sharp swords to the soul of Abraham; they must have pierced his heart, even as his knife was to pierce the body of Isaac. It would be difficult to imagine a greater accumulation of affectionate terms for testing parental love. But we must not suppose that God did this "to tempt" Abraham in the ordinary meaning of the word tempt. The word is here used in the sense of *try*, *prove*, or *test;* in the Revised Version the word is correctly translated "did prove." The ordinary meaning of tempt is to solicit to evil, and in this sense, as the Apostle James teaches us, God tempteth no man. The Hebrew word *nissah* is, without doubt, correctly translated *tried*, *tested*, or *proved*. All God's children must pass through severe trials of their faith, and Abraham can be no exception. God had only one Son without sin;

but God did not have even one Son without suffering. But God graduates our trials according to our strength. Abraham is now able to endure a trial of great force, for he has already developed a sublime moral heroism. The language of the command must have been so understood by Abraham that Isaac was to be offered, not simply as a spiritual self-surrender, but really as a burnt-offering. Sublime, indeed, was the faith which did not stagger at this command! It is true that at this time no formal prohibition, like that of the Mosaic code, had been issued against human sacrifices; but every instinct in Abraham's heart, as the father of Isaac and as a son of God, must have opposed his obedience to the command, except for his triumphant faith in God's wisdom, love, and power.

The divine origin of the command adds to the severity of the trial. It is distinctly affirmed that it was God who proved Abraham's faith. Could a God who was just and holy issue such a command? This question might well tax Abraham's faith; it sometimes taxes the faith of men even to this hour. This command has been a fruitful theme of cavil with the enemies of divine revelation through all the centuries. It is positively affirmed by some that it is utterly inconsistent with the attributes of a holy God. Some have endeavored to remove the difficulty by declaring that the entire narrative is mythical; some that it was merely a subjective impulse on the part of

Abraham; and others that it was directly inspired by Satan. But it is not too much to say that these suppositions are more difficult of belief than is the plain statement of the narrative. God as the Author of life can take it away as it pleases Him without any shadow of injustice. He did not give life to Isaac upon the condition that it was to be taken away only by the event which we call death. The conduct of Junius Brutus, who passed the sentence upon his own children that before his eyes they should be beaten to death with rods, has been justified by reputable historians and moralists, because of the circumstances of the case. Brutus owed this duty to his country. Did Abraham owe less duty to his God? Abraham seems now to have been on intimate terms with God; he readily distinguished the voice of God from all other voices. It is the high dignity of a moral being that he is placed in circumstances of moral probation. God had a lofty purpose in applying this heart-searching test to Abraham, and only He who knows the heart and who is holy, just, and good, can determine the right tests which are to be employed for reaching the highest moral ends.

The event does present many and great difficulties, but it also suggests reasonable explanations. We cannot suppose that Abraham was in error in believing that God called for the actual sacrifice, but we know that this was an exceptional command for a unique occasion. We know also with absolute certainty that this command does not authorize human sacrifices; on the contrary, the result shows that God virtually prohibits human sacrifice. We must bear in mind also that God never intended that the command would be literally executed. He knew from the beginning what the result would be; He foresaw the faith of His servant, and He knew when He gave the command that He would intervene at the right moment to save the father's heart and the boy's life. His purpose was to test Abraham's faith. This signal instance of unquestioning submission to the will of God has been a shining light upon the path of many to cheer them in the way of obedience. Had the impulse been from Abraham's own mind, desiring to rise above his heathen neighbors in the value of his offering, the narrative would not represent God as giving the command. Abraham is to rise to loftier heights of faith than he had yet attained; his faith is to be perfected. He must not trust in the life of Isaac, but rather in the promise of God. He must give his son up as if he were dead, so that he may receive him as a gift from God, who, as the writer to the Hebrews tells us, Abraham believed could raise him from the dead.

But there is a still higher thought which must enter into this whole discussion. The difficulty is largely removed when we consider that there is here a typical reference to the sacrifice of Christ. When the heathen practised human sacrifices their act implied their sense of the insufficiency of animal sacrifices. The true idea of sacrifice was fulfilled in Christ of whom Isaac was only a type. Isaac's sacrifice was not accomplished; it foreshadowed its completion in Jesus Christ, who in the fashion of man became obedient unto the death of the cross. We must see, indeed we cannot help seeing, this fuller meaning in this ancient narrative. In John viii. 56, Jesus, when addressing the unbelieving Jews, said: "Your father Abraham rejoiced to see my day; and he saw it, and was glad." On what occasion in Abraham's life could these words so fittingly have their application as in his constructive offering of Isaac? It is not here said that Abraham rejoiced to see Christ Himself, but to see His day. This must imply that it was the peculiar day or hour in Christ's life which gave that life its essential character, which Abraham actually saw. What was that day or hour but the one to which Christ so often referred as "my hour—the hour," the time when he was betrayed into the hands of sinners? The laying down of his life constituted Jesus the Redeemer of the world. When Abraham constructively sacrificed his only son, he saw Christ's day as at no other time in his life. This is the natural interpretation of our Lord's reference to Abraham. If the entire significance of this mysterious command of God was a trial of Abraham's faith, that result could have been secured without directing Abraham to the place which later was the site of Jerusalem, and to offer up his sacrifice on or near the very spot where afterward the Son of God gave His life for the redemption of men. Without at all forcing the natural meaning of Scripture, we cannot help seeing in Abraham's sacrifice a suggestion of the love of God which led Him to give His "only begotten Son" for a lost world, and in the obedience of Isaac we cannot fail to be reminded of Him who bore His cross to Calvary and died thereon as a willing sacrifice for the sins of men.

THE TRANSCENDENT VICTORY OF FAITH.

This was the grand crisis, the crowning event, the glorious victory in the history of the patriarch. He was called to a high destiny; he has already been taught to believe in God on His bare promise; and he has been taken into covenant with Jehovah. More and more does the glory of God shine in his faith and devotion. He is now to show that he is as one born again, that he is dead to self and alive to God. But he would have been less than human if this terrible test did not cause him indescribable pain. But his obedience was prompt; he rose up early in the morning and prepared for the journey. What a morning that must have been in Abraham's tent! See him starting with his young men and Isaac, the wood being prepared for the burnt-offering! Did he tell Sarah of the command? Perhaps he had not the courage; her affection for Isaac might have overpowered Abraham's faith. What wonderful thoughts must have been in his tender, obedient, brave, but breaking heart! The brief, sententious, and somewhat broken clauses of the narrative at this point finely set forth his calm deliberation and his unflinching heroism. No one better than he could have appreciated the apparent inconsistency between the divine precept and the divine promise concerning Isaac; but faith gloriously triumphed. Still the moral difficulty of offering a human sacrifice remained; and its only solution was in the divine command. The divine Creator, within the limits of absolute rectitude, will do right even though human reason cannot understand the divine action. The story is told with exquisite simplicity. The distance from Beersheba to Moriah, the Salem of Melchizedek, is about forty-five miles. Perhaps the first day was somewhat broken by the necessary preparations; we may, therefore, assume that they travelled fifteen miles that day, twenty on the second day, and on the third day they would come early within sight of the appointed place. Jewish tradition tells us that the place was indicated by a cloud of glory or a pillar of fire. Behold the solemn procession! Was there ever such a journey taken on this earth? Abraham commands his young men to remain behind while he and the young lad go forward to worship. He dare not open his heart in speech in the presence of his servants. They might have interposed to prevent the execution of his purpose; they might have believed that he was actually beside himself. On what grounds did Abraham intimate that he and the lad would return to the servants? Was this an act of pardonable dissimulation? Was it a somewhat confused utterance? Was it not rather an unconscious prophecy? Was it not still more fully the voice of his all-conquering faith? He must conceal his full purpose from his servants. There is wonderful pathos in the words of the seventh verse, "my father" and "my son." Did not Abraham even now account that God was able to raise his son even from the dead? Behold Isaac with the wood of the burnt-offering upon his shoulder! Josephus reports the tradition that he was now twenty-five years old; he certainly was old enough and strong enough to resist if his spirit had not been sweetly obedient. We cannot help beholding in him a type of our blessed Lord bearing His cross, perhaps to the same place. A silence, both dreadful and mysterious, must have fallen on both father and son, which was broken by Isaac's question regarding a lamb for a burnt-offering. This question must have gone to Abraham's heart with terrible pain. If his heart could have relented, that question from his beloved and innocent boy would have melted it into compassion. Only the scenes of Gethsemane and Calvary surpass in pathos and tenderness this journey to the sacrificial altar. Surely it must have dawned upon Isaac that he was himself to be the sacrificial victim. Wonderful is Abraham's reply, "God will provide Himself a lamb for a burnt-offering." This is the utterance of heroic faith and not pious dissimulation. Silence then seems again to have fallen upon both as they went on together; it was a terrible moment for father and son. Isaac seems to have assisted in all the affecting preparations for the proposed sacrifice. Then he is bound, and the mighty secret, which must have been suspected by himself and with difficulty was concealed by his father, is fully divulged. Isaac now knows that he is the destined victim. As noble as is Abraham's faith, so heroic and divine is Isaac's obedience; truly he also "was led as a lamb to the slaughter." We are grateful that the sacred historian has drawn a veil over this affecting scene; we shall not rudely lift that veil; we shall not coarsely describe this painful, solemn, and sublime event. We cannot but see illustrations of the unspeakable love of God and the unresisting obedience of the Lamb of God as the sacrifice for sinners. Abraham is thoroughly in earnest. With unhesitating promptness he stretches forth his hand to slay his son. We almost shudder as we approach the terrible crisis, and nature shrinks back at the fearful spectacle. At this crucial moment the Angel of Jehovah interposes for Isaac's deliverance. In this fearful moment the awful mandate is countermanded. The title given to this divine messenger shows that he was not a created being, but a divine personage, who often appears in the narrative under the title of Angel of Jehovah, or the Angel of the Covenant.

Just then a substitute is found in the ram caught in the thicket by his horns; thus God provided Himself with a burnt-offering. We cannot help seeing here a foreshadowing of Christ, who was the true sacrifice, even from before the foundation of the world. Faith in God was the secret of Abraham's great triumph. There was danger lest he should trust in Isaac rather than in God to fulfil all of God's great promises. He now shows that his faith rested on the bare word of God as the ground of all his hope. Such an act of self-sacrifice is of the highest value. It teaches lessons of the utmost importance. It has proved a school of faith throughout all countries and centuries. From the terrible ordeal Abraham came forth like gold tried in the furnace. We may almost hear God addressing him in these suggestive words:

> "All thy vexations
> Were but my trials of thy love, and thou
> Hast strangely stood the test."

The Divine Approval of Faith.

The voice from heaven declares that God does not accept human sacrifices. Man is rather a doomed culprit than an appointed victim. The intention was enough to show Abraham's faith, and that test had been conspicuously given by actual experiment. Abraham's voluntary surrender was the keystone in the sublime arch of his faith, which still stands before the world giving Abraham praise and God glory. God interposed at the right time. It has been well said, that if His interposition had been sooner, Abraham's faith would not have been fully tested; and had it been later, Isaac's life had not been saved. God accepted the will for the deed, the arresting voice being heard when the knife was ready to strike. The ram was then substituted for Isaac. Abraham rises here almost to a divine height, for in his intent he withheld not his only son, and yet in fact he offered a substitute. We may well see in Abraham's act a shadow of the love of God who spared not His only Son; and in the substituted ram we see an emblem of Him who, as the Lamb of God, gave Himself as an offering for sinners.

God's approval was shown in the new name given to the place—Jehovah-jireh, the Lord will provide, or will see. The name was thus changed from Moriah, which by interpretation meant "the land of vision," a name probably given from this event, in reference to the remarkable vision or manifestation of God which was there made, and to which fuller allusion is found in the new name Jehovah-jireh. There are many interpretations of both these names; the latter name is in some sense a proverb; it declares that on the mount of Abraham's sacrifice Jehovah would afterward reveal a greater sacrifice for the salvation of His people. It clearly suggests that "man's extremity is God's opportunity." This prophecy had many fulfilments and applications, but it was literally fulfilled in the manifestation of the divine glory in Solomon's temple, and later in the incarnation, death, resurrection, and ascension of Jesus Christ. Some believe that Calvary and Moriah were identical; this we cannot affirm with certainty, but the lessons taught by both are substantially similar. He who provided a ram has since provided the atoning Lamb, of whom this ram was a type. Thus it was that Abraham saw Christ's day and was glad. In the Mount, in the highest experience of trial, God will appear to deliver His saints. Abraham has now reached a great moral elevation; the angel of the Lord, therefore, confirms with great solemnity all the special promises already made. Abraham's offspring, instead of being cut off by the death of Isaac, will be as the stars of heaven and the sand of the seashore. He shall also have a great territory and vast temporal power and influence. He takes his place at the head of the faithful and as a type of the justified. He shows that he deserves the twofold title, the father of the faithful and the friend of God. Thus it comes to pass that the lessons of Moriah and Calvary sweetly blend. East of the Church of the Holy Sepulchre a spot is pointed out with the idea of connecting the sacrifice of Isaac with the crucifixion of Christ.

Just at hand there is an ancient thorn-tree, which is usually covered with the rags of pilgrims, and tradition affirms that it is the thicket in which the ram was caught. Some writers have gone so far as to see in the thorn-tree a shadow of the crown of thorns. We need not dwell upon these fanciful allusions, but we can rest securely upon the great fact that the deepest significance of this offering of Isaac is found in the sacrifice of Jesus.

Additional Teachings.

We may learn from this most interesting history that trials are sure to come to the greatest as well as to the humblest of God's saints. All God's children must pass through deep waters; but God has promised that the waters shall not overflow them. They all must go into some fiercely heated furnace; but it is certain that a divine presence will be with them, so that the flames shall not consume even their garments. God has not promised to save His people from trial, but to make them victorious over trial. Sanctified trials separate the chaff from the wheat; they consume the dross and so purify the gold. They develop character, ennoble life, and prepare for heaven.

We see also in studying this narrative the blessedness of trusting God. It is evermore true that the time of greatest trial gives the opportunity for exercising the sweetest trust. Abraham would never know the blessedness of receiving Isaac as one raised from the dead had he not trusted God with unquestioning faith. Not until the summit of the mountain is reached can we behold the grandest display of God's glory. He who withholds nothing from God will by a blessed experience realize that God withholds nothing from him.

We here behold with new beauty and radiant glory the true Lamb of God provided as an offering for sin. Abraham may not have understood this great truth in all its fulness, but he certainly had some glimpses of the glory that was to be fully revealed. In some sense Isaac bound and laid upon the altar was a type of man's helplessness; in another sense he was the type of Christ as the deliverer. All the sacrifices of the olden time pointed to Jesus as the Lamb of God, who taketh away the sin of the world. Past every type and shadow, past every symbol and offering, let us look away unto Jesus, the author and finisher of our faith.

XIV.

DID REBEKAH AND JACOB CHEAT ISAAC AND ROB ESAU?

XIV.

DID REBEKAH AND JACOB CHEAT ISAAC AND ROB ESAU?

We now enter, in the twenty-seventh chapter of Genesis, upon the study of one of the most picturesque and pathetic stories in the Bible. It is a story which at one time makes the eye moist with tenderness, and at another time makes the heart throb with indignation. But whether it excites our praise or blame, it never fails to secure our interest. It attracts childhood and old age with equal force, and holds both with a resistless charm. The inspired historian tells the story fully and frankly, but without any comments of his own. A thoughtless reader might suppose that the sacred writer considered the conduct of Rebekah and Jacob to be simply a dexterous trick, not involving any great moral delinquency. But the later development of the story shows plainly how a just God punished the sins of all concerned; and we thus learn instructive lessons as to the baleful results of fraud and deceit. We see plainly that no one can oppose God and prosper.

Preparations for the Paternal Blessing.

Isaac was now growing old. He evidently had fallen into physical, mental, and spiritual feebleness. It is clear that Rebekah anticipated his speedy death, but he surprised her by living still for more than forty years. He did not seem to understand that in the purpose of God Jacob was heir to the promises. He seems to have been stricken with some sharp malady, as well as increasing blindness; and, like most other men, he was unduly alarmed by his physical symptoms. Perhaps he had not fully learned of the command of God to Rebekah concerning her sons; neither may he have known of the transference of the birthright of Esau to Jacob. He therefore makes arrangements for bestowing the paternal blessing on Esau; and so he called Esau to him—*Esau beno haggadol,* "Esau his son the great"—meaning the greater or older of his sons. Notwithstanding Esau's undutiful conduct in marrying into the people of Canaan, his father still treated him with great and even culpable partiality. He directed Esau to take his weapons, *kele,* a word signifying implements or utensils of any kind; and it is probable that our English word weapon originally had this broad meaning, and was not limited to instruments of warfare. He instructs Esau to go out to the field and secure some venison. The expression in the original, as Dr. Bush has pointed out, is striking; Esau is to "hunt me a hunting," *tzudah li tzayidah*—that is, game of whatever kind. The result shows that a kid of the goats might have sufficed, but a cunning hunter like Esau would naturally prefer game to kids. The Orientals were and are fond of highly flavored and luxurious dishes, and this is implied in the Hebrew which we translate, "savory meat." The original is *matammim*, from a word meaning to taste. There is almost no end to the salts, spices, garlics, and onions of Oriental dishes; thus sweet and sour, oil and acid, combine to mystify the dish and to enhance its value in the judgment of the Oriental palate. This Hebrew word means delicacies of any kind which would be grateful to the taste of Isaac, whose appetite, as the result of his illness, needed tempting. There is little doubt but that there was also a religious significance in the meal of which he desired to partake. It was probably part of a religious solemnity; it was in some sense a sacrifice offered by the recipient of the blessing, and thus it would be considered as a ratification of the proceeding. Thus Jacob killed two kids of the goats, although one would have been sufficient for the meal. In addition to the religious idea involved, Isaac's spirits would be revived and his vigor increased by the delicacies, for the solemn work of bestowing the parental blessing. We thus see Isaac preparing to perform his part in discharging the solemn obligations which belonged to his position. As Elisha demanded the influence of music before speaking the word of the Lord, so Isaac sought to secure the necessary physical vigor and inspiration for this great occasion.

Rebekah's Wily Stratagem.

Rebekah overheard Isaac giving his instructions to Esau. She, doubtless, was greatly excited. A crucial moment in the family history had arrived; a sad domestic drama is to be enacted; plotting and counter-plotting are to be the order of the hour. When Rebekah sees Isaac about to bestow the blessing on Esau, she determines to trust her own skill and deceit rather than God's wisdom and purpose. Perhaps she thought she was justified in using deceit to forward God's plans; perhaps she saw no other way to prevent Isaac from thwarting the divine purpose; and perhaps there was a strange mingling of blamable maternal jealousy and commendable faith in the divine and prenatal oracle. It is possible that she did not clearly distinguish between the good and evil in her motives. She is a resourceful woman; she is master of the duplicity characteristic of her family. She braves the indignation of Isaac, the anger of Esau, and the displeasure of God. Her course was deplorably wicked; it ought never to have an apologist. It was an act of cruel deceit toward her husband, of great guilt toward Esau, and perhaps of even greater wrong toward Jacob; but it was most of all a signal offence against God. Her conduct has found apologists, but the result showed that it never received the approval of God. She was equally weak and wicked in supposing that the fulfilment of God's promise required treachery on her part. Her policy was hopelessly crooked, and wholly at variance with the trustfulness and honesty of a true child of God. She distrusted God, and endeavored to accomplish His purpose by utterly unrighteous means. She is a proficient in the arts of dissimulation; she adopted the satanical and Jesuitical maxim that the end justifies the means. She was impiously daring in commanding Jacob to obey her voice, and in her willingness to assume God's curse. One is startled at her words and acts. She loved Jacob unwisely; she rightly recognized that he was the birthright son, and she also remembered Esau's reckless and contemptuous treatment of the privileges of the birthright; but nothing could justify her in the wrongs she did. She was the cunning mother of a cunning, though cowardly, son.

Progress of the Plot.

Esau has now gone to the field to hunt for the venison; the way is therefore clear in the home for the course of deception which Rebekah has determined to pursue. Jacob, in harmony with his timorous nature, views the matter more coolly than does his mother; he sees and rightly estimates the dangers in the way, but he is far more concerned that he may be safe than that he may be right; he cares only for the risk, and not for the sin of the course proposed. He is not concerned with the enormity of his offence against God. He fears that he shall seem to his father as a deceiver, *kimtataa*, as one that causeth greatly to err, as a very deceiver. The original is most emphatic; perhaps it includes the idea of despising or mocking another. He may have no objections to the imposition on his senile father or his open-hearted brother, but he is greatly alarmed lest he should be detected in his frauds, and so a curse and not a blessing should come upon him from his father. Rebekah might have gone to Isaac, if she found that he was determined to give the birthright to Esau, and might have urged him to follow the counsels of God. The temptation which came to her was in its essence that which came to our Lord in the wilderness, when Satan offered Him the kingdoms of the world if he would give Satan His homage; it is the temptation which comes to all of us in every walk of life; it is the temptation which we must resist with holy indignation, or before which we shall fall in hopeless subjection.

Jacob's Acquiescence.

Rebekah assured her son that she would take the curse upon herself. She ran a fearful risk in making such a declaration, and she thus manifested a low tone of moral sentiment. She could not take Jacob's curse, even if she would; only the compassionate Saviour of sinners, who bore our sins in His own body on the tree, can take the curse upon Himself. Her words, perhaps, show great faith in the divine prediction, but they magnify rather than minify the fraud which she purposes to practise upon Isaac.

It is simply astonishing that in the form of solemnization of matrimony in one of the prayer-books, a petition is offered that the man and woman entering into this sacred relationship should live together as did Isaac and Rebekah. Doubtless this petition is based upon the monogamy characteristic of Isaac and Rebekah, as distinguished from the polygamy of that day; but it is, to say the least, a most unfortunate prayer to be offered at the marriage ceremony. When one remembers the domestic drama in that ancient family, and the painfully unwifely conduct of which Rebekah was guilty toward her invalid and blind husband, one would surely prefer some other prayer on such an occasion. Rebekah's greater force of character entirely overcame Jacob's hesitancy. He goes to the flock and secures two kids of the goats, and Rebekah determines that with all the witchery of her cookery she shall make Isaac believe that the delicacies which he desired are now prepared. She is thoroughly master of the situation; and Jacob was both her tool and accomplice. She prepares goodly raiment, *hahamudoth*, desirable garments, with which to impose further on her husband.

She also will cover Jacob's hands and neck with the skins of the kids so as to make him appear the more like Esau. It is well understood that the Oriental camel goats, as they are called, furnish a wool that is soft and silky, and of a much finer texture than that of the European goat. This wool was often used as a substitute for human hair. Rebekah will leave nothing undone to carry out her plans. She could readily impose upon the dim sight and the dull touch of the blind invalid.

A Dramatic Scene.

The scene at this point is as striking as it is sad. It is difficult to surpass the spirit of deception practised by Jacob at this point. The father wonders at the haste with which Esau has returned; he wonders, also, whether this can really be his son. And now Jacob deliberately and repeatedly lies to his father, at this solemn hour and in connection with this solemn event. We must call things by their right names; we need not be more solicitous for the character of Jacob than is the Bible. Doubtless by some mental and spiritual legerdemain he justifies himself. Augustine and others attempt to justify his conduct on the ground that he already had purchased the birthright. We do not wish to criticise with undue severity a fallible man whom God designed greatly to honor; but none of the patriarchs can be taken as models for our conduct. They lived under a primitive and very imperfect code of morals. The Bible nowhere justifies the conduct of Jacob and Rebekah; if the Bible had been written by uninspired men, this story had never been told. Uninspired writers often magnify and even create the virtues of their heroes; and they often minify and even deny the vices of their heroes. But while the Bible sets down naught in malice, it dares tell the truth and the whole truth. Jacob even went so far as to bring in God as sharing in the deception he had practised. He found the venison so soon "because the Lord thy God brought it to me." The original is here very striking, *hikrah lephanai*, made it to occur, or caused it to come before me. Jacob here uses language expressive of a special interposition of Providence on his behalf. But Isaac is not yet through with Jacob, and his falsehoods must be repeated. Isaac's ear denotes the difference of tone, although his eyes give no testimony. A thrill of alarm must have filled Jacob's soul as Isaac commands him to come near. Martin Luther strikingly says: "I should have probably run away with horror and let the dish fall." Isaac feels the hairy skin, and it resembles Esau's; still he has a lurking doubt, and in response to his question, Jacob affirms that he is his very son Esau. Had there been a failure at this point, the whole scheme would have failed, but Rebekah guarded against this danger. Jacob was afterward the victim of the deceits which his sons practised upon him in connection with the coat of Joseph.

True religion is not responsible for Jacob; it was the lack of true religion which made him deceitful. He had not yet passed through that experience which we understand by conversion, but which was his at the brook Jabbok. True religion was no more responsible for this act than it was for Paul when he persecuted the believers in Jesus. In Jacob we find the quiet patience of his father, and the grasping selfishness and unholy acquisitiveness so characteristic of his mother's family. It was diamond cut diamond when these two Hebrews, Laban and Jacob, were driving a bargain. We ought ever to remember that God's promises and purposes never necessitate, certainly never justify, fraud and falsehood on the part of men. God can accomplish all His purposes without wrong-doing on the part of His creatures.

The Paternal Kiss.

In verses 26 to 29 we see that the paternal kiss is given and the paternal benediction bestowed. One would think that the father's kiss would have burned the son's cheek. Isaac smelled the smell of Jacob's raiment. We know that often in blind men the sense of smell helps them to recognize objects. As Jacob was supposed to have returned from the field, it was expected that his garments would smell of the chase. It is still common in many parts of the Orient to distinguish persons by smelling the crown of the head or other parts of the body; of an amiable man it is often said: "How sweet is the smell of that man; the smell of his goodness is universal." Thus Isaac smelled and kissed him. The kiss was the sign of affection, the token of friendship, and, in some sense, a symbol of homage. And while he kissed Jacob the odor of Esau's garments, impregnated by aromatic herbs, excited the sensibilities of the aged man and inspired him to pour forth his benediction. Jacob was to receive the fatness of the earth, the dew of heaven, the homage of nations, and to exercise lordship over his mother's sons.

Esau's Return.

A thrilling scene comes before us. Esau unexpectedly returns. Clandestinely Jacob had received the blessing. No wonder we read: "Isaac trembled very exceedingly." The painful illusion is dispelled, the abominable deception is discovered, and the guilt of wife and son is revealed. Isaac's emotions must have been absolutely overwhelming. A just indignation must have filled his soul. He must at the same time have been conscious of his own wrong in allowing his unwise love for Esau to lead him to disobey God. Years before, he was willing to trust God, even to laying himself upon the altar of sacrifice. But the benediction had been given, and it cannot be recalled. He now saw that it was God's purpose that the blessing should continue in the line of Jacob rather than in that of Esau. Esau's grief is distressing; and we cannot but sympathize with him in his terrible disappointment, even though we blame him for despising his birthright. There is an obvious reference to Jacob's name when Esau said: "He hath supplanted—*yakebani*—me these two times." Jacob's name, *yaakob*, Esau here interprets, and it can not be denied that there was ground for these reflections upon Jacob the supplanter. But Isaac has a blessing for Esau also. With his name was long associated dominion by the sword and great power among the people. To him a pastoral life is distasteful, as it was afterward with his race. The Edomites were long independent, but were conquered by David and others. Rebekah is obliged to urge her beloved Jacob to flee to Laban, her brother, and there remain until Esau's wrath shall abate. She was the cause of much of the sorrow in her family, and she suffers retributive chastisements. She parts with Jacob, not to see him for twenty years, if ever after; and even in this parting with him she artfully plans so as to conceal from Isaac the worst features of the case.

Lessons.

We see by this ancient story the danger that men may sin even while seeking a worthy end. All the parties to this domestic tragedy sinned against one another and against God. Isaac sinned by striving to set aside the will of God, because of his unwise partiality toward Esau. Rebekah sinned by distrusting God, and by practising abominable deceptions. She did evil that good might come. Her course was evil, and that continually. Jacob sinned in a most revolting way, in the transaction by which he secured the birthright.

He took a mean advantage of Esau's hunger, and robbed him of that which should have been dearer to Esau than life itself. He sinned in obeying his mother rather than God, and one sin led to another, until his falsehood became profanity, making God a partner in his crime. Esau sinned in despising his birthright and also in his marital relations. We have no right ever to make God's supposed designs the rule of our conduct. God does not give us His prophecies as maxims for the government of our actions. We are simply to do right, even though the heavens should fall. Parents are in danger of cherishing an unwarranted partiality for sons or daughters, and against this tendency they must ever be watchful.

We learn, also, that sin must evermore be punished. Punishment followed according to the most natural laws all concerned in this guilty transaction. The best men and women are compassed with infirmity; sinless perfection does not belong to this life. The old Greek tragedies show us the close relation between crime and punishment, between sin and sorrow; they teach this lesson as truly as it is taught even in the Bible. In the end wicked schemes prove abortive; in the end the deceiver is himself deceived; "the engineer is hoist on his own petard." Jacob suffered from the cupidity of Laban, and afterward from the deception of his own sons. Terrible was the sorrow of Rebekah as she parts, probably forever, from her beloved Jacob. As the chief offender, she probably was the chief sufferer. Whatsoever we sow that shall we reap; that is one of the most solemn statements in the whole Bible. As God lives, the man who sows the wind shall reap the whirlwind. Thank God! there is forgiveness with Him, if we but turn to Him in penitence and faith.

We read that "Esau found no place of repentance, though he sought it carefully with tears." We must not suppose that Esau, wishing to repent, could not; the meaning clearly is that he sought for his father's repentance, in the sense of a change in his purpose; but all his tears could not change that purpose. He sowed to the flesh, and he could not expect to reap the fruit of the spirit. We sympathize with him in his great and bitter cry, and in contrast with his dashing conduct we stigmatize the mean cupidity and commercial sharpness of Jacob; but Esau's cry is simply that of one who did not heed God's warning, and who despised God's gracious gifts. He threw away his blessing for a mess of pottage, and he cannot now get it for a flood of tears. Happy are they who know the time of grace, and who do not despise the opportunity of mercy. Esau's tears are too late; he must reap as he sowed. We also have a great and glorious birthright, and we also may lose it for some temporary pleasure. Adam and Eve sold theirs for a little fruit. God help us not to choose baubles for diamonds, earth for heaven, time for eternity, and self for Christ!

XV.

WHO WAS THE WRESTLER WITH JACOB AT JABBOK?

XV.

WHO WAS THE WRESTLER WITH JACOB AT JABBOK?

In the 32d chapter of Genesis we have an account of the turning-point in the life of Jacob. We here see another wonderful event in the stirring career of this historic patriarch. Before this period we observed his cunning devices, his numerous artifices, and his intense selfism, growing out of a weak and defective faith. But after this period we shall notice his great humility, commendable resignation, and beautiful confidence as a child of God and a patriarch of Israel. The old Jacob, with his desire to supplant his brother and his uncle by his commercial shrewdness, disappears; the new Jacob, who is now Israel, appears and remains ever afterward on the historic page. It required much sorrow, many trials, and severe chastisements to eliminate Jacob and to introduce Israel. All the previous events in his life were but the divine preparations for his change of heart and of name. Hitherto his conduct was that of a clever, self-reliant, and not over-scrupulous man; hitherto he has fought with the weapons of human shrewdness and unholy cunning. Now we are to see him relying on God and doing his duty as a follower of the holy One, and as the head of a great race. We are now to enter upon the period which marks his conversion, his regeneration, his consecration as a true servant of God.

Preparing to Return.

His departure from Canaan to Aram was marked by a crisis in his life; so now is his return from Aram to Canaan marked by another and even greater crisis. We are told that on his way a vision of the heavenly host was granted to him; we do not know just how this apparition of angels was made to Jacob. We are, however, fully to believe that these angels, *malakim*, messengers, were not merely human, but truly the angels of God. We may well believe that the occasion was sufficiently important to justify an angelic manifestation. Jacob now has to pass through the land of Edom, which was in possession of his brother Esau. He also had every reason to believe that Esau might be as hostile as he was powerful. God's angels thus came to quiet his fears and to strengthen his hopes. A glorious physical prospect is here before him; fresh verdure and rich pasturage are about him, and as he enters the land the heavenly messengers give him greeting. He now sees that his late deliverance was due to God's providence, and that his future welfare is also under God's watchcare. Twenty years before when, fleeing from his angry brother, he had arrived at Bethel, the mystical ladder, reaching from earth to heaven, and upon it angels ascending and descending, he beheld; and now, as he returns, angel hosts come to defend him should dangers arise. He rightly called the name of that place Mahanaim; this Hebrew word is a dual term implying two hosts or camps. Years before he saw the angelic messengers in a dream, but now he sees them when awake. He recognizes them as the messengers of God, and he names the place Mahanaim from the double host. This place has been identified with Mahneh, and the name was handed down to after ages as a place of sanctuary for the trans-Jordanic tribes. Jacob is still on the heights of the trans-Jordanic hills. These messengers do not seem to have given him any verbal communication, but he could readily infer the object of their mission and so become assured of God's protecting providence. This was truly a glorious vision which was granted Jacob at this crisis of his life. In Psalm xxxiv. 7 we read, "the angel of the Lord encampeth round about them that fear him." The word angel in this passage without doubt means "angelry," the collective multitude of angels. Such a multitude we may well believe Jacob now saw. They surrounded his camp, and their presence and the events which there occurred have made the place historic and even immortal. He is by the brook Jabbok, a word which probably means "pouring out," or "flowing forth," or it may be connected with the word in verse 24, rendered "wrestled." It is now the Zerka, a perennial stream which flows into the Jordan, between the sea of Galilee and the Dead Sea, after a westerly course of about sixty miles. Penuel, where Jacob wrestled with the angel, was a fording-place of this brook. This stream divided the territory of Og from that of Sihon, and it flowed through the region afterward assigned to the tribe of Gad.

Sending Messages to Esau.

Verses 3 to 9 give us the account of the message sent to Esau informing him of Jacob's arrival. We now, again, have the word *malakim* as in the first verse of the chapter, but now referring to human and not divine messengers. This mission was obviously a very wise precaution, for Jacob fears the wrath of his justly incensed brother. Jacob is ever skilful, cautious, and crafty; he knew something of the temper of his brother, and he now knows also something of hi great power. We do not know why or when Esau had removed to the land of Seir. This was Arabia Petrea on the east and south of the Dead Sea, and inhabited originally by the Horites, or "troglodytes," who excavated the singular rock-dwellings found in the vicinity of Petra; this was a place with which Esau had become connected by marriage with a daughter of Ishmael. Probably the gradual enlargement of his domestic establishment and the unfilial deportment of his wives made it fitting that he should not live near his parents; we may also believe that there was a divine purpose in his departure from the land of promise, thus making room for his brother, its divinely appointed possessor. Esau thus acted with the utmost freedom, and yet he was fulfilling the divine purpose in the course he adopted. He had a force of four hundred men with him, and this is a truly formidable company of dependents. He has begun to live by the sword; and, being associated by marriage with Hittites and Ishmaelites, he has become a powerful sheik. What was his purpose in thus approaching Jacob? Perhaps he generally travelled with a large escort; perhaps he is not openly hostile to his brother, but is just in that state of mind when a slight word or act may inflame his wrath.

Jacob approaches him with marked respect and deference; his instructions to the messengers are conciliatory in the extreme. He does not avail himself of the honor of precedency as given in the paternal blessing, but he calls Esau his lord and speaks of himself as "thy servant." He takes great pains to suggest—a very important matter, doubtless, to both—that he does not come in poverty asking help, but in wealth, and so is able to bestow favors. He wishes Esau to know that he has not come to claim "the double portion," and this statement would certainly tend greatly to conciliate Esau. Doubtless it was a time of great anxiety to Jacob; we are told that he was "distressed," *yetzer*, straitened—this term implies that the distress of Jacob was very real; and, without doubt, God intended thereby to quicken His servant's fervency in prayer, and to lead him to cast himself unreservedly upon divine help. We now see Jacob exercising the utmost precaution as he divides his flocks, herds, and camels into two bands; he has determined to prepare himself for the worst while he trusts for the best. If Esau should smite one band the other may escape by flight. We ought not to blame him for taking these precautions; we ought not to say that he ought to trust God without adopting wise measures to help himself. His prudence was as commendable as it was considerable; and he can the more truly trust God after he has wisely helped himself. We see also that he manifested the utmost skill by placing spaces between the droves of cattle. He would thus make the number appear as large as possible, as do the adroit managers of political processions in our own day. He wished Esau properly to estimate the value of the gift. The announcement of the gift to Esau and the expressions of his regard for his brother are repeated in the most artful manner possible. It is asserted that Jacob is Esau's servant, and "behold thy servant Jacob is behind us." Jacob makes sure that nothing shall be neglected which shall appease Esau. Truly Jacob was a Hebrew of rare wisdom, skill, and foresight. These qualities would give him great success to-day in America; he would doubtless take high rank among his fellow Hebrews amid the exciting competitions of our day. Our thoughts turn for the moment from Jacob thus making careful preparation, to his open-hearted brother approaching him with his large escort. Probably Esau had an almost pardonable vanity in showing Jacob how powerful he had become; possibly, also, he wished to protect him from danger on the journey. Esau was always dashing, startling, and chivalrous. There was a decidedly spectacular, and a somewhat Napoleonic, element in his character, an element which almost, in spite of our better judgment, wins our undue admiration. This is the picture of the two brothers. One is planning on the banks of the Jabbok to appease his brother, while that brother approaches him with a powerful company of retainers.

Prayer Following Effort.

Jacob now prays as well as plans for deliverance. He not only uses all his own skill, but he seeks help from God. We have here really a remarkably fine model for a special prayer to God; this is one of the best, as it is one of the most ancient, intercessions with God which we have in the Bible. This successful prayer deserves particular notice. Jacob approaches God pleading his promises for the protection of his people. He lays hold of God's faithfulness as a God in covenant with his people; and thus he appeals to God as his own God in covenant with Abraham and Isaac. He also lays claim to personal mercies and promises. Most beautifully also does he manifest a spirit of deep humility and self-abasement; the prayer is literally steeped in humility; and yet it is as urgent as it is humble. He does not forget in his pleas for deliverance his own unworthiness and God's greatness and holiness. It would be difficult to emphasize unduly the excellence of the spirit which he here manifests. He frankly confesses his sin and invokes God's mercy as an unmerited boon while he prostrates himself in the dust at God's feet; then he earnestly prays for deliverance, making tender reference to "the mother with the children." He identifies himself thus with the entire company, as he was its leader and head. He then pleads God's promise that He would grant him prosperity and crown him with blessing. We have often thought of Jacob, as he has been perhaps unkindly called, as "the father of Jewish guile"; that element, doubtless, was in his nature, but we ought not to forget that he was a faithful lover and a tender father, and that he is now to rise to be a majestic man of faith, and to have his name written with honor upon the imperishable pages of sacred story. Thankfulness was one of the striking characteristics of his faith and his prayer. He traced all his success to God's loving care and gracious providence. We thus see him alone engaged in communion with God on the bank of the Jabbok.

The Mysterious Wrestler.

Jacob is thus alone, as all the others of his company have passed over. We now approach the crisis of the crisis in his life. God has marvellous honors in store for him, and he must be prepared for their reception. He is to have a new name and a new nature; he is to be made worthy of his great place in the Kingdom of God. He has hitherto been a very unsaintly saint; but he is now entering upon a new life and a new consecration to God. Old things are passing away and all things are becoming new. Hitherto he has been self-reliant, self-righteous, self-seeking; thus he bargained and plotted for the birthright; thus he bargained with God at Bethel; thus he higgled with Laban, cheating and being cheated. Just at this crisis, when, perhaps, he had passed over the ford and was seeking a little rest, a strange Being wrestles with him. The word wrestled, *yeabek*, a term occurring only here, is perhaps derived from *abak*, dust. It is supposed by some authorities to be applied to wrestling because of the dust which was excited by the exertions of the wrestlers. The combatants in the Grecian games were glad literally to raise the dust, because thereby they could grasp more firmly the naked bodies of their opponents, which were besmeared with oil. Jacob is still true to his old nature, which has not yet fully passed away; he will fight it out on the line of self-confidence if it take all night to reach a conclusion. He has been a taker-by-the-heel, a supplanter, all through his life; and, true to his character, he closes in with this great Unknown. But this mysterious One touches the socket of his hip-joint, and immediately it is wrenched out of joint. The thigh is the pillar of the wrestler's strength, and now Jacob is absolutely helpless, he can only hang in his helplessness on his conqueror, and thus he will sweetly learn that when he is weak he is strong. He clings to his conqueror and begs for a blessing. His action at this point is profoundly suggestive in its spiritual instruction. Jacob is in the mighty hand of his almighty Vanquisher, who will overthrow the self-trustful Jacob, but who will not deny the prayer of the helpless and trustful supplicant. We know from other Scripture, Hosea xii. 4, that he wept and made supplication, throwing himself in importunate prayer upon the mercy of God.

Who was this mysterious wrestler? He does not give his name to Jacob, but he changes Jacob's name to Israel. In the passage before us the mysterious One is termed a man, but in Hosea xii. 4 he is called "the Angel"; this reference clearly shows us that he was not a human antagonist. In verse 30 he is virtually called God in connection with the name of the place Peniel. Thus he who is at one time called "a man" and "the Angel" is afterward designated by the august title of God. There is not the slightest doubt but that this mysterious wrestler was none other than the Angel of the Covenant, none other than the Son of God, none other than Jesus the Christ. No longer is the patriarch to be Jacob the supplanter, but Israel, a prince and a prevailer with God. Jacob is no match in a contest with God as a wrestler, but as a suppliant he prevailed. The new name and the new nature go together. Jacob needed both, and Jacob now received both. He has now learned that the contest with Esau was nothing, but the contest with Jehovah was everything. Hitherto he had been a clever and pertinacious man; henceforth he is to be the humble suppliant, the devout believer, and the faithful servant. The transaction was profoundly real in Jacob's experience, and was symbolic of Jacob's past, present, and future.

The Face of God.

The word *Peniel* means "the face of God." Jacob so named the place because he had seen God face to face, "*raithi Elohim panim el panim*" ("I have seen the Elohim faces to faces"), had seen him fully and completely, and still lived. He carried ever after the marks of this conflict, for we are told that "he halted upon his thigh." When the Apostle Paul, in the abundance of his revelations, was exalted to the third heaven, he received a thorn in the flesh to humble him; so Jacob received, perhaps, in the sciatic nerve, "the tendo Achillis of the Greeks," a token for a like purpose which he should carry with him to his grave. The Jews to this day abstain religiously from eating of the sinew which shrank, or became feeble, a custom which is a monument to the historical truth of this remarkable event in the life of Jacob.

All true Christians have their remarkable spiritual experiences. The artist has his times of glowing enthusiasm and of almost superhuman inspiration, historians and artists love to visit places historic in their respective departments of genius. The man of letters lingers with fondest enthusiasm on moments of history and art in the world's great historic and artistic capitals. The Christian has his Bethlehems and Gethsemanes and Olivets. All along life's pathway he has his Peniels, times and places when the glory of God shines upon him and the peace of God fills his soul. Peniel may be found in secret prayer, in sacred communion, in the study of the Bible, or in the assembly of God's people. Happy are they who know these experiences which are foretastes of heaven itself. We may yet see God in the face of Jesus Christ and thus find our true life. He who walked in the garden in the cool of the day, who guided Noah, who visited Abraham, who delivered Lot, came finally as the Son of Man to dwell with men. The same mysterious One pronounced the word "Mary," as this devoted woman wept at His sepulchre. It was He who walked with the two disciples on the way to Emmaus. It is He who walks and talks with His children to this blessed hour. It is well for us when we receive some wonderful honor from God, to receive also some memento of humility lest we be unduly elated by our spiritual exaltation. As men heard Jacob's new name and saw his lameness they would be reminded of the spiritual honor which he had received. May our humility ever testify to the reality of our communion with a risen and exalted Christ!

Great trials are necessary to the purification of our faith. But for Jacob's utter helplessness he had never become the prevailer with God. When trials are sanctified they are the richest proofs of God's fatherly love. Let us not hesitate to go into the furnace, if only the Son of God go with us.

He who prevails with God can never be overcome by men. Success in life must depend, as its deepest source, upon the favor of God. What is the mightiest power of our adversaries compared with the almighty power of our God? The might and the wisdom of man are weakness and foolishness with God. Christ's real triumph was in Gethsemane; our greatest triumphs are to be in our closets. If we be victorious there, men will not be victorious over us in the public walks of life. We pray too little. Let us wrestle in fervent prayer with God and we shall never be vanquished by men. The man who fears God so much that he has no fear of men will triumph over every foe. If we be wrestling Jacobs we shall become prevailing Israels. Never was a more glorious night than that of Jacob's on the bank of Jabbok. As the morning dawns the unknown wrestler disappears and the triumph of Jacob is complete. Esau, as the impulsive hunter, passes away. But Jacob, purified by trial and cleansed by grace, transformed from the supplanter into the prince of God, still stands before the world crowned with glory and honor. Let us not be weary in our supplications. Upon us, as upon him, the Sun of righteousness will rise with healing in his beams and undimmed glory in His rays, and we, too, shall be transformed from supplanting Jacobs into prevailing Israels.

XVI.

DID GOD OR PHARAOH HARDEN PHARAOH'S HEART?

XVI.

DID GOD OR PHARAOH HARDEN PHARAOH'S HEART?

Few subjects in biblical interpretation have given rise to greater controversies and more conflicting opinions than the hardening of Pharaoh's heart. This subject has greatly perplexed the devoutest believers, and it has given infidels of every class supposed materials for criticism of God and His holy Word. If we understand the subject rightly, we shall clearly see that neither God nor his Word needs apology on the part of any class of believers. This discourse is in no technical sense a theodicy; theodicean alleviations of this difficult narrative are not really necessary if only our interpretation be correct, if only it be truly biblical. If professional interpreters and all readers would only look at the entire narrative concerning the hardening of Pharaoh's heart in the light of common sense, of daily experience and observation, and especially in the light of a fair interpretation, instead of through the medium of traditional conceptions and unauthoritative creeds, they would have no difficulty in discovering the truth without any intermixture of error. Such an interpretation of God's Word will clearly show that God was no more responsible for the hardening of Pharaoh's heart than He is to-day for the hardening of the hearts of all men who shut their eyes to the light of His Word, and who sear their consciences against the influence of His Spirit.

It will be readily admitted that there are things hard to understand in the statements made concerning Pharaoh; there are also facts difficult of explanation in every man's resistance to the claims of God upon his mind and heart. Unfortunately, the Scripture narrative respecting the Egyptian king has been so interpreted as to cause many to stumble thereat, and others to become fierce opponents of God's way and Word. But it is absolutely certain that a correct understanding of the narrative will greatly lessen the inherent difficulties of the case, and will bring God's treatment of this proud and stubborn king into line with the laws which govern men to-day in their rejection of truth, and in their refusal to do justly toward God and men, and into line also with the natural and inevitable effect of such conduct on their hearts and wills. In speaking of the hardening of Pharaoh's heart, the Bible simply states facts and suggests processes which we are daily witnessing among men now, as in the case of Pharaoh in that ancient day and remote land. A careful study of the texts in which reference is made to the hardening of Pharaoh's heart will show that there was no other influence at work than that which proceeded from his own determination not to lose the services of the Israelites by obeying God in letting them go, as God through Moses had commanded; and that there was no other control over his heart than the action of laws still operant on the hearts of men who refuse to obey God, and whose hearts become hardened by the rejection of the Holy Spirit even to this hour. We are still taught to command men not to refuse to hear God's voice; and we are still taught that by refusing to obey they harden their hearts as truly as Pharaoh hardened his.

Prophecy of the Hardening.

When we turn to Exodus iv. 21, we learn that before Moses had returned to Egypt God had declared of Pharaoh, "I will harden his heart, that he shall not let the people go." At first blush these words surprise us, and suggest that God, by an act of arbitrary and sovereign power, had made it impossible for Pharaoh to obey the divine command given by Moses. We must, however, remember the purpose for which this statement was made to Moses. It was needful that he should be strongly impressed with God's providence in all the events which were to occur; thus the result in regard to Pharaoh is stated at the outset for the encouragement of Moses. This statement was not so much causative as it was predictive. This statement of God resulted from His omniscience, He thereby knowing what would be true in regard to Pharaoh, rather than from God's omnipotence, he thereby being able to cause this result to be true. The purpose of the statement was to prepare Moses for the final result lest he should become discouraged upon a first and second failure, and should renounce the solemn mission upon which he had been sent by God. He is prepared for Pharaoh's repeated refusals, and for the dread ultimatum which finally he will announce to Pharaoh. Moses is to understand that the heart of Pharaoh and of all kings is in the hand of the Almighty who sent him upon this mission.

It is important at this point that we should carefully observe that the Bible, in speaking of the hardening of Pharaoh's heart, employs in the Hebrew original three distinct words differing in meaning from one another, but which, unfortunately, are all in the common version of the Scriptures indiscriminately rendered "hardened." It may be permitted, even in a popular discourse, to explain the diversity of the import of these words. In Exodus iv. 21, the passage already quoted, we have the expression *chazzek eth libbo*, "I will strengthen his heart." The Hebrew word *hazak*, which our version translates harden, literally signifies to strengthen, confirm, embolden, make courageous; it is translated by such words as to excite to duty, to be strong, to persevere. It is placed by Hebrew compilers at the end of some of the books in the Bible to encourage readers to proceed with their study of the sacred writings, and to render the obedience which they require. It is a part of the exhortation of God to Joshua, Joshua i. 7, *rak chazak*, "only be thou strong." It is also found in Joshua's dying exhortation to the people (xxiii. 6) *ve-chazaktem*, "be ye therefore very courageous," etc. No one would think of translating the original in these cases by the word "harden"; perhaps, indeed, the word "hardy" would not be inappropriate to the meaning of the passage before us and its context. If we carried over this meaning to God's words to Moses concerning Pharaoh in the passage under consideration, the thought would simply be, "I will make Pharaoh's heart daring, presumptuous, hardy"; the principle which acts in harmony with God's holy law, and which is rightly termed courageous, becomes presumptuous, dangerous, and defiant when it is opposed to God's will as revealed in His Word. Another one of the three words which is used to describe the condition of Pharaoh's heart is *kabad*, this means "to make heavy"; and the third word is *kashah*, meaning "to make hard" in the sense of difficult, intractable, immovable, stiff, or rigid. We thus see that these three original words differ considerably from one another in their primary significance. When, for the second time, God says (Exodus vii. 3), "I will harden Pharaoh's heart," the announcement was made to Moses just before the beginning of the ten plagues. Moses is thus informed that the course which God would pursue with regard to Pharaoh would harden, and not soften, his heart, would simply make him more obstinate in his refusal that Israel should not go. The result of this process on the part of Pharaoh would make it necessary that Moses should make before the Egyptians still greater exhibitions of the divine might and majesty. The purpose of this announcement to Moses, as before, was to assure him that in assuming these enormously difficult tasks God was with him, and would overrule all things for the deliverance of his people. In these statements regarding the process of petrification of the heart of Pharaoh the statement by God is again predictive rather than causative. The whole purpose, at this point, is to strengthen the faith, quiet the fears, and multiply the hopes of Moses by the assurance of God's presence in the vast undertaking commanded by God and assumed by Moses. When God is spoken of as hardening the heart of Pharaoh, the language simply implies that without the exertion of any positive divine influence Pharaoh should so treat God's command as inevitably, by the operation of perfectly natural laws, to confirm, to strengthen, and to harden himself in his opposition to God. Instead of being humbled by the wonderful displays of divine power, he should be, by his resistance of light and by his wilful opposition to truth, the more determined in his opposition to the mandate of Jehovah. God is said to have done this simply because He permitted it; in no other sense can it be said that He was the author of this hardening. In some sense, as Augustine long ago suggested, God may be said to harden those whom He refuses to soften. If men will not walk in the light that God gives them, they become blind; if they will not listen to God's call, they repel God. Nowhere does God, by an exercise of arbitrary power, make it impossible for men to see the light, to walk in the truth, and to believe the right. When men grieve God's spirit, that spirit withdraws from them, and they are thus left to the consequence of their own wilful and sinful act. In Deut. ii. 30, language is applied to Sihon, King of Heshbon, similar to that here used with reference to Pharaoh, and in both cases we have simply the statement of the result of the disobedience of these two men to the plain commands of God. In Joshua xi. 20, like terms are employed of the enemies of God. They had sinned against the light they had received, and God justly left them to the pride and obstinacy of their own wicked hearts. They chose to retain their idolatry, and God permitted them to be destroyed. Similar sad experiences are being enacted in the history of every congregation, and in the lives of thousands of men to this very hour. We have in the Bible the statement of the operation of these laws; we have all around us to-day the operation of these laws, and if we had its inspired history, the language of the Bible regarding

Pharaoh would be repeated to-day regarding tens of thousands who hear and who reject the gospel of salvation. In the Bible we have a flash from the X-ray of divine truth; that truth is still operant, but we do not see its processes. Any one who will take the pains to examine the use of these Hebrew words in other parts of the Bible will see that they are employed with different shades of meaning, as suggested in this discourse; and he will see that there is a solemn personal danger which still warrants the solemn exhortation of the Psalmist (Ps. xcv. 8), "Harden not your heart." This hardening is here spoken of as a voluntary act on the part of those who reject God's Word, an act for which certainly God cannot be responsible, except He should deprive men of the freedom which is the inalienable right and great glory of manhood.

Pharaoh's Responsibility.

Attention frequently has been called to the fact that while in the narrative in Exodus the hardening of Pharaoh's heart is ten times ascribed, in the sense now explained, to the Lord, it is also several times ascribed to Pharaoh himself (Exodus viii. 15, 32; ix. 34); it is also several times stated that his heart was hardened, without naming the author of the process. We can readily see that the fact when ascribed to God, and then to Pharaoh, is so ascribed in different senses of the word, so that there is no contradiction between the two assertions. It can be ascribed to God only in one of two senses: first, in that He permits it to occur; or, second, in the sense that He is the Designer, Creator, and Supreme Governor of the entire universe, and that the acts of all His creatures may, in some sense, be carried back to Him, either as permitting or causing their occurrence. In the early day God was so constantly thought of as present and active in the government of the world and the control of men that it was natural to refer to Him as the author of all events of whatever kind. But in no respect was God the author of Pharaoh's sin; in no respect is He the author of the sins of men to-day. God does not interfere with the freedom with which men are endowed; if He did so interfere there could be, on the part of men, neither right nor wrong, neither virtue nor vice, neither personal sinfulness nor holiness. It is unfortunte that in our common version only the word "harden" is used to translate the three different Hebrew terms now given and explained; had their various shades of meaning been properly expressed in English many of the difficulties which have arisen would be unknown. The same three terms are used when the hardening is ascribed to God as when it is ascribed to Pharaoh, or when its author is not distinctly stated.

The Progress of the Hardening.

Pharaoh resisted the reasonable demands of Moses for the deliverance of the people, notwithstanding all the wonderful signs which Moses had given him. The hand of God became more and more clearly revealed; finally Pharaoh confessed his wrong. His magicians could, in a measure, convert the rod into a serpent; still they must have felt Aaron's superiority as his rod swallowed up their rods. Before the ten plagues the heart of Pharaoh was hardened; and after each of the first five plagues the hardening is expressly attributed to Pharaoh himself, or is named without specifying the author (vii. 22; viii. 15, 19, 32; ix. 7). After the sixth plague, Pharaoh still resisting, we read for the first time (ix. 12) that "The Lord hardened the heart of Pharaoh." This word really means that "the Lord made firm the heart of Pharaoh; the Hebrew is *jchazzek*. Space for repentance was then given Pharaoh, for after the seventh plague we read (ix. 34) that Pharaoh "made heavy his heart." The third plague utterly overmatched the skill of Pharaoh's magicians; they owned their powerlessness, and confessed the presence of the finger of God. After the fifth plague Pharaoh discovered that not one of the cattle of the Israelites was dead. This difference between the Israelites and Egyptians ought to have removed Pharaoh's last doubt. It did produce a marked impression on the minds of some of the Egyptians, and when the seventh plague was announced, they took steps to protect their cattle against the predicted storm of hail and fire. After this plague Pharaoh owned his sin, acknowledged the righteousness of God and the wickedness of himself and his people (ix. 27); but when the severity of the plague was over he hardened his heart again (ix. 35). The sun of prosperity once more shone forth; and, as the natural sun hardens the clay that had been saturated by rain, so Pharaoh's heart was hardened by the removal of the plague and the occurrence of the respite. He was thus preparing himself and his people for the final catastrophe. He was, by his own voluntary, deliberate, personal, and wicked acts, fitting his heart for the judicial and divine hardening as the natural and inevitable result of the laws of freedom with which he and we are endowed. The progress of evil in the human soul is one of the most solemn facts in human existence. Men who will not use their limbs will one day find that they are virtually unusable; men who will not exercise their memories practically lose their memories; men who will not speak and pray in religious services will largely lose the power of speech and prayer. A species of eyeless fish is found in dark caves; having no use for eyes, they soon have no eyes to use. These are tremendously solemn realities in the experiences of men to-day as well as in the judicial judgment on Pharaoh. These great moral laws sweep through the universe; they are irresistible as gravitation and universal as God. No one can escape their operation. If we come into line with them, they will help us in the development of character for useful lives on earth and for admission into heaven; if we oppose them, they will, by all the might of infinity, utterly destroy us.

Human Disobedience and Divine Hardening.

Let us bear in mind that the words referring to God's agency in the process of Pharaoh's hardening were for the encouragement of Moses, and that the words referring to his own action show his determination to resist God. The wonders and signs performed by God through Moses acting on a better man with a better heart would have secured obedience; but acting on Pharaoh with his haughty heart, cruel nature, and mistaken notions of political economy, simply produced hardness and rebellion amounting to moral insanity. But for his sullen obstinacy, his determined disobedience, and his wilful blindness, his heart had never been hardened; the responsibility of this hardness, therefore, rests with him, and not with God. The same sun hardens clay and softens wax. Do we blame the sun because the clay is hardened? The differences between the two results in the clay and the wax are due to the differences between the two substances, and not to the sun, although it apparently produced these opposite effects. God's providences were by Pharaoh's disobedience the occasion of his hardening; but his own stubborn will and wicked heart were the cause of his hardening. God did not purpose the hardening, in the sense of causing it;

God permitted it, in the sense of letting natural forces and wholesome laws bring about their usual and inevitable result. God uniformly performs good; God may occasionally permit evil. Men may, in the exercise of their God-given freedom, so misuse God's good gifts that they result in evil, and not in good, so far as the will of man is concerned.

Let us thus clearly understand that God's announcement to Moses of the hardening of Pharaoh's heart was not causative, but simply predictive. The fulfillment of the prediction was suspended to give Pharaoh an opportunity to turn to God in penitence, and to the enslaved people in justice. We have seen that five plagues occurred, and still Pharaoh resisted all these remarkable proofs of the divine presence and power; and not until then was the divine prediction against him fulfilled. God restrained His punishment until the cup of Pharaoh's guilt was full. Pharaoh hardened his own heart in determined sin before God hardened it in righteous punishment. Pharaoh was by his own will an obstinate, impenitent, and abominable sinner, before God by His sovereign permission allowed him to be judicially, in harmony with the law of his own conduct, a doomed reprobate.

Practical Applications.

These great truths have their practical applications in the lives of men to-day. The Bible simply declared the process of hardening in the heart of Pharaoh; but a similar process is taking place to-day in the hearts of thousands who listen to the gospel of Christ. If God should fully write the history of many in our congregations, it could be said of them, as truly as of Pharaoh, that they hardened their own hearts in their guilt, and that God permitted this hardening in their guilt, and also that God permitted this hardening in punishment for their wicked unbelief. We know that in the exercise of their freedom men now resist, despise, and oppose God; out of this conscious, obstinate, and determined resistance comes hardness of heart. The moment a man knowingly and willingly disobeys God, that moment the process of hardening begins. God's calls are numerous, tender, and varied. As truly as did Pharaoh harden his heart, so do men harden their hearts at this hour. Their act is voluntary; it is chargeable to themselves, and not to God. In God's name you are exhorted to-day, "harden not your hearts as in the provocation."

The Gospel never leaves men as it finds them; it must either harden or soften. It must either be a savor of life unto life, or of death unto death; and the savor which is life to one, or death to another, is according to the manner in which the Gopsel is received. It is never the intention of God that the Gospel should bring death; but, like every blessing which is rejected or perverted, it works the greater evil when rejected. Pharaoh's heart was once relatively susceptible; then he rejected and opposed God, and so his heart became a stone in his bosom. The Bible tells us that God hardened it, and it also tells us that he hardened it himself; and both statements are true in the senses already explained. When we neglect light and knowledge, they add to our condemnation. Men may to-day pass over into the power of Satan as truly as Pharaoh was in his grasp.

We do not so much need greater proofs of God's will as we need greater willingness to obey His will. Men do not need greater light so much as they need better eyes; the light may be strong enough wellnigh to scorch their eyes, and yet they pretend that they do not see the path of duty. The most astounding miracles could not subdue Pharaoh's heart. Christ could not convince men who would close their eyes to His miracles and their ears to His words. He assured us that some men would not believe, though a preacher to them rose from the dead. The historic Lazarus rose from the dead, and some strove to put him to death. Christ rose from the dead, but some men to-day are so hardened in heart that they will not believe Him.

God will assuredly in the end come off victorious. Resistance to Him will end in our utter defeat. Each pleading invitation rejected will add to our guilt; each gentle admonition refused will increase our insensibility. The Apostle Paul tells us of certain persons who were "past feeling." Open your hearts to-day to listen to God's call, lest the time may come when God will say, "Because I have called, and ye refused; I have stretched out my hand, and no man regarded"; "I also will laugh at your calamity; I will mock when your fear cometh." God forbid that it should be said of any who hear or read these words: "Then shall they call upon me, but I will not answer; they shall seek me early, but they shall not find me: for that they hated knowledge, and did not choose the fear of the Lord."

XVII.

WAS THE PASSAGE OF THE RED SEA SUPERNATURAL?

XVII.

WAS THE PASSAGE OF THE RED SEA SUPERNATURAL?

This is an interesting and practical question; it has its relations to the wonderful events which mark the deliverance of Israel from the bondage of Egypt. The fourteenth chapter of Exodus records the miraculous passage of Israel through the Red Sea. By remarkable signs God attested the commission of Moses to Pharaoh. The number of these signs was ten, expressive of their completeness. The hour was now near when deliverance for Israel should come. God was not deaf to the cry of the oppressed which went up to His ear. Brave and wise leaders were needed; and the heroic Moses and the eloquent Aaron are the men for the hour. When the tale of bricks was doubled, then came Moses. When the knell of liberty seemed about to ring, then the song of hope sounded forth. If Moses and Aaron shall fail in reaching the heart of Pharaoh, the Almighty One, whose name is Jehovah, shall make him hear.

The Deliverance.

Probably the Pharaoh of the exodus was Menephtah I., the son and successor of Rameses II. This Rameses was called by the Greeks Sesostris; he was the most famous of all the Pharaohs, being a mighty conqueror in Africa, Asia, and Europe. His statues and temples are found throughout the Nile valley, from Zoan to Nubia. His mummy was found in 1881, in a rock chamber on the west bank of the Nile, near Thebes, and was transferred to the Boulak Museum at Cairo. His son, Menephtah I., appears to have been inglorious, and to have died without finishing his father's tomb. With him probably Moses was familiarly associated in childhood within the palace. It must have been a startling experience to be authoritatively addressed by the friend of his boyhood, now the leader of the captive people, and the representative of Jehovah. But a greater than Moses is here; the Almighty is the leader of this deliverance. Moses knew, and Pharaoh was soon to learn, the truth of which Lowell has sung:

> "Right forever on the scaffold, Wrong forever on the throne—
> Yet that scaffold sways the future, and, behind the dim unknown,
> Standeth God within the shadow, keeping watch above His own."

God has now made bare His arm for the deliverence of His chosen, and no power of Egypt can resist the onward march of the Almighty. The plagues followed each other in quick succession; then came the last terrible night. Jehovah passed through the land of Egypt, and the midnight echoed with the loud wail of a nation's woe. The gods of Egypt, one by one, were utterly overwhelmed, and Jehovah is triumphant. The king seeks Moses and Aaron, and the people cry out in their bitter grief that he should permit Israel to go. Finally, Pharaoh says "Go"; and the great exodus is begun. Egypt's slaves have become men and women; a nation is born in a night. The journey to Canaan is begun, and Jehovah goes before His people. The pillar of cloud and of fire was more to Israel than was the brazier of the great Alexander to Greece. For a time all went well, for water and food were abundant, and the hearts of the people beat high with patriotic hope. But Israel had many lessons to learn—lessons as to the value of liberty and the necessity of righteousness to the preservation of liberty. These are lessons which we have not fully learned even to this hour. The people journey onward to Etham, on the edge of the wilderness. Should they continue their journey in that direction, they would pass immediately into the wilderness, and Pharaoh, pursuing them, would soon overtake and recapture the imperfectly armed fugitives. The Lord would not conduct them by the straight road into the land of promise lest the appearance of war should discourage them; still less might he carry them into the wilderness, where they might be readily overtaken and entirely overcome by well-disciplined soldiers. The order is therefore given to change the line of march, and soon they are encamped before Pi-hahiroth, the last encampment before crossing the Red Sea. They are between Migdol and the sea. Perhaps it is impossible, after the local changes of more than three thousand years, to determine these sites. Baal-ze-phon was over against Pi-hahiroth. Thus the Israelites had mountains on the west and south, and sea on the east.

Pharaoh repented of his leniency in having let them go. The wound in his heart is healing, and the old satanic spirit is returning. When sick, he would be an angel; when well, he was a devil. He believed that the fugitives were entangled in the land and shut in by the wilderness. God has already been honored by His victory over Pharaoh, and His glory will be still more signally displayed. We now have an account of the pursuit of Pharaoh; the third day has now arrived, and pride, ambition, and revenge fill Pharaoh's soul. Orders for instant preparation are given, and soon six hundred chosen chariots, belonging to the state, are pursuing Israel in hot haste. The pride and chivalry of Egypt are in Pharaoh's army; his knights are men-at-arms ready for any chivalrous and heroic service. Finely bred horses drew his war-chariots, and in each chariot was a warrior and a charioteer. The days of mourning over the dead first-born added to the fierceness of the attack on Israel. Terrible was the situation of Israel at this moment. The sight of the well-appointed soldiers of Pharaoh filled them with alarm. They forgot the wonderful interposition by which they had escaped thus far; for the sight of their former masters amid the splendor and pomp of chariots and horses caused their hearts to fail with fear. On the west and south mountains frowned; on the east rolled the sea, and yonder on the north the war chariots of Egypt, with apparently resistless might, were approaching. Though comparatively few in number, these horsemen and chariots had conquered mighty foes, and had given Egypt glorious victories. Shame on Israel's cowardice in the presence of Egypt's chivalry! Shame on Israel's meanness toward the heroic Moses! The prolonged period of slavery had robbed them of bravery. In the agony of their distress they charged Moses with having brought them into the wilderness to die. This is the treatment which this heroic and perplexed leader receives from the cowards whom he is striving to rescue. This is evermore the fate of noble-hearted souls, who strive to lift the down-trodden into fuller light, larger liberty, and nobler manhood. Never was cynicism more cynical; never cowardice more cowardly. Slavery made these Israelites cravens; it transformed men into soulless things. The heart of Moses must have been touched to the quick with their cowardice;

from some part of the great host there ought to have been heard this brave voice:

> "Though love repine and reason chafe,
>   There came a voice without reply,
>   'Tis man's perdition to be safe,
>   When for the truth he ought to die."

These men knew but little of the infinite resources of the Almighty! Though hemmed in on every earthly side, one way was opened to Moses— the way upward to God's throne and heart. Moses is strong in faith. He assures the people that they shall see their enemy no more forever. He affirms that Jehovah shall fight for His own. Only God could deliver a defenceless people from an armed and infuriated foe. God's voice comes to Moses, "Why criest thou unto me?" Then the command is given to stretch the rod out over the sea and divide it. God gives the assurance that again the heart of Mizraim shall be hardened, and that the people shall know that the Lord is God. We behold the cloud between the camp of Israel and the camp of Mizraim, light to one and darkness to the other. Now we behold Moses stretching his hand over the sea. A strong east, or northeast, wind blows all that night, and behold! the waters are divided, and the sea is made dry land. Thus the waves rolled back, and thus Israel marched forward. In dashed the pursuing Egyptians; their hosts are soon in the midst of the waters. We are told in language of mysterious majesty, that "the

Lord looked" in the morning watch into the host of Egypt. It was a marvellous moment. Other Scripture clearly teaches that a storm burst upon the sea, that flash after flash of lightning shot through the midnight darkness, and peal after peal of thunder rolled over the heads of the bewildered Egyptians. Their chariot wheels are removed, and, as the morning dawns, the hand of Moses is stretched once more over the sea. The waves roll backward. The chariots and horsemen, and all the army of Pharaoh sank like lead in the midst of the sea. Glorious was this display of almighty power. At one fell sweep the chivalry of Egypt is laid low. Soon the dead are cast upon the shore of the sea, and the song of Moses, one of the most triumphant pæans ever heard by human ears—more glorious than the Marseillaise of France, the "Ein' feste Burg ist unser Gott" of Germany, the noblest songs of Puritanism in England, and the most patriotic hymns of America—is sublimely chanted, with the music of the stormy sea as its divine accompaniment.

The Red Sea.

This is the substance of the miraculous story told by the inspired penman. In order more fully to understand it, a few facts regarding the Red Sea may appropriately be given. The Red Sea is known by various names. Sometimes it is called simply the Sea; sometimes the Sea of Suph, and sometimes the Egyptian Sea. The

Egyptians called it the Sea of Punt, that is, of Arabia; its Arabic name is Bahr-el-Hedjaz, from a province on its eastern coast, or Bahr-el-Ahmar, meaning "the red." The Erythrean, or Red Sea, was the Greek and Roman name. The word Erythrean means the same in Greek that Edom does in Phœnician and Hebrew. Suph denotes the wool-like seaweed found on its shores. The name "Red" Sea probably is from Edom, its northeast part having washed the country possessed by the Edomites, or from the color of its corals, or possibly from the red zoophytes found at times floating on its surface. But the better opinion is that which gives the name "Red" from the pink colors found at times on the mountains on the shores; but the best explanation of the name is that which finds it in the word Edom, which means red. The Greeks borrowed the name from the Phœnicians. The name Edom was taken for an appellative instead of a proper name, hence the name Red Sea to this day. The sea is a beautiful green or blue. The Black Sea is not black, the Blue Danube is not blue, the Yellow Sea is not yellow, and the Red Sea is not red. It is really an arm of the Indian Ocean. On the east is Arabia, and on the west is Egypt. The straits of Bab-el-Mandeb, or Gate of Tears, connect it with the Indian Ocean. This writer will never forget the scorching heat which he experienced when he sailed over this historic sea. Since November, 1869, the Suez Canal has connected it with the Mediterranean. The sea is about fourteen hundred and fifty miles long, with an average width of one hundred and fifty miles. The north end divides into the Gulf of Suez on the west, the Gulf of Akaba on the east; and between these two bodies of water lies the peninsula of Mount Sinai. There is no doubt but that the sea was anciently connected with the Nile by a canal used by the Pharaohs, fifteen centuries before Christ. Recently this canal was restored, and it is now the Sweet-water canal, giving water to the stations between the Mediterranean and the Red Sea, and causing fertility in many parts of the country which otherwise would be deserts. The sea is difficult of navigation because of submerged coral reefs; it receives no rivers, but many rain torrents.

The Natural and the Supernatural.

There is no doubt but that in the time of Moses the sea extended at least fifty miles farther north than to-day. It is believed that this change has taken place within the historic period. If so, this is a fulfilment of the prophecy of Isaiah xi. 15; xix. 5: "The Lord shall utterly destroy the tongue of the Egyptian sea," etc. Probably the "Lake of the Crocodile," the Birket-el-timsah, indicates the old bed.

Where did the Israelites cross the Red Sea? This is a perplexing question. We follow them from Rameses to Succoth, then to Etham, " in the edge of the wilderness." Probably each place of encampment marked the close of a day's journey. The last camping-place was Pi-hahiroth. But where was that? Probably it was the name of a natural locality, and it seems to have been near the sea. How far was the passage of the sea natural, and how far supernatural? It is quite certain that the ten plagues, or at least several of them, were just what might have been expected in Egypt. It is equally certain, also, that the order in which they occurred is the normal order in which the natural phenomena would operate. Thus the corruption of the river was naturally followed by the plague of frogs; and thus, from the dead frogs, gnats and flies were bred, and from these painful and poisonous insects came, in turn, murrain among the cattle and boils among the people. These plagues, in kind though not in degree, are actually experienced to this day in Egypt. Travellers there even now, when a southwest wind is blowing, observe swarms of locusts, and in the spring of the year they are known to come with an east wind. Lepisus speaks of a "regular snowdrift of locusts." He also says "that they fell down in showers, and this continued for six days." Even during the last few years, great storms of hail have occurred in Egypt, and thousands of cattle have been carried off by murrain. It was, therefore, to be expected that God would use material immediately at hand for the punishing of the Egyptians. The natural element was in the presence of common plagues among the people; the supernatural element was in the extent, fierceness, and succession of these plagues for the accomplishment of God's purpose in humbling the heart of Pharaoh and breaking the power of Egypt.

The inspired narrative teaches us that there was a like commingling of the natural and the supernatural in the passage of the Red Sea. Travellers and scholars of many centuries and countries have given their best thought to this great event. Strabo, Josephus, Diodorus, Niebuhr, Stanley, Robinson, Professor Palmer, Sir J. W. Dawson, and many others, have carefully studied every spot in the entire neighborhood, and every scrap of information on this important subject. But they contradict one another as to the place of the passage. Sir J. W. Dawson many of us are accustomed to follow with great readiness and satisfaction, but it is difficult to be sure regarding the authority which we should follow touching these much debated historic conclusions. There is no doubt, as already suggested, that the waters of the Red Sea once occupied a much larger area than at present. There is no doubt but that a strong east or northeast wind would produce a great effect upon the ebb and flood tides. The Seventy has south wind instead of east wind; the Bible word is not definite, for *kadim* may refer to any rough wind; the term is generic rather than specific. The statement that the place of passage must have been broad, as the whole Egyptian army perished, is not well founded. The force employed against the Israelites was not large. There were only six hundred chariots, each carrying two men. This was probably only the advance guard of a much larger army which later would join these chariots. We do not know how many chariots went abreast. It is difficult, indeed it is impossible, to calculate the space which would have been taken by the Israelite multitudes. No doubt Moses calculated these details with the utmost care. He was as wise as he was brave, and as practical as he was prayerful. To this hour the wind often drives out the water from parts of the Red Sea; islets thus appear, which look like huge stepping-stones; and so, at the head of the arms of the sea sandbanks and fords are found, which may have literally been trodden by the escaping Hebrews. Diodorus says that at times "the whole bay at the head of the sea was laid bare." Doubtless Moses, like the skilled leader he was, like the man who was master of the learning of the Egyptians, including geometry, surveying and hydraulics, and with a knowledge of the tides, took advantage of that knowledge at this critical hour. He would have been unworthy of his great responsibility had he not done so. Even though the whole event may have been in due course of nature, we must still see that God's will and purpose were thereby accomplished. All the processes of nature, ordinary and extraordinary, are under God's control. There is a region in which in God's thought there is no distinction between natural and supernatural; we make such distinctions, but to God all is natural, and all is supernatural. We have seen that in all the miracles in Egypt there was a union of the natural and supernatural. This was not otherwise in the miracles of our Lord. He took advantage of the water when He made wine; He availed Himself of the loaves and fishes in the hands of a boy when He performed a miracle to feed hungry thousands. Doubtless this is God's usual method. In the Bible the spiritual is the antithesis to the natural; the word supernatural is a human rather than a divine word.

By admitting, nay, by insisting on, the presence of the natural in this passage of the Red Sea, in harmony with the distinct statement of the inspired historian regarding the strong wind that blew that night, we are very far from rejecting the miraculous element in the great event. All the resources of the universe are God's. It was He who caused the wind to blow; it was He who made the sea roll back in obedience to His will. The use of a natural wind gives additional honor to God in this event.

His power and purpose are seen in that the wind blew at the right time and in the right direction to deliver the Israelites, and to destroy the Egyptians. If we reject the miraculous element in this marvellous event, how shall we account for the shallower waters for Israel, and the deeper waters for Egypt? We affirm with undiminished emphasis our faith in the reality of this miracle, and our increasing honor to God because of His ability to use natural forces at the right time, and with the necessary volume, and under the appropriate control for the accomplishment of His divine purposes. If the crossing took place near Suez—as probably, notwithstanding all that has been said in favor of other localities, it did— the strong wind acting on the ebb tide could drive the waters from the arm of the sea near Suez, and possibly even from the end of the gulf. Thus the shallower parts would become dry, while, as Dr. Edward Robinson has suggested, the northern part of the arm would still remain in its normal condition. The waters would thus be divided, and so would be a wall—in the sense of being a barrier—to the Israelites on the right hand and on the left. The miracle was thus natural as to the means employed, and supernatural as to the application of these means for a divine and glorious end. Recent surveys clearly show that the narrator must have traversed the country, and have been an eye-witness of the events which he thus records. The narrative seems to have been a daily journal.

Paul refers to the passage of the Red Sea as a type of baptism, as it marked the beginning of a new era in the life of the Israelites. It was the crisis of the exodus; no event comparable to it is found in all the pages of that divine history. It gave inspiration to the genius of the psalmist, and the song of Moses on the Arabian shore is the prelude to that more triumphant pæan, which shall be chanted by the redeemed, standing on the sea of glass, having the harps of God and singing the song of Moses and the Lamb. There is no difficulty in life too great for God. If we move forward in the performance of duty, every form of opposition will disappear, every foe will be overthrown, and victory from the hand of God shall assuredly be ours.

XVIII.

WHAT WERE THE SYMBOLS CALLED THE URIM AND THUMMIM?

XVIII.

WHAT WERE THE SYMBOLS CALLED THE URIM AND THUMMIM?

What were the Urim and Thummim? It would not be easy to ask a question to which a conclusive reply is more difficult. It has been suggested by some writers on this subject that as the Jewish exiles on their return from Babylon postponed the settlement of a difficulty till there should rise up "a priest with Urim and Thummim," so we may not be able to answer this question until a priest comes with Urim and Thummim to give us the answer as to what both were. Many learned scholars of different countries and centuries frankly confess that they do not know what these symbols were; and some declare that, in their judgment, it is impossible ever to know, and that God probably meant that this discovery should never be made.

But no earnest student of the Bible can ever be satisfied to pass the subject over in silence as the result either of indifference or cowardice; we are under solemn obligation to learn all which the Bible, rightly interpreted, can teach us. Both nature and revelation are constantly giving up knowledge which had remained quite mysterious or utterly unknown for ages. We must modestly and reverently strive to master every kind of knowledge which our minds are capable of receiving, and which the divine storehouse contains for our instruction. Out of this treasury are to come things old and new. It is, of course, frankly admitted that all kinds of knowledge are not of equal importance. What is necessary to our knowledge of salvation in Christ is simple; what is essential to our growth in grace is comparatively plain. But, while thankfully and joyfully partaking of the sincere milk and also of the strong meat of the Word, we may profitably attempt to understand some of the things in different parts of the Bible which the Apostle Peter, referring to parts of the writings of his brother Paul, describes as "things hard to be understood." But in so doing we shall not forget the plainer and weightier matters of the law. Matriculates in Christ's school may, with the angels, desire to look into the profound mysteries both of redemption and revelation, and the Urim and Thummim belong to this class of mysterious and sacred things. Rightly studied, we shall find that even this subject is not without great value to us in our practical and spiritual lives; we shall clearly and joyously see that these mysterious symbols direct us to Christ, who is the world's true Light and glorious Perfection.

Various Theories.

Various theories, as was to be expected, have been suggested in explanation of these remarkable symbols. Indeed, the literature of the subject would make a library of considerable dimensions, for the solution of the problems connected with these symbols has proved to be as fascinating as it is confessedly difficult. It would be a comparatively easy matter to give a summary of these various hypotheses; but it will be more profitable to follow a correct historical method, which shall account with reasonable fulness for the discoverable facts of Scripture regarding these symbols. The terms themselves we are able to understand without much, if any, doubt. To discover their meaning is a fair starting-point in our discussion. The Hebrew in Exodus xxviii. 30 is *Urim ve-eth hattummim*, the " Lights" and " Perfections." The Greek version makes the clause mean, " The Manifestation and the Truth." Other versions give it as " Enlightenings and Certainties," " Elucidations and Perfections," " Illuminations and Certainties," the "Lucid and the Perfect"; the Vulgate gives it as " Doctrine and Verity," and Luther, in his later translations, gave it as " Light and Right."

Let us look carefully at the Hebrew terms in their order. Hebrew scholars are nearly unanimous in making Urim the plural of Ur, light or fire; but, as we have seen, the Septuagint and other versions give a slightly different meaning to the word. The literal English equivalent is "Lights." Regarding Thummim there is also great unanimity of opinion in deriving it from the Hebrew word *tom*, meaning perfection or completeness. Some would derive the word from the Hebrew *amen*, to be true, but the majority, as already stated, from the word *tom*, some finding in it the meaning, "a twin," they imagining that the two groups of gems, six on each side of the breastplate, constituted the Urim and Thummim. The best English equivalents of these Hebrew words would be, *light* and *perfection;* for there is a traditional belief among the Jews, and a virtual consensus of opinion among all scholars, that the plural forms do not imply numerical plurality. This plural is probably what is called the *plurales excellentiæ*, denoting the things or modes through which the oracle of God was given. Some have assumed that there is here what the rhetoricians call a *hendiadys*, making the two words equivalent to perfect light; but, perhaps, the weight of authority is in favor of regarding the words as referring to distinct things. This latter idea is certainly suggested by the fact that in Numbers xxvii. 21, and 1 Sam. xxviii. 6, Urim is found alone. And in Deut. xxxiii. 8, the usual order is inverted, Thummim being given first. It is stated that, with the probable exception of Psalm xvi. 5, Thummim is never given alone. It is not surprising that different versions slightly vary the meaning of these words; but the variations in meaning are more apparent than real. In Scripture language perfection and truth, and light and truth are practically identical; that which is perfect is truly performed, and that which is truly performed is necessarily perfect. In Joshua xxiv. 14 we read: "Fear the Lord and serve him in sincerity and in truth"; the Hebrew is, *betummim ubeemeth*. We can see at a glance that here the idea of our obscure phrase is not remote from the thought of this exhortation. It is also in harmony with the thought expressed in 1 John iii. 18, "But in deed and in truth"; neither is it far removed from Psalm cxix. 130, "The entrance of thy words giveth light." We are also reminded of Psalm xliii. 3, "Send out thy light and thy truth." It is true that the words Urim and Thummim are not here found, but it is perfectly obvious that the psalmist has in mind the very thought which probably these symbols set forth; and, indeed, his thought may be literally an echo of the high-priest's prayer when he went before God with the Urim and Thummim on his heart.

Some Other Scripture References.

These wonderful words come before us first in Exodus xxviii. 30. They are introduced in the account of the high-priest's apparel, and they are mentioned without a single word of explanation, as if they were already quite familiar to the writer and its readers. The breast-plate was a piece of embroidery about ten inches square and of very elaborate work, which the high-priest wore on his breast. The front was set with twelve precious stones, on each of which was engraved the name of one of the tribes. Inside the breast-plate, we are told, the Urim and Thummim were to be placed; and they were to be on Aaron's heart when he went in before the Lord. How we wish that at this point a few words of description and explanation had been given, but not a word is written. It certainly seems as if it were assumed that both Moses and the people would understand what was meant when the symbols are named. Joshua, when he became the successor of the heroic lawgiver, is commanded to stand before Eleazar, the priest, "who shall ask counsel for him after the judgment of Urim," and this counsel is to determine the course that Israel shall pursue. The Urim and Thummim are mentioned with the blessing of the tribe of Levi; and they are mentioned in the history of the Judges, and Saul is left in darkness, being answered "neither by dreams nor by Urim nor by prophet." They are referred to also in other Scriptures directly or indirectly. Some have supposed because they are introduced without any explanation that they were of supernatural origin, and were unlike anything upon the earth. They are thus suddenly brought to our notice on the sacred page. So far as we can discover, no order was given for their construction; and no hint is given that these names were to be employed for any of the articles which Moses was to make. This obscurity has led many to suppose that God never intended that we should endeavor to solve this mystery; but there is no warrant for this opinion, any more than regarding a thousand things in nature and revelation which once were impenetrably mysterious, but which now are exhaustively understood.

Various Opinions.

Were the Urim and Thummim the same as the Teraphim? This theory would make them nothing more than small divining images put into the lining or the folds of the breast-plate, and which miraculously spoke with an articulate voice uttering the oracles of God. This view distinguishes them from the twelve stones and from each other, and it makes them to have been placed in the *chosen*. It is not impossible that there are certain passages of Scripture which show that the Teraphim were used as a substitute for the Urim; but it is almost certain that if such were the case the substitution was the result of conformity to heathen ideas, and was not authorized by God. The Mosaic system was intended carefully to guard the people against the danger of image worship; but such a conception of the Urim and Thummim would make them contribute directly to the indorsement of heathenism.

Others make the Urim and Thummim bright stones, perhaps diamonds, in the form of dice.

They suppose that a number of them were carried in the pocket of the high-priest's *chosen,* and when he wished for a divine response they were thrown on a table, or on the ark of the covenant, and as they fell their position, according to laws understood by the priests, enabled them to discover the answer which God intended to give. But this view robs the whole proceeding of dignity and propriety, and brings it into the category of the rules or tricks of fortune-tellers; it is also without due Scripture warrant. Another theory makes these symbols a stone or plate placed in the middle of the ephod or within its folds, on which plate or stone the sacred name of Jehovah was engraved. By gazing on this the priest became capable of prophesying and listening to the divine voice communicating the will of God. This name of Jehovah is the *Shemhammephorash* of the Jewish Cabbalists; this is sometimes called the "Tetragrammaton," or four-lettered name of God, by the mystic virtue of which name the priest was enabled to pronounce luminous and perfect oracles. This conceit is now largely relegated to the figments of the Talmudical rabbins, figments as numerous as they are childish and fantastic.

Another view makes the Urim and Thummim identical with the twelve tribal gems, and makes the two words equivalent in meaning to, Perfect Illumination. We know that on these twelve stones the names of the twelve tribes of Israel were engraved, and when the high-priest went before the Lord he bore "the judgment of the children of Israel upon his heart." According to Josephus and the Seventy, these jewels were the twelve precious stones of the breast-plate. This theory supposes that they revealed God's purpose by emitting an extraordinary lustre, or by an arrangement of letters forming the divine response, the letters necessary for that purpose being distinguished from the other letters. This theory has various modifications in its essential features, and also in its incidental details. Some authorities would make the letters bright when victory was at hand, and dark when disaster was near. It is difficult to distinguish between the subordinate theories of different interpreters which have for their fundamental basis this general conception of the precious stones in the breast-plate as the Urim and Thummim. Probably these jewels still exist somewhere as symbols of the eternity and fidelity of God. It would be fascinatingly interesting and equally instructive if they should some day be discovered and the mystery of centuries resolved. Some of those who hold this general view believe that as the high-priest fixed his eyes and concentrated his thought on these jewels and on the great attributes which they represented, he was able, partly by well-known laws as illustrated in hypnotism, and partly as the result of an immediate divine influence, to pass at once into communion with God and into a true prophetic vision.

The Probable Explanation.

Most of the theories now named may at once be eliminated from our discussion. There are but two which seem worthy of consideration. The first of these is that which identifies the Urim and Thummim with the twelve tribal gems and which regards the two words, by the figure of hendiadys, as equivalent to perfect illumination. This is the view which the author had strong prepossessions to adopt. There is much to be said in its favor. If the words were regarded merely as epithets applied to the stones in the breast-plate they would seem to be especially appropriate. These stones were intrinsically brilliant, splendid, and luminous, and thus they might apparently be termed with propriety Lights and Perfections. It is fair for us to assume that these stones were the most perfect of their kind. Then, again, if the Urim and Thummim were not identical with the gems of the breast-plate, it seems difficult to explain the fact that the inspired historian gives no account of their preparation and of their religious uses. All other parts of the ritual are described with the utmost carefulness; every pin of the tabernacle and every thread of the priestly garments had to be made according to divine direction; and yet here are symbols of the utmost importance in obtaining responses from God, and no account is given of their preparation or consecration for this sacred function. The silence of the historian, it is natural to believe, gave a strong presumption that the Urim and Thummim were identical with the brilliant gems of the breast-plate.

But there is an objection to this view suggested in Leviticus viii. 8, "And he put the breast-plate upon him; also he put in the breast-plate the Urim and Thummim." This passage clearly speaks of these symbols as being put into the breast-plate; this seems to be also the clear meaning of the words in the verse, which is really the text of this discourse (Exodus xxviii. 30), "And thou shalt put in the breast-plate of judgment the Urim and the Thummim." Other passages might be quoted illustrative of the force of the word "in" in this case (Exodus xxv. 16, 21), "And thou shalt put into the ark the testimony which I shall give." This latter verse shows that the testimony was distinct from the ark into which it was put. It would, therefore, seem a natural inference that the Urim and Thummim were in like manner distinct from the breast-plate, and that they bore to the breast-plate a relation similar to that which the tables of testimony bore to the ark of the covenant. It would thus seem that Moses, after inserting the precious stones in the "pectoral," was commanded to put the Urim and Thummim into some fold or pouch of this same pectoral, even as he put the tables into the ark. It seems impossible to avoid the conclusion that these symbols were in some way put into the fold or lining of the breast-plate. Dr. Bush in his comments on this verse strives to break the force of this reasoning by stating that the stones of the breast-plate might not have been attached externally, but that the pectoral was of the nature of a bag or pocket in which the stones themselves may have been deposited; but his reasoning fails to carry conviction.

The Most Approved Theory.

Modern Egyptology furnishes us with a clew to the true explanation. All intelligent students will admit that there are many points of similarity between the Jewish and Egyptian systems of worship. For a long time both Jewish and Christian scholars were slow to recognize this fact. They feared that by admitting this similarity it would militate against Judaism as a divinely revealed religion. It was long believed that no custom, rite, or symbol was introduced into Judaism from any system of heathenism. Sometimes the transference to Judaism of things common to it and to Egyptian heathenism was affirmed as a divine condescension to the superstitious notions of Israel when in a condition of ignorance and debasement, but that view is not considerate or even tenable. Fortunately the prejudice of earlier times in this regard is now passing away. It may be true—it certainly is true, in some respects—that the Egyptians got many of their rites and symbols from the Hebrews, and no doubt the law of reciprocal influence was in operation. In quite recent years so many new sources of knowledge on this subject have been made available that now the interchange of religious ideas and symbols is not a question of argument, but of fact. The ancient paintings and sculptures not only give instruction regarding the nation in peace and war, but also concerning its social customs and religious rites. We now fully know much which half a century ago was entirely unknown regarding the garments worn by the priests, and the ceremonial observances in their religious services. There is a striking similarity even between the Egyptian ark borne by the priests and the ark of the Covenant as described by Moses; the similarity is found even in the manner in which both arks were carried. Did the Jews borrow from the Egyptians? Did the Egyptians borrow from the Jews? Did both derive their ideas from some common and patriarchal source? This latter is the most probable view; doubtless, many ideas came down from remote antiquity as the sons of Noah were scattered to different lands. At the moment, we are stating the fact of this similarity and not attempting to account for it. The earliest religious ideas were preserved among the Jews in comparative purity, while among the nations which knew not God they were gradually corrupted and mingled with abominably idolatrous practices, but many essential truths still remained. Ideas, rites, and symbols would not be adopted by the Israelites from the Egyptians merely because they were Egyptian; but they might be adopted because they were right, were primitive, were divine in their origin, and thus they might again be ordained by Moses. That in a corrupted form some of them were observed by the Egyptians is no reason why in their religious meaning and true form they should not be observed by the Hebrews. This consideration deserves emphasis; it has been too much overlooked in past years in studying the Bible.

Egyptian Teachings.

Bearing these great principles in mind, we are prepared to see their illustration in connection with the Urim and Thummim. The Egyptian paintings show a pectoral ornament somewhat corresponding to the Jewish *chosen* or breast-plate. In addition to this discovery, two Greek historians call attention to the fact that the Egyptian arch-judge, who was always a priest, venerable in age, distinguished in learning, and commendable in character, always wore a gold chain around his neck—a gold chain to which was suspended an image made of a sapphire stone which was called in Greek *Aletheia*, meaning "Truth," when he officiated in civil and religious functions. With this image he touched the litigant when a suit began, and he permitted the winner to look upon it or to kiss it when he had gained his cause. It is believed that this image was a representation of the goddess Thmei, who was worshipped as "Truth and Justice," and it is not a little remarkable that the very name of this Egyptian deity suggests the word Thummim. A mummy was found at Cairo around whose neck was found a chain, to which was attached a plate or symbol with the figure of a bird, which suggested Truth and Justice. It is interesting also to know that traces of a similar custom are found among the Romans, for among the Vestal Virgins she sat who was called "Maxima," and who assisted in the trial of causes. To this hour a triangular mirror is found in courts of law in Russia which in some mysterious way symbolizes the presence of the Czar and through him the presence of God. As one looks into the mirror and sees himself, so it is believed the Czar, and above him God, look into the heart. This mirror, indirectly at least, implies the presence of Justice, and the necessity of truth. Something similar is also known among the Japanese, and it is an interesting fact that to this hour in Great Britain "the royal mace" is borne by, or carried before, a magistrate as the symbol of his authority, and it must be laid upon the table of the clerk when the House is in session. It was long believed that the Egyptians derived the custom under discussion from the Jews after Solomon's marriage with the daughter of Pharaoh; but it is now quite certain, as the result of comparatively recent studies, that these resemblances to Hebrew customs belong to a much earlier period. This representation of the Egyptian goddess expressed the notion of two truths, or the double character of Truth and Justice. Before the election of a king among the Jews the chief priest was a civil officer as well as a religious functionary; in this respect the analogy between the two peoples is all the closer. It has been reasonably suggested that the touch of the successful litigant with the image in the Egyptian court bears some relation to Isaiah vi. 7, " Lo, this hath touched thy lips; and thine iniquity is taken away, and thy sin purged"; also to Jeremiah i. 9; Esther v. 2, and many instances in the Bible in which touching represents the impartation or possession of miraculous power or virtue.

If we were to carry out the similarity still further it might be found that the Urim and Thummim, as signifying Light and Truth, bear some analogy to the two figures of *Ar*, the Sun, and *Thmei*, Truth—figures worn by the Egyptians in their breast-plate. Often Thmei is represented by a figure wearing two ostrich feathers. It is known also that in the final judgment Osiris is represented as wearing around his neck this double image of Justice and Truth.

It is not forgotten that there have been arguments used against the Egyptian origin of the Urim and Thummim; but these arguments have already been virtually named in connection with our discussion of the tribal gems in the breast-plate as the Urim and Thummim. It is known that in the early days, as even now, peculiar virtue was often attributed to gems as amulets and charms; thus jasper, amethyst, emerald, and all stones were supposed to have a peculiar significance and to be influential in warding off evil and in bringing good. We cannot suppose that God would indorse any heathen or superstitious ideas in the use of such a symbol, but He could exalt it, purify it, and glorify it, and make it a part of true worship. We know that in Egyptian thought the mystic Scarabaeus was an emblem of profound significance; as it came out of the dark earth after the flood of waters it was therefore the symbol of life out of death and of transformation and resurrection. In many countries various symbols came to be virtually thoughts and words in painting or sculpture. Thus some symbol, whether or not suggested to the Hebrews by the Egyptians, seems to have been placed in the *chosen*, setting forth the great and glorious fact that Light and Truth were a blessed revelation from God, were the centre of the nation's life, the guiding star of the nation's progress, and the glorious ideal of the nation's hope. This was the Urim and Thummim.

Typical Significance.

There is not space to discuss the process of consulting Jehovah by Urim and Thummim; there is, perhaps, even greater doubt regarding the method of consultation than regarding the Urim and Thummim themselves. It seems certain that these symbols were closely connected with the theocratic government of the Hebrews, and that after that government passed away this method of consulting God seemed also to have passed away. All pertaining to the office of the high-priest was typical of the Christian dispensation and of the office and work of Christ. This is, doubtless, true also of the Urim and Thummim. Christ is the glory of the old dispensation. He is the very heart of the Bible. He was and is the true Urim and Thummim; He was the end of the law for righteousness; He was the reality of every symbol, the substance of every shadow, the desire of every longing heart. He was Light, Perfection, and Truth. He was "the true light which lighteth every man that cometh into the world." He was Perfection, "being made perfect, he became the author of salvation to all that obey Him." He was Manifestation: "He was God manifest in the flesh." He was also "the Way, the Truth, and the Life." Through the Urim and Thummim a measure of the Holy Ghost was granted to the Jewish high-priest; but Christ is a high-priest who possesses the Holy Ghost without measure. Christ is a high-priest "who put on righteousness as a breast-plate." Christ is the glorious Luminary of the new Jerusalem. He is its Perfection. Perhaps the Urim and Thummim are suggestive also of "the white stone" which is beautifully symbolic in the Christian mysteries as set forth in the book of Revelation. We are thus sweetly led by the Lights and Perfections, the Urim and Thummim, to the cross, to the feet and to the heart of Jesus Christ, the Light of all dispensations, of all religions, of all philosophies, of all civilizations and of all experiences, and the crowning glory, cloudless beauty, and ineffable bliss of the heavenly city, the new Jerusalem.

XIX.

DID BALAAM'S ASS LITERALLY SPEAK WITH MAN'S VOICE?

XIX.

DID BALAAM'S ASS LITERALLY SPEAK WITH MAN'S VOICE?

The narrative in Numbers the twenty-second chapter, and the allusion to this narrative in 2 Peter ii. 15, 16, have been regarded by most Bible readers and commentators as fraught with great difficulties. In the minds of some Christians these difficulties are so great that they are disposed to reject the entire narrative as fictitious, or at least as utterly inexplicable. It is, therefore, of very great importance that an interpretation shall be found which is true to the original narrative, and which at the same time relieves it from difficulties which many consider to be insuperable. It is believed that a genuinely alleviative interpretation can be given which is also thoroughly loyal to the inspired record, more loyal, indeed, than the traditional interpretation.

Balaam is a profoundly mysterious and a strangely interesting man. He comes suddenly into the sacred narrative, and his name reappears in the Book of Revelation. It is evident that in the church at Pergamos, Rev. ii. 14, there were those who taught, as did Balaam, so as to lead men into idolatry and the gross sins of the flesh.

The teachings of the Nicolaitanes were of like character and tendency. Much of mystery attaches to the name, which means "conquerors of the people." Perhaps both names, Balaam and Nicolaitanes, are used symbolically, like the name Jezebel, to designate certain types of false teachers. Balaam's first appearance is as abrupt as that of Elijah the Tishbite, and is as mysterious as it is abrupt. He is at the same time a truly instructive historical character. He is almost as mysterious as Melchizedek, and yet his life is full of lessons of the greatest practical value. Both in his virtues and his vices he is thoroughly human. He is richly endowed with the gift of prophecy; and he utters sentiments worthy of the heartiest commendation. The words which he spake to Balak, as recorded by the prophet Micah vi. 6-8, are not surpassed in loftiness of thought and eloquence of speech by any words of man recorded in the Bible. These noble sentiments are an anticipation of the Sermon on the Mount; they are worthy to stand beside the sublimest truths uttered by the Apostle Paul. The man who spoke these great truths was fully inspired of God, so far as concerns their utterance. God used Balaam in wonderful ways in connection with the progress of true religion; and his name is thus perpetuated through all generations. There is no literary honor so great as a place in the divine library which we call the Bible. Compared with this honor all the glory of human fame is less than nothing.

In the Book of Numbers xxii. 5, Balaam is introduced as the son of Beor, who in 2 Peter ii. 15 is called Bosor. This form of the word may be a Chaldaism; for many believe that the Apostle Peter was in Babylon at the time of this writing. But the change in the form of the name may be due to the transmutation of the letters with the desire of softening the sound of the original Hebrew word. Among the Midianites, to whom Balaam belonged, he seems to have exercised an authority not unlike that possessed by Moses among the Israelites. In Numbers xxxi. 8 his name is mentioned in connection with the five kings of Midian, indicating that he possessed high rank and exercised great authority. His home was at Pethor, a city of Mesopotamia and probably on the banks of the Euphrates, although its exact site is entirely unknown. Some have supposed that as Pethor is derived from the word *pathor*, to "interpret," it is the name of a place which was the chief resort of men who professed to explain occult arts and to interpret the will of the gods. The name Balaam may mean "lord of the people," but others understand it to be "the destruction of the people," with an allusion to his supposed supernatural powers; and it is also suggested that his father's name probably comes from a root meaning to consume or destroy. God now and then chooses out persons dwelling among the heathen and endues them with remarkable and unexpected knowledge of Himself for the accomplishment of His great and holy purposes. Balaam belonged to this class of divinely chosen instruments in God's method of dealing with men. He certainly was a man of high intellectual attainments; indeed, he was in the true sense of the word a genius of a rare order. He had poetical and prophetical gifts as great as they were rare then and now; he was literally a seer and a poet. He possessed remarkable intuitions of spiritual truth; and he also recognized God as the author of his unusual endowments.. He thus stood on that mysterious borderland which overlaps true religion on the one side and gross heathenism on the other. Ever and anon in different ages and lands inexplicable men of this character are found. Some of these men are partly deceived, and are partly deceivers; and often the most analytic historian cannot draw the lines of separation between these two conditions. Indeed, often the men themselves could not always tell when they were acting under high motives and when impelled by the grossest ambitions. The great plays of Shakespeare finely illustrate the apparently contradictory elements in the lives of men. Now Dr. Jekyll comes forward and now Mr. Hyde appears in many lives in many lands and at various times; it is not otherwise in some measure in the lives of all men. There were times when the Apostle Paul was distinctly conscious of these contradictory elements in his deepest nature.

Historic Glimpses.

Balaam's natural and acquired gifts gave him great influence among his contemporaries. It was believed that he had power not only over temporal, but, to some degree at least, over eternal destinies; and also that his blessing or curse had the approval of God. Josephus calls him an "eminent diviner." He has been well called by Bishop Newton "a strange mixture of a man"; for while he practised an art expressly forbidden to the Israelites, he possessed some true knowledge of Jehovah, rendered Him worship, and received from Him divine communications. Balaam finally came to believe that his great gifts were his own, and that he might use them to advance his personal interests. The Israelites were now marching to the occupation of Palestine; on the plains of Moab, on the east of the Jordan, they were encamped. At that time Balak was king of the land. He had heard of the wonderful manner in which the Israelites had overcome the Amorites, and he is filled with alarm. He knows that he has no chance whatever in fighting these victorious invaders; he feels that if they come to battle he had better surrender at once. He puts the case very strongly when he declares that the Israelites can "lick up all that are round about us, as the ox licketh up the grass of the field." What shall he do in his great distress? He hears of Balaam, the soothsayer of Pethor. He will now have recourse to the supernatural. He will enlist divine power against his foe. Here a great truth is suggested; here an important lesson may be learned. It is eminently wise to invoke supernatural aid, but we should be quite certain that the aid invoked is truly supernatural. We ought not to be satisfied with appealing to Balaam or Simon Magus. Balak entered into a league with the Midianites against the Israelites. He also hastily sent messengers to Balaam in his remote home with rich rewards to secure his help in divination. At first Balaam refused with emphasis; but later he hesitated, and expressed a desire to seek wisdom from God in prayer. He ought to have known better than to pray in those circumstances. His duty was clear; he ought not to ask God to help him in compromising right with wrong. Other messengers came to Balaam with promises of greater gifts and honors. Again he juggled with right and endeavored to cheat God. God finally granted him his desire, but assured him that in the end his plans would be frustrated. The narrative at all these points is remarkably suggestive and instructive. It deserves to be more fully studied at these points than the purpose of this discourse will permit.

We now see Balaam starting on his journey with the messengers of Balak, king of Moab. God was much displeased with Balaam's importunity, and yet He granted him in some sense his desire. On the journey he met the angel of the Lord, who stood before him, *lesatan lo*, for a Satan to him, or an adversary against him. Now comes the remarkable narrative, Numbers xxii. 23-35. This entire narrative is worthy our most careful thought. We are here told that the dumb brute spake with a human voice. The animal seemed to have a deeper spiritual perception than its rider. The ass saw the angel standing in the way with drawn sword in hand. Balaam smote the creature that he might induce it to continue the journey. It is a strange story. What is its true interpretation? Is it a narrative of events which literally occurred as here stated? There is not space to go, in the effort to answer this question, into all the details of the narrative; but two possible interpretations can be given, and only two views can well be taken, and the reason for the adoption of one and the rejection of the other will be stated.

Two Interpretations.

Is this narrative literal history, or is it merely a vision? Is this a description of an objective or a subjective experience? Did the words ascribed to the ass proceed literally from its mouth, or was the scene transacted in the mind of Balaam in a condition of ecstasy or trance? These are the questions to be answered; let them be kept distinctly before our thought. Either answer might be given with certain modifications by those who fully believe in the authenticity of the narrative; the correctness of the narrative is not to be called in question whichever of these interpretations may be adopted, for the question is simply one of interpretation. Those who believe that this is a literal narrative affirm that the incidents recorded must be assumed to be literal, so long as no information to the contrary is given. They claim that it would be unnatural to expect any of the occurrences to be a vision, except a statement to that effect was made; and that if the visionary element were introduced it would be difficult to tell where it ended and where the historical narrative began; and they claim, finally, that the language of the Apostle Peter, in his second Epistle ii. 16, favors the literal sense. Are these claims well founded? We may say in reply that we know with absolute certainty that there are numerous instances in the Bible where we have abrupt transitions from one style to another, and that no mention of the transition is made. The Bible supposes some degree of sanctified common sense on the part of all its readers. The sacred writers, therefore, slide frequently from events in the natural world to the relation of a vision or dream wherein notice of the transition is given.

In Genesis xv. 1 we are told that the word of the Lord came to Abraham in a vision. In the fifth verse Abraham is asked to look toward heaven and to tell the stars, and he is assured that like to their great number shall be his seed. In the twelfth verse we see, as Dr. Bush in his comments on the narrative especially under discussion reminds us, that it was the daytime when Abraham saw the stars, indicating that this sight was a vision and not a literal reality. In Jeremiah xiii. 1–7 we see that Jeremiah was commanded to go to the river Euphrates and hide his girdle; but at the time this command was given the prophet was in the land of Canaan, hundreds of miles from the Euphrates. It was clearly a command given in a vision. So Ezekiel when in the land of Babylon, Ezekiel viii. 1–12, was ordered to dig a hole in the wall at Jerusalem; and he was then shown the abominations of the house of Israel, a transaction which certainly must have taken place in a vision. The voice addressed to Samuel when he ministered unto the Lord before Eli, 1 Sam. iii. 1–10, was clearly of the character of a vision; and in the fifteenth verse of that chapter we distinctly read, "Samuel feared to show Eli the vision," *march*, a word always, or generally, used of internal visions. In John xii. 28, 29, we are told of the voice which came from heaven, and it is quite evident that it was addressed to the inner sense of those for whom it was especially intended; for others heard it only with the outward ear, and to them it was simply a meaningless noise, or the voice of an angel. In the narrative of Paul's conversion, Acts ix. 3–8, there is no suggestion that the leading events were simply or chiefly internal or subjective; but when we compare with that account Acts xxii. 9 we are inevitably forced to the conclusion that, in its deep significance, it was to the Apostle Paul a vision. Other instances might be furnished leading to the same conclusion. The language of the Apostle Peter does not forbid this interpretation. In quoting a passage from the Old Testament he does not necessarily confine himself to any one interpretation which we may give of that passage. He takes the passage as he finds it. In like manner we could refer to a character in Shakespeare or in any great writer, and we might use the language of that character without entering into a full discussion as to various interpretations of the language, or of the relation which the character sustains to the original author's purpose. Could not the Apostle Peter, or any other apostle, have referred with perfect propriety to the Lord's call to Samuel, although it was in a vision? Was not that call just as real when addressed to the inner ear as it would have been if addressed to the outer ear? It is not a question of the reality of the divine communication, but only of the method which God chose to employ.

Positive Evidence.

We have only to turn to Numbers xii. 6 to see that dreams are designated as the usual mode of divine communication to the prophets. This fact certainly goes far to confirm our belief in the subjectivity of the incident under discussion. We there read: "Hear now my words: If there be a prophet among you, I the Lord will make myself known unto him in a vision, and will speak unto him in a dream." Balaam belonged to the class of whom this affirmation is made. Why should we doubt the correctness of this positive affirmation of Scripture? Is not the narrative before us in perfect harmony with this divine promise? When we look at chapter xxiv. verses 3, 4, 15, 16, we see that Balaam speaks of himself as the man "which heard the words of God, which saw the vision of the Almighty, falling into a trance, but having his eyes open," etc. Perhaps we ought not to quote the words "into a trance"; the Hebrew may admit only of the translation "falling," or "falling down"; but the statement has its appropriate application to the incident recorded in the narrative whose true interpretation we are aiming to give. Was not that the occasion when Balaam was in this condition of prophetic ecstasy? To what other occasion can these words be so well applied? That condition was the appropriate one for a seer like Balaam. Those who deny the application of this statement to this incident should clearly establish the correctness of their denial. It is difficult, if not impossible, to name another event in the life of Balaam to which this language so fittingly can be referred. It seems almost certain that the appearance of the angel was to the inward and not outward eye; and just so the voice of the ass was intended for his spiritual and not physical ear.

Another argument in favor of this view is that Balaam expresses no astonishment on hearing the ass speak; neither do his servants; neither do the Moabitish princes who accompanied him. They seem to have heard nothing unusual and to have seen nothing supernatural. If Balaam had heard the ass speak, we might expect him to have been struck speechless with astonishment at so unusual an event. But he goes on speaking almost with petulancy, chiding the brute as if it had been a disobedient servant. His language certainly is not what we might expect from one who had witnessed a prodigy so remarkable as an ass speaking with a man's voice. It is also to be said that the drift of Jewish interpreters, as well as that of many great Christian scholars, favors the subjective explanation. Maimonides leads off with an indorsement of this interpretation; Leibnitz, Hengstenberg, and Tholuck, and among comparatively recent American scholars Dr. George Bush, and the writers in Smith's and other Bible dictionaries, earnestly support, or at least incline to this same view.

This view does not in any way deny the historic reality of the event; it nowhere denies, or even depreciates, its miraculous occurrence and its divine influence. God is seen to exert such an influence on Balaam that the reproof which he received sank deep into his heart. He saw this wonderful sight with the eyes of his soul, and he heard this powerful rebuke with his spiritual ear. The angel was revealed to him in his prophetic or ecstatic state. Which ever view we adopt we see that the occurrences were realities to Balaam. The subjective view does not make the events to be less real. In any case there was a direct communication from God to Balaam. God could have put the sound of words into the mouth of the beast, or into the ear of Balaam; and in either case it would be equally the work of God, and would be equally effective. We may readily believe that all the incidents narrated actually occurred on the natural plane, with the exception of the angelic appearance and the miraculous speech, which were perceived by the spiritual eyes and ears of Balaam. To him it was all a terrible reality; to him this was a real theophany, a genuinely divine interposition. It was just as real as if it had all been a literal sight and sound. Why should we doubt the correctness of this interpretation? Certainly it is in harmony with God's usual method of revealing Himself in that age; for no one can doubt that His revelation was, for the most part, by dreams and visions. Balaam's history in this connection shows that in two cases, at least, he waited until night, the usual and natural season for dreams and visions. There is no certain evidence that God ever revealed Himself otherwise to Balaam, unless this case be an exception. Why should we introduce a new method on the part of God? Why insist on a needlessly difficult interpretation when an easier one is in harmony with God's ordinary mode of communication? None of those present, as already suggested, seem to have been cognizant that any communication was made to Balaam. No wonder is expressed; no alarm was experienced; no comments were made. Let us adopt an interpretation which fully meets all the requirements of the case, which relieves the narrative from the enormous difficulties of the literal interpretation, and which is in perfect harmony with God's usual method of communicating His will to Balaam, and to other Old-Testament seers, which is in harmony with the statement in Numbers xii. 6, and in equal harmony with the words of Balaam in the twenty-fourth chapter. Why refuse to accept the teachings of these Scriptures? Why create difficulties? Why not believe the Bible, letting Scripture interpret Scripture?

Additional Teachings.

God can and often does reach out His hand and choose His servants from among idolatrous peoples. Perhaps reports of the miracles attending the exodus had reached Balaam in his own land; perhaps he was a descendant of Shem, and the germs of religious truth may have lingered long among the people. Perhaps Jacob's residence for twenty years in Mesopotamia disseminated the elements of true religion, though mingled with much superstition. God can still select His great instruments out of the most unfavorable environments. Balaam even spoke of God as "the Lord my God." Balaam's sin was great. He dared, for the reward which Balak offered, to abuse his office as a prophet, and to think that his divine gifts were his own, and to call down curses on God's people. He admired righteousness, but he loved the wages of unrighteousness. The bearer of sublime messages of Jehovah, he still counselled that the young women of Moab should lead the Hebrews to worship Baal-Peor, and as a result twenty-four thousand Israelites were slain. His conduct in this regard was abominable in the extreme.

But even Balaam, as he himself frankly confessed, could speak only as God ultimately directed. He was powerless in the presence of the Almighty. He was obliged to bless those whom he wished to curse. It is glorious to serve a God who can make even the wrath of men contribute to His praise. The fearful doom which befell Balaam warns us against seeking gain in ways of sin. If we are to die the death of the righteous, as Balaam hoped he might, we must live the life of the righteous as God commands us, and as our highest interest here and hereafter requires.

God still speaks.

XX.
DID THE SUN AND MOON STAND STILL?

XX.

DID THE SUN AND MOON STAND STILL?

Many persons are greatly troubled by the difficult miracles and histories recorded in the Bible. There was a time when the miracles were supposed to be of great evidential value. At that time, the greater they were in number, and the more stupendous they were in character, the greater was their supposed value. But that day has passed away, and it is not likely to return. Now the miracles themselves, in the judgment of many critics, need the support of alleviative explanations. Many persons turn away from the Bible, not because of what it really teaches, but because of what they suppose that it teaches. We ought always to bear in mind that to believe the Bible is one thing, but to believe all the interpretations of the Bible which some persons choose to give is quite another thing. Miracles performed by God we joyfully receive; but miracles imagined by commentators we certainly are at liberty to reject. Unfortunately, to doubt the interpretations of Scripture given by some men is to lead these men to declare that you doubt the revelations given by God; but one must be loyal to God's truth even at the expense of losing the good opinion of traditional interpreters of that truth.

No one who really believes in God can doubt the possibility of miracles. We know that God metes out the heavens with a span; we know that he holds the waters, even of the mightiest oceans, in the hollow of His hand. We must firmly believe that, by introducing laws now unknown to us, He could stop the clock of the universe without jarring its mechanism. The question before us is not, Could God perform the stupendous miracle of causing the sun and the moon to stand still? The simple question is, Did God cause the sun and moon to stand still at the command of Joshua? Does the account in Joshua x. 12-14 declare that the sun stood still? It may be unhesitatingly affirmed that it is not so stated in this Scripture, nor clearly in any other portion of God's Word. We know well that a man can arrest the progress of a machine many thousand times greater than himself; and we may confidently affirm that God could arrest the progress of the world in its course around the sun. All the discoveries of modern science, when rightly understood, make it easier to believe in God, in prayer, and in all spiritual realities. Let us clearly understand that the only question before us in regard to this passage is a question of fact. Was the writer speaking in impassioned and figurative language, or speaking in the language of sober and literal truth? These, let it be repeated, are simply questions of fact. This passage, it is frankly admitted, has given great difficulty to many commentators, and to all apologists of revealed truth. God for wise purposes has introduced miracles into both the Old and the New Testament, but for equally wise purposes He has apparently reduced them to a minimum. Let us look at some of the interpretations which have been given to this vexed passage.

Different Interpretations.

Many of the early rabbis and Christian fathers took the literal view of the passage. They supposed that the sun actually stood still in the heavens. The sun was then believed to revolve around the earth; thus these interpreters were ignorant of the diurnal motion of the earth, which has been wellnigh the universal doctrine since the time of Galileo and Copernicus. This view was held even after the reception of the Copernican system of the universe; but it was then explained as optical rather than strictly literal. It made, in this later modification of the view, the earth and not the sun the stationary body at the command of Joshua. These interpreters, however, differed among themselves as to the length of time during which the sun or the earth was stationary; some said forty-eight hours, some thirty-six, some twenty-four, and some twelve.

Another class of interpreters, led perhaps by Spinoza, affirmed that the miracle was caused by refraction and reflection. This view made the sun to appear above the horizon after the usual time of setting. We know that we get the afterglow of sunset in the diverse forms familiar to travellers in lofty mountains and in high latitudes. This result might be caused by a change in the atmospherical medium, and so the sun might appear to be above the horizon even after it had set. This explanation makes the miracle much less formidable than the literal view necessitates. It makes, as we have seen, a change merely in the atmospheric medium, and it leaves the rotatory motion of the earth undisturbed. The sun always is set before it appears to us to have gone below the horizon; by the law of refraction it appears to us to be above, when really it is below the horizon. According to this interpretation, all that it was necessary for God to do was to increase an effect observable in our daily experience. We would then have visibly the same result as if the earth had actually paused in its revolution round its axis. This explanation will relieve the minds of many readers of the Bible, and it will account for the phenomenon which some believe they find in this famous passage in Joshua. But is it necessary to introduce even this modified view? The real question before us, as already remarked, is simply one of fact. A third view is related to the one just given; it is what is called the subjective prolongation of the day. According to this interpretation, the day was not really lengthened, but was supposed by Joshua and the Israelites to have been prolonged. They were so busily engaged in conflict with their enemies, and they accomplished so much in the time, that they did not take accurate account of the time. It seemed to them that the day had been prolonged, and the writer simply records the popular opinion. This interpretation will relieve some minds of the stupendous difficulties inseparable from a strictly literal interpretation of the passage. There is a fourth interpretation which, it has been well said, is among the curiosities of biblical exposition. This view supposes that the lightning which accompanied the hailstorm was prolonged far into the night, and that thus the darkness was so illumined as to appear like daylight.

The Better View.

Is there not a more satisfactory explanation than any of those thus far given? The view presented first by Maimonides, the learned Jew born at Cordova, March 30th, 1135, a master in the Hebrew Scriptures, the Talmud, and Jewish literature generally, is that the passage is simply a poetic way of saying that the Israelites won their sublime victory before the setting of the sun. Before the day closed five kings with their armies were utterly vanquished. This view is indorsed by Hengstenberg, and by many other commentators, Jewish and Christian, Roman and Protestant.

It is very doubtful whether a strict interpretation of the words will warrant us in making Joshua's language a prayer to God. Are we obliged to regard his words as more literal than the apostrophe of Isaiah, "Oh that thou wouldst rend the heavens and come down, that the mountains would flow down at thy presence"? Are the words to be taken as more literal than the statement of Deborah and Barak that, "The stars in their courses fought against Sisera"? Are they more literal than the words of the psalm, "The hills melted like wax at the presence of the Lord"? Or the words of the other psalm, "The mountains skipped like rams"? Are they more literal than the words of Isaiah, "All the trees of the fields shall clap their hands"? Joshua's words remind us of the words of Wellington at Waterloo—"Oh, that Blücher or night would come!" There is in the "Iliad" a prayer by Agamemnon not unlike the words of Joshua on this occasion:

"Jove greatest, Jove most glorious sky-dweller, cloud bedight,
 Let not the sun nor darkness fall and wrap the world in night,
 Till Priam's stately palace I cast in ruin low."

It is to be said in general that the words in the original have been greatly misunderstood. The author's meaning is very obscure. The language attributed to Joshua is abrupt, broken, impassioned. It is absolutely certain that literally rendered it does not assert that the sun remained in the heavens a day, nor an hour, longer than its usual time. The passage simply affirms that the sun stood still long enough for the people to be avenged upon their enemies; it did not set until the great work of that heroic day was completed. A people, unused to the appliances of war, overcame with great slaughter soldiers fully armed and trained to military exploits. The sun and moon were witnesses of the valorous deeds of God's people; they held their courses until the triumph was complete.

It is fitting that we should look at the words a little more closely; a careful examination will show that even a tyro in Hebrew poetry can see that the words will not bear the meaning usually given them by traditional interpreters. It is very doubtful whether the language attributed to Joshua is, in any real sense, a prayer. No Hebrew scholar will deny that here nothing is said of a direct address *to* Jehovah; the address is not to *God*, but to the *sun and moon*. We see at once that the language in the original properly means, not *to* Jehovah, but *before*, or *in reference to* Jehovah. The verb translated "stand still" in the original is "*dōm*," and it generally means "cease," "rest," "be still," "keep silent." The meaning "stand still" seems to be an inference from the thirteenth verse, and not a translation. In Exodus xv. 16 and in Lamentations ii. 10 this verb signifies to be dumb with terror. It is often used figuratively to signify a silent or submissive frame of mind. See Psalms lxii. 11; iv. 4; xxxvii. 7, and Isaiah xxiii. 2. It is thus certain that the meaning is very indefinite. We have positively no right to make this word certainly mean that the sun's course was arrested in the heavens. It is also to be observed that the phrase in the thirteenth verse, "hasted not to go down about a whole day," is a mistranslation. The Hebrew *keyōm tâmim* means *as at the perfect day*. This says nothing whatever about the sun's remaining in the heavens for a whole day. If we compare Exodus xxxi. 18, and other scriptures in which a similar expression is found, we shall have full proof of the correctness of the interpretation now given.

It is distinctly stated in the thirteenth verse that this account is written in the Book of Jasher. The *sēpher hayâshâr*, or the "Book of the Upright," appears to have been a collection of eulogistic odes in praise of national heroes. This quotation is thus a part of a triumphal song, like that recorded in the fifth chapter of Judges, where in the twentieth verse there is a very similar thought, which has already been quoted in this article. The Book of Jasher is mentioned in 2 Samuel i. 18, where reference is made to teaching the use of the bow. There it is said the David's lamentation is partially an extract from this book. Some have supposed that this book refers to some book or books of the Bible itself, but that is not the common opinion. No one can read Joshua x. even in English without feeling that verses 12-14 are a quotation, if not an interpolation. No allusion is found in the Scriptures to this event, except in an obscure passage in Habakkuk iii. 11; and Josephus makes but a slight reference to this supposed miracle. A vast structure of argument has gathered around this passage, and it is now time that it should fall to the ground. The importance of the passage has been greatly exaggerated both by the friends and the foes of revealed religion. It is certain that in our version the passage is somewhat of a mistranslation; it is also equally certain that it is a quotation, and it is possible that it is an interpolation. In no case ought this uncertain passage longer to trouble devout students of the Word of God.

Josephus simply says in referring to this incident: "The day was increased, lest the night should check the zeal of the Hebrews." We have seen that if we accept the historicity of the narrative, it can be explained by the recognized laws of refraction and reflection without involving the tremendous consequences not only upon the globe itself, but upon the entire solar system, and even upon the equilibrium of the whole material universe, which the traditional interpretation necessitates. The Copernican system as set forth by Galileo invested the passage, interpreted literally, with alarming importance. Around it fierce ecclesiastical battles have been fought. The Vatican has had a conspicuous share in these battles, and has had often to confess its defeats. The explanation of Kepler is deeply interesting: " They will not understand that the only thing Joshua prayed for was that the mountains might not intercept the sun from him. Besides, it had been very unreasonable at that time to think of astronomy, or of the errors of sight; for if any one had told him that the sun could not really move on the valley of Ajalon, but only in relation to sense, would not Joshua have answered that his desire was that the day might be prolonged, so it were by any means whatsoever?"

In writing a history of the Civil War one might well quote Whittier's words in " Barbara Fritchie":

> "'Shoot, if you must, this old gray head,
> But spare your country's flag,' she said,"

without becoming responsible for the exact and literal truth of the story of this woman's loyalty. It is affirmed that history will not indorse the details of the poem. The writer of the Book of Joshua quoted from a book of poems; he so informs us in connection with the quotation. Why can we not believe him? Why must we create difficulties which the writer takes pains not to suggest? Let the battle over this vexed passage cease; let us take its own explanation of itself. Let God's Word interpret itself, although it prove many human interpretations to be erroneous. God's Word will stand forever.

XXI.

DID JEPHTHAH REALLY SACRIFICE HIS DAUGHTER?

XXI.

DID JEPHTHAH REALLY SACRIFICE HIS DAUGHTER?

This question has for many generations perplexed Bible students. The fact that Jephthah, in the eleventh chapter of Hebrews, is mentioned as one of the heroes of faith, has led many persons to doubt that he really offered his daughter in sacrifice. Volumes have been written on the subject of his rash vow; and many writers have stoutly maintained that his character should be relieved from the dark stain of having offered his daughter as a sacrifice in consequence of that vow. The account is found in the eleventh chapter of the book of Judges.

Jephthah was the ninth judge of Israel, and was of the tribe of Manasseh. His father's name was Gilead, and he was born out of wedlock. His father having died, his brothers, who refused him a share of the heritage, expelled him from his home. He then withdrew to the land of Tob, which was beyond the limit of Hebrew territory. He was distinguished always by great bravery of character and by equal skill in arms. After his banishment by his brothers, a number of desperate men gathered about him, and he became the leader of this reckless band. In this respect his life was not unlike that of David after his withdrawal from the court of Saul. Jephthah and his companions thus resorted to a life of brigandage; but such a life was not deemed dishonorable in the East in those days, nor in very much later times, especially so long as freebooters preyed simply upon public or private enemies and were not guilty of needless cruelties in their brigandage. They might rob and possibly murder, but they must do both with delicacy and despatch, and, according to the rules of their order, with some degree of gentlemanly deportment. This class of men were the Robin Hoods of that early day. We well know that in the border wars between England and Scotland a class of men of similar character long flourished with some degree of governmental authority and general approval. We also know that Columbus in his early life, and Drake and Raleigh, the naval heroes in the time of Elizabeth, and others of this general character, were really pirates. Jephthah was a freebooter of this class, and his aggressions were confined to small neighboring nations, who were in some sort the enemies of Israel even when a nominal peace was observed.

The Deliverer and Judge of Israel.

The Ammonites and their allies had held the country east of the Jordan in subjection for eighteen years. Once more the people turned in penitence to Jehovah, and once more He heard their prayer and sent them deliverance. The daring deliverer at this time was Jephthah, the rugged chieftain and reckless freebooter. His dashing exploits and successful enterprises gave him the reputation of great bravery and superb heroism. Notwithstanding that his brothers had driven him from home, when his kindred were groaning under foreign oppression, the people generally looked to this lawless compatriot for deliverance. It must have been a proud day for him when the deputation was sent to invite him to take command. He did not quite forget the treatment he had formerly received, but after some demur and delay he consented to be the leader of Israel's faithful band, who determined to return to God and to overthrow the enemies of the nation. The Ammonites were assembled in force when Jephthah sent to them demanding a reason for their invasion. His whole procedure was marked by a certain kind of rude dignity which we cannot but admire; it shows that even in that early day some provocation was required before any war was considered justifiable. The spirit of our own time in this regard was thus early anticipated. There is no nation to-day in Christendom that would declare war except it had grounds for the declaration which other nations might be expected heartily to approve. This fact makes nations extremely slow in our day to issue the final declaration making war inevitable. This principle seems to be deeply rooted in human nature. Jephthah recognized the propriety of this procedure; and the Ammonites also felt obliged to justify their aggressive operations by affirming that the land beyond the Jordan belonged to them rather than to the Israelites. The Ammonites were its owners before it was taken from them by the Amorites, from whom, in turn, the Israelites had captured the territory. On these grounds they attempted to justify their effort to recapture the soil. Jephthah laid down in his reply a principle which has been observed through the centuries among civilized nations—a principle which the great writers on international law have repeated and emphasized. It is most interesting to discover in this remote country and time the germs of international law as it has been fully developed in our own time. It was here affirmed that by right of conquest the Israelites secured the territory from its actual possessors; thus the Israelites could not recognize the claim of any former possessors, who had rendered them no assistance in securing the territory, but who had rather opposed the claims of the Israelites. The Ammonites, however, continued to assert their claims to the soil, and thus the issue was joined, and finally resort was had to the arbitrament of war. Jephthah thus saw that all negotiations with the king of the Ammonites would be fruitless. The Spirit of the Lord, as a spirit of strength and bravery, came upon him, and he at once prepared for war. The Gileadite elders consented—and their consent was solemnly ratified before the Lord in Mizpeh—that in the event of being victorious Jephthah should be considered as the head of the nation.

His Solemn Vow.

The war on which he entered was likely to be severe and deadly. Jephthah was under profound emotion; and he, in a spirit of reckless daring not unmingled with religious devotion, solemnly vowed to the Lord, "If thou shalt without fail deliver the children of Ammon into my hands, then it shall be, that whatsoever cometh forth of the doors of my house to meet me, when I return in peace from the children of Ammon, shall surely be the Lord's, and I will offer it up for a burnt offering." The word here rendered "whatsoever" in the authorized version may be rendered "whosoever," as it is without distinction of gender.

Jephthah girded himself for war. He burst upon the enemy with terrific fury. He drove the Ammonites before him, capturing twenty towns from Aroer on the Arnon to Minnith and to Abel Keramim. The Ammonites thus sustained a terrible overthrow. Jephthah was thus victorious, and he returned in peace to his house in Mizpeh. The news of his glorious victory preceded his own return to Mizpeh; but instead of being met by an animal or by a slave, his only daughter, in whom his heart was bound up with peculiar tenderness, filled with pride because of her father's splendid victory, came forth with timbrels and with dances to meet the triumphant hero. Her fair companions joined her in this hour of gladness and glory. But the sight of his daughter, dancing in the joy of her heart, was enough to freeze the blood in the father's veins and to stop his heart in its beating. What can it all mean? No sooner did he see his daughter than he rent his robes and cried, "Alas! my daughter, thou has brought me very low; for I have opened my mouth unto the Lord and cannot go back." The music is hushed; the maiden draws near in silence. The hero of the hour is the picture of despair. The wretched man forgets all the victories of the battle in this moment of domestic tragedy. Nobly does the heroic maiden speak: "My father, if thou hast opened thy mouth unto the Lord, do to me according to that which has proceeded out of thy mouth; forasmuch as the Lord hath taken vengeance for thee of thine enemies, the children of Ammon." Her beautiful young life is the awful price of his great victory, and the noble but misguided young woman insisted that he should not disregard his solemn vow. The bearing of both is equally striking in this sad calamity in their family life. Must she die—she, his only child, and so young and beautiful? The greatness of the sacrifice he must make almost crushes his life; but the brave-spirited maiden rises with a noble grandeur above her own sorrow, and above her father's grief, with her mistaken conception of God and duty; she glories in her father's and her nation's victory, even though it be at the price of her own beautiful young life. She is calm when rough-cheeked warriors turn pale and quiver with sorrow. She merely asks for a short period to be given her, which she will spend in the lonely depths of the mountains bewailing her sad fate—bewailing, as did the Antigone of Sophocles in her special grief, that she must die without the hope of becoming a bride or mother in Israel. No doubt all eyes were turned in admiration on the heroic girl. Then came the last sad scene, for "he did with her according to his vow."

The Daughter's Fate.

What was the fate of Jephthah's daughter? What did he do unto her according to his vow? Volumes have been written in answer to this question. It has been stoutly maintained that he did not offer her in sacrifice, but that she was simply doomed to a life of perpetual celibacy. Others, as Professor Bush, have affirmed that a human sacrifice was contemplated, but that during the time when the maiden bewailed her virginity upon the mountains, Jephthah obtained better information respecting the nature of vows, and that finally he redeemed his daughter at a legal valuation. As between this view and that of perpetual celibacy the idea of legal redemption is more probable; but neither view meets the conclusion that "he did with her according to his vow." If she were preserved from death there would be no significance in the lamentations of the daughters of Israel, and to make the word "lamentations" mean "celebrations" is certainly a forced significance. There is really no difficulty in the text; the entire difficulty arises from our unwillingness to accept the text in its natural meaning. Commentators have, therefore, invented a new thing in Israel, both in ancient and in modern times, that a damsel should be consecrated to perpetual virginity in consequence of a vow of her father. All unprejudiced interpreters must admit that nothing of this kind is contained in the vow; they must also admit that this idea is utterly foreign to all Hebrew notions regarding wifehood and motherhood. If commentators are at liberty, because of their dislike to accept the teaching of any part of Scripture, to inject into a given passage what, naturally interpreted, it clearly does not contain, then Scripture can be made to mean anything which commentators desire. Many Jewish interpreters admit that Jephthah sacrificed his daughter, and affirm that she was not devoted to perpetual virginity or to any form of religious service. It is even alleged that the dynasty of the house of Eleazar was passed over to that of Ithamar because the high-priest

permitted this horrible sacrifice to be performed.*
We do not know where the immolation took place,
but probably on some altar in the wild region beyond the Jordan. The painters represent it as
having taken place at the altar of the Tabernacle,
and Jewish authority can be quoted for this view,
but it is utterly impossible to believe that such a
terrible sacrifice could have taken place at the
altar of God, and a high-priest as the sacrificer.

The Horrible Sacrifice Hateful to God.

The story of this sacrifice lingered long in the
memory of the people; and for generations afterward Jewish maidens, in sympathy with the self-sacrificing spirit of Jephthah's daughter, bewailed
her fate. The story brings us into the atmosphere of classical times. We are reminded of the
sacrifice of Iphigenia, the daughter of Agamemnon and Clytemnestra. Agamemnon having
vowed to offer her, and having failed to keep his
vow, the Grecian ships could not sail from the

---

* Joseph Kimchi is especially the author of the interpretation that the maiden was shut up in a house which her father erected for this purpose, and that she was there visited by the daughters of Israel four days in each year while she lived. It is true that Hebrews such as Levi ben Gersom and Bechai, and Christian scholars such as Grotius, Bishop Hall, Dr. Hales and some others of earlier and later times have adopted this view. Lightfoot for a time held this view, but more careful study led him to abandon it and adopt the interpretation which the story naturally teaches.

port of Aulis against Troy until the offended gods were propitiated by the sacrifice of the maiden. There is thus often a close likeness between the Hebrew story and those of the heathen nations of nearly contemporaneous times. It was an age of rash vows. The whole nation made a vow against the tribe of Benjamin, and King Saul made a vow which nearly cost Jonathan his life. Jonathan would have been slain but for the interposition of the army; but there is no mention of an interposition on behalf of the heroic but misguided maiden and her brave but superstitious father. Without doubt the darker view of this tragedy is the correct one. It is true that human sacrifices were forbidden by the law; but Jephthah lived in Gilead, and Gilead adjoined the countries of Moab and Ammon, where human sacrifices were common. In the unsettled times in which the Judges lived many Israelites adopted the cruel practices and superstitious customs of their heathen neighbors, even good men performing acts as truly forbidden by the law as were human sacrifices. Thus an altar was set up by Gideon at Ophrah against the distinct law on that subject. It cannot be denied that human sacrifices were in these rude times often considered meritorious and propitious by some Israelites, as by almost all the heathen peoples. This was the first and last human sacrifice offered in a mistaken interpretation of the will of Jehovah. We must constantly bear in mind that this was a time of anarchy, ignorance, and superstition. Vows of celibacy were then entirely unknown among the Hebrews; the idea of nunnery belonged to a much later period, and to a different condition of society. It is affirmed that the maiden could not be dedicated to the services of the high-priest, for he and the ark were then at Shiloh in the territory of Ephraim, and Jephthah was then at deadly war with that tribe.

There is something peculiarly painful in the idea that this maiden, perhaps crowned with flowers and led forth with music and song to the altar, could have been a sacrifice pleasing to God. This act was the result of a false principle and a foolish vow; it was an act utterly hateful to God and utterly repugnant to all the finer feelings of human nature. Let us in no way hold God or true religion responsible for so cruel, abominable, and wicked an act. Such an act was not performed because its perpetrators had true religion, but simply because they were utterly lacking in true religion. It was not performed because God commanded it or approved it, but because its perpetrators, living in a heathen atmosphere, were ignorant of God's will, and so committed an act unspeakably displeasing to God and dishonoring to man. Tennyson in his poem, "A Dream of Fair Women," gives a glowing picture of this maiden lifted above herself in her desire to bless her country, assist her father and honor her God; but her mistake was as great as her self-sacrifice was heroic.

XXII.

DID SAMUEL APPEAR WHEN SUMMONED BY THE WITCH OF ENDOR?

XXII.

DID SAMUEL APPEAR WHEN SUMMONED BY THE WITCH OF ENDOR?

SAUL, the first king of Israel, is one of the most romantic and tragic characters of history. He was the son of Kish of the tribe of Benjamin, and his name means "the desired one." Zelah was probably the place of his birth. His father was a wealthy and powerful chief; and Saul while searching for lost asses found a kingdom. A "seer" was met on the journey, and he was none other than the prophet Samuel, who after a little time poured over Saul's head the oil of consecration. Saul was an unusually attractive man at that moment, as he towered head and shoulders above average men. He received both an inner and an outer call to the new life which awaited him by the ordainment of God. The latter call was given him at Mizpeh, when in his modesty he was hidden in the circle of the baggage which surrounded the encampment. His great stature aroused the utmost enthusiasm of the people; and soon they shouted, "Long live the king." This was the first time this shout was ever heard in Israel, and perhaps in the world—a shout later so often heard both in ancient and modern times in scenes of joy and sorrow, of comedy and tragedy.

Later, when Saul had apparently returned to private life, he heard as he drove his oxen near Gibeah those wild lamentations peculiar to Eastern towns when some great calamity has come. Soon he learned that Nahash, king of the Ammonites, had issued a terrible threat against Jabesh Gilead. The Spirit of God came upon Saul, as upon the Judges in an earlier day; and the shrinking and timid man was immediately transformed into the brave patriot and heroic leader. The bones of two of the oxen which he was driving were sent through the country as a suggestive message. The people came in a body to meet Saul at Bezek. The Ammonites were totally routed. Soon under the direction of Samuel at Gilgal the monarchy was inaugurated anew, and Saul was recognized with solemn sacrifices as the victorious leader in the kingdom, and was publicly installed and anointed. Samuel virtually gave over his own administration to Saul, whose military successes produced a profound impression on the people, and thus the monarchy was fully established.

Saul's First Transgression.

We are passing over great movements with only the briefest mention. We see Samuel gradually withdrawing from the responsibility of leader until Saul fully assumed that position before all the people. God was the true King, and

Saul simply His lieutenant. This relation was well understood both by Saul and the people. This is the true idea of the theocracy; but unfortunately when Saul was put to the test of this idea he proved unfit for his high office. The first trial led to the threat which ended in his rejection by God; for Saul forgot that he was only the servant of Jehovah. In the second year of his reign, as it is believed, he strove to shake off the heavy Philistine yoke. This yoke was peculiarly grievous in his own tribe, over which a Philistine officer exercised some degree of authority. Soon he raised a small army, which under the leadership of the noble Jonathan took a fort of the Philistines. Saul later was reduced to a great extremity, and the seventh day having come, whose expiration Samuel had enjoined Saul to await, Saul ordered sacrifices to be offered. Whatever was the exact nature of this act, the fact was soon recognized that Saul in performing it had greatly sinned against God. Saul's conduct at this point virtually involved a rejection of God, and the assumption of the claim to conduct the war according to his own will rather than God's command. Upon Samuel's arrival after the completion of the sacrifice he pronounced a curse on Saul's thoughtless zeal. Soon after, largely through the bold exploits of Jonathan, aided by a panic of the enemy, Saul effected a great slaughter; but his rashness led almost to the death of Jonathan. The reckless vow of Saul regarding this truly heroic son was the first appearance of Saul's madness. The Philistines, however, were driven to their own country, and for a time were confined within its limits. Great honor thus came to Saul, as no previous ruler had reached so high a position and had won so striking a triumph. Now he began the organization of a royal establishment, and we soon see the beginning of the institutions which marked the monarchy. There is the nucleus of a standing army; there is a bodyguard of young, tall, and handsome Benjamites; and there are official runners and messengers. David and Abner are the two principal officers at court, and they sat with Jonathan at the king's table. Another officer was the keeper of the royal mules. The king now appears in state. His tall spear became the symbol of his office; and it is still the mark of the dignity of the Bedouin sheik. It was reproduced in the great iron staff always carried by Ivan the Terrible of Russia as the symbol of the Czardom. This spear was ever after associated with Saul in battle, at his meals, and in his repose. It is as inseparable from his name as is the harp from David's name. We now see Saul with a diadem on his head and a bracelet on his arm. He has become an autocratic rather than a theocratic king.

Saul's Second Transgression.

The years pass. There is war with Amalek; and in sparing the conquered king and retaining the spoil Saul disobeyed the command of Samuel. Thus he failed a second time in the trial of his obedience to God and to His prophet. He failed to extirpate the Amalekites, whose hostility to the people of God was so old and so fierce. Saul probably spared the king in order to make a greater parade at the sacrificial thanksgiving. Josephus expressly says that Agag was spared for his stature and beauty; such a prisoner would greatly grace Saul's triumph. At southern Carmel he set up a monument, probably a triumphal arch of myrtles, olives, and palms, to commemorate his victories. His spirit of rebellion against God led to his final rejection; and his disobedience led Samuel to withdraw all approval from Saul. The separation between them was indicated by the rent in Samuel's robe of state, as he tore himself away from Saul's grasp. He was thus left to his sins and their inevitable punishment; and we read that "Samuel mourned for Saul."

His Last Offence.

From the time of Samuel's rejection of him Saul's life is one long tragedy. Doubtless at times he was mentally and morally insane. The frenzy which occasionally only touched him lightly at other times controlled him completely. He became at times the victim of melancholia; and then the subject of fierce and uncontrollable passion. David's harp temporarily chased away his sorrow; but soon it came back associated with the savage madness which broke out against David and Jonathan. The monarchy which he had organized was breaking down at every point. The Philistines were again in the land, and their chariots and horses swept over the Plain of Esdraelon. Near Shunem their camp was pitched. On the opposite side, on Mount Gilboa, was the army of Israel, clinging to the heights for safety against the resistless chariots of the Philistines. Great events are rushing on apace. Saul's army is near the spring of Harod, or the Spring of Trembling, a name which assumed an evil omen in connection with this sad history. The cup of Saul's iniquity is fast filling; he is to perform just one more act of open rebellion against God and that cup will be full. It is a solemn moment in Saul's checkered life. He is crossing the boundary line between God's patience and His wrath. God help us all when that terrible crisis comes, as come it may, in our lives!

Saul had driven out those who practised necromancy; perhaps his act was intended in some sense as an atonement for his many forms of disobedience to God. As we now see him his condition is desperate. He is forsaken of God and of men. No oracles now give him any communications of God's will. Samuel is dead, Samuel on whom he had leaned in so many crises for help, and had not leaned in vain. David is now alienated, David whose dash and bravery, love and loyalty had so often spared or delivered Saul in times of great danger. There is one witch left in the land; and we are now to see in Saul a strange mixture of superstition and religion at this trying moment. He asks his attendants to seek out for him a woman who had a familiar spirit, as the vague phrase in the narrative describes her. The expression more literally is "a mistress of the Ob," a name which is derived from the leathern bag, sometimes called a bottle, used in magical incantations, and it may suggest the practice of ventriloquism; the Septuagint translates the word "a ventriloquist." Probably the name "Ob" is so given because it was supposed that the spirit or demon which possessed the necromancer inflated the body so that it protuberated like the skin used as a bottle. The Ob of the Hebrews was thus exactly similar in conception to the Pytho of the Greeks, and the name might be used both for the performer and for the spirit which was supposed to possess him. Saul's act was positively forbidden by the law, Lev. xx. 6, which sentenced such pretenders to death, and Saul himself had recently enforced this law.

Her Residence.

Near Endor such a woman lived. There is a Hebrew tradition, mentioned by Jerome, that she was the mother of Abner, and that because of her relationship to him she escaped the general massacre of the necromancers at the hands of Saul. Let us get the scene clearly in mind. The armies are in full sight of each other; between them lies a part of the historic plain of Esdraelon. The sight of the Philistines filled Saul with fear, and so we read that "his heart trembled greatly." He is alone in his camp. Neither David, Samuel, nor God was now on his side. Neither by dreams, Urim, nor prophets would the Lord give him any answer. His suspense was terrible. If an answer will not come from heaven, perhaps one will come from hell. Look at the place as travellers see it to-day. A short ride from Nain brings us to Endor; the word means the "Spring of Dor." This spring has made the place habitable through all the centuries. Here are found to-day a few squalid people in their huts of stone and earth. Here are also some remarkable caves; enter these caves. Behold this one; it is roomy, and in it observe almost at any moment women filling their water-skins or jars. The walls of this cave are old, seamed, and weird. It is the traditional place of the abode of the witch of Endor, whom Saul came to consult. Wretched old women may still be seen coming out of their holes or caves to stare at strangers as they approach. It is no difficult task to imagine that one of these hags represents the old witch, who has made the place famous through all the centuries since Saul's visit. Saul's journey was a perilous one; but the outward danger was nothing compared to the horror of great darkness which filled his soul. We can still trace the road which he took. He must have crossed the plain, gone round the left flank of the enemy, ascended the ridge of Little Hermon, and then have gone down a steep descent to Endor.

Meaning of the Appearance.

Was the scene which followed a genuine apparition or a vulgar imposture? Volumes have been written in answer to that question. Many circumstances suggest that it was an imposture. Saul was in exactly the frame of mind which exposed him to an imposition; he was weak, excitable, and superstitious. He came to this woman by night; he sees her alone, his attendants being absent although near at hand. It is easy to suppose that one of his servants had agreed with the woman to personate Samuel. The narrative shows us that Saul did not see any appearance of Samuel. From this supposed ghost he learned nothing which he might not have learned from his attendants, except the words: "To-morrow shalt thou and thy sons be with me"; and attention has been called by several critics to the fact that the word translated "to-morrow" is very ambiguous, and often means the future indefinitely.

But others believe that Samuel did actually appear to Saul; and possibly it will be admitted that the narrative suggests the hypothesis of some kind of apparition. Josephus pronounces a labored eulogy on the woman. But the literal appearance of Samuel, it may be said in reply, is inconsistent with all which we know of the dead. Can the dead assume a corporeal shape? Can they converse and perform other acts of living beings? Can we suppose that the spirits of departed saints are amenable to the call of every old witch who chooses to dupe gullible men and women? Such a thought is incredible. Heaven would offer few attractions if saints like Samuel are to be called back to earth by witches like the woman of Endor. Others have suggested that the woman induced Satan or some other evil spirit to personate Samuel. But what right have we to assume that any person has such power over Satan? What right have we to assume that Satan has any power over, or any relation to, departed saints like Samuel? This theory is not encouraging to saints as they leave this earth.

Is it not better to suppose that God permitted a divine impression to be made, partly upon the senses of Saul and partly upon those of the woman, that Saul might be once more rebuked for his many departures from God? As we carefully read the narrative we discover that Samuel appeared before the woman had performed any of her tricks of jugglery. When she saw Samuel she was utterly amazed and cried out with a loud voice; and thus she appears to have been as much startled as was Saul himself. There seemed to have been no magical formulæ employed to cause the appearance, or to give her ground to affirm an appearance. God for wise purposes seems to have interposed, and to have given the woman a vision of the presence of Samuel; in this sense that presence was real to her, and through her statement real to Saul. God in a similar way moved upon the mind of Balaam so that he was obliged to bless those whom Balak desired him to curse. The hearts of all men and women are under the power of God; and He can overrule the evil of men for good. The woman believed that she saw Samuel, but Saul saw nothing. He simply listened to the woman's description of a god-like figure of an aged man wrapped in the royal cloak or sacred robe, an appearance like that of gods, and then Saul fell the whole length of his gigantic stature on the ground, and so remained until the woman and her servants forced him to take nourishment. The woman was an impostor, and Saul was in a sense her victim, but God overruled the duplicity of the one and the superstition of the other for the accomplishment of His divine purposes.

The Sad Ending.

Thus Saul heard his death-knell rung from the world of spirits. Back through the darkness he goes with his sorrowful heart wellnigh broken in his bosom. What a night he must have passed! The day dawns, and soon he is rushing into battle. The Philistines poured down the hill on the one side, and the Israelites were forced up the hill slopes. The battle was sore against Saul; the archers hit him, and he was mortally wounded.

He fought with the valor of despair. At his feet Jonathan and his other sons lay dead. Saul sought death, but it came not to his relief. He is faint and dizzy with the darkness and weakness of the approaching end. Fearing that he might be the sport of the Philistines if captured, he begs his armor-bearer to thrust him through with the sword. But respect for his fallen master prevents the servant from granting this boon. Behold Saul fixing his sword into the blood-stained ground, and see him falling upon it with the courage of despair! Now he lies in pain smeared with his own blood. A wild Amalekite, wandering over the upland waste seeking plunder, sees the dying king and at that king's request he puts him out of pain, giving him the *coup de grace*. He then took off the royal diadem and bracelet and carried them with the news of Saul's death to David. The Philistines found the body on the morrow, and stripped and decapitated it. The armor was sent into the Philistine cities, and apparently deposited in a temple at Bethshan; and on the walls of the same city was hung the naked and headless body of Saul, together with the corpses of his three sons. The body was removed from Bethshan by the gratitude of the inhabitants of Jabesh Gilead, who did not forget the kindness done them by Saul in the beautiful days of his early kingship. They came over the Jordan by night, took down the bodies, burned their flesh, and then buried the bones under a tamarisk at

Jabesh. David finally removed Saul's ashes and those of Jonathan to their ancestral sepulchre at Zelah in Benjamin.

There is no more melancholy character in Bible history than that of Saul. There was in him much that elicited admiration and evoked enthusiasm. But his rashness was controlled neither by sense nor conscience. The naturally fierce spirit of the tribe of Benjamin developed in him into uncontrollable ferocity. The naturally strong affection manifested toward David and Jonathan was perverted into bitter wrath, which finally developed into insanity. The zeal which was uncontrolled became disobedience toward God, and this disobedience was the cause of all his disasters. Those who reject God will believe in witches. Men who are too incredulous to believe in the Bible will believe in the ravings of ignorant, vulgar, and lying spiritual mediums and fortune-tellers. There is no depth too low for men who turn away from God, from purity, from truth, and from the Bible. The whole law of God is summed up by the divine Lord in the two great principles which are universal as gravitation and eternal as God: "Thou shalt love the Lord thy God with all thy heart, and with all thy soul, and with all thy might. This is the first and great commandment. And the second is like unto it; thou shalt love thy neighbor as thyself. On these two commandments hang all the law and the prophets."

XXIII.

DID TWO SHE-BEARS DESTROY FORTY-TWO CHILDREN?

XXIII.

DID TWO SHE-BEARS DESTROY FORTY-TWO CHILDREN?

The narrative of this incident in the life of Elisha is found in 2 Kings ii. 23-25. The belief that two she-bears, as a part of the curse of Elisha on the derisive children at Bethel, utterly destroyed forty-two of these young people has greatly perplexed many Bible readers, and has utterly offended others, who desire to accept unquestioningly the Bible narrative. Recently at a great assembly of Sunday-school teachers in this city a rector of one of the churches unreservedly affirmed that this incident was not authentic, that it was an interpolation, and that, without the slightest doubt, the event never occurred. His affirmations and the doubts engendered in the minds of many Christian people are largely, if not entirely, caused by a misinterpretation of the ancient story. It is most unfortunate that many readers of the Bible have confounded false interpretations with true revelations; it ought to be clearly seen that their objections are not really against the Bible narrative, but against incorrect explanations of that narrative.

Let us "fetch a compass" and approach this incident so that its salient features may be discovered and emphasized. Elisha was the successor of Elijah as the leader in the prophetical office. As such a leader it was fitting that he should visit the school of the prophets which was at Bethel. This place, it will be remembered, was then a chief seat of the illegal and idolatrous calf worship. Elisha is on his way from Jericho to Mount Carmel as he visits Bethel. In company with Elijah he had made his last visit to that historic town, when these two famous men were taking their memorable journey before Elijah's translation. We now approach the story at which many have taken offence. They have considered it unworthy of the great prophet; they have even declared that it was immoral on Elisha's part to pronounce a curse on these derisive youths. As Elisha approaches Bethel we see these youths clustered near the entrance to the town, as is the manner of the idle crowds in Palestine to this day. The incident which is about to occur is recognized at once as altogether unlike the life and spirit of Elisha, and as more nearly resembling those of Elijah. We have here the one case of severity in a life remarkable for its gentleness and beneficence; but a clear understanding of the facts in the case will remove many of the difficulties with which the story is associated in the minds even of devout readers of the Bible.

Not Irresponsible Children.

We are not for a moment to suppose that these derisive youths were little boys, merely irresponsible children, indulging in a childish prank as Elisha approached the town. If we examine closely the words which they uttered, as well as the conduct which they manifested, we shall clearly see that their abusive epithets were not born of a mere childish freak. They knew well what they were doing; they belonged to a city which was the centre of an abominable apostasy. Because of its bad pre-eminence Bethel, meaning "house of God," was called Bethaven, meaning "house of the idol." These youths incarnated the spirit and manifested the temper which we might naturally expect from the offspring of confirmed and aggressive apostates from God. They were not, as already affirmed, irresponsible little children. The objectors to this narrative generally assume that these were children, perhaps from six to ten years of age; but nothing could be farther removed from the facts in the case. The original terms are *nearim ketanim*, which may mean young men in the strength and vigor of their early manhood. *Naar*, the singular form of the word of which *nearim* is the plural, signifies not only a child, but a young man, a servant, a soldier, one actually fit to go out to battle. Isaac is called *naar* when it is believed he was twenty-eight years old; and Joseph was also called by this name when, according to some authorities, he was thirty-nine years old. The word is applied to the soldiers who served as a body-guard to Ahab. It is also applied to Solomon when he was at least twenty years old, at the time when he began to reign; and Jeremiah uses the word of himself when he was called to be a prophet. Those who translate the original terms by the phrase "young people" are probably entirely correct. It is quite certain that the terms could appropriately be used of those who had reached the period of early manhood, and who might be of different ages within that limit. We still speak of the Hebrews as the "children of Israel"; and different words in the Hebrew translated children have a great breadth of meaning.

It is thus evident that those who mocked Elisha were fully accountable for their abusive and irreverent language. If this fact had been held constantly in mind it would have entirely disarmed many of the severest critics of this ancient story. They have, as already implied, supposed that these were thoughtless, sportive, prankish, and merely fun-loving little children. Because of this misconception as to their age the critics have been disposed to consider that their offence was very light, and so their punishment was extremely severe. Thus the opposers of the narrative have affirmed, because of these misconceptions, that there was no proper proportion between the crime committed and the punishment inflicted. It has thus come to pass that rather than believe that divine revelation was responsible for so great an injustice many earnest Christians, as well as hostile critics, have rejected the narrative as an unauthoritative tradition or an unfortunate interpolation.

Meaning of the Insolent Epithet.

"Go up, thou bald head; go up, thou bald head." The original words thus translated are *aleh kareach*, and they are the language of grossest insult. Some have supposed that these words are equivalent to, "Ascend, thou empty skull, to heaven," implying that these youths knew of Elijah's translation. If this be the meaning, their language was blasphemy against God, and the punishment of these Bethelite idolaters was light compared with their crime. If this be the significance of the language, then great scorn is cast upon the ascension of Elijah. But this is probably not the correct interpretation. Many authorities affirm that the word translated "go up" does not mean "ascend," in the sense in which the ascension of Elijah took place. In addition to this consideration, it is not at all probable that these young people could have heard at this time of the ascension of Elijah. The language of the sixteenth verse clearly suggests that even the disciples of the prophet had not yet learned of the translation of their great master.

Let us get the scene clearly in mind. We see these young Bethelite defamers clustered about the entrance to their city. They behold Elisha at a distance as he approaches; they recognize him by the prophet's mantle. It was probably the mantle which Elijah had worn, and which he had left behind him as he ascended; it was, therefore, in a peculiar sense the symbol of the prophetic office. They recognized Elisha as an earnest opponent of the calf worship to which they were devoted, and of which Bethel in a special sense was the headquarters. They watch Elisha ascending the hill and approaching their city. They have come out probably as an organized band; they certainly were a numerous group, for if forty-two were injured by the bears there must have been more than that number in the entire company. They now call to Elisha in mockery, *Aleh kareach*, "Go up, thou bald head." It is as if they had said, "Be off, thou prophet of God; we do not want your presence in our city; let us be rid alike of God and His prophet." The word which is here translated "bald head" is a peculiar term, and it strictly describes shortness of hair at the back of the head; it is distinct from another term which describes baldness at the front of the head. The term does not necessarily affirm actual baldness. These youths could not notice the condition of Elisha in that regard, as they were now seeing him at a distance. It is true that Elisha might have been prematurely bald. We know, however, that he lived long after this event; but his baldness, if it existed, as already suggested, could not have been observed by these youths when they uttered their opprobrious language. It is quite well known that there could have been no artificial baldness of the head caused by shaving, as the law forbade those who were consecrated to the service of God from shaving the hair of the head. Probably the language attributed some form of moral culpability to Elisha; for baldness was often regarded as the sign of leprosy, or as the result of some form of moral dishonor. The epithet was, therefore, implicative of moral disgrace, and was thus a great reproach to Elisha as a man of God. Attention has been called to the fact that the tonsure among the Roman priests was long considered in many countries not as a mark of consecration and holiness, but rather as a symbol of moral impurity. It is absolutely certain that the language applied to Elisha was the keenest sort of scornful epithet when uttered against him as a prophet of the true God. We have not, therefore, here an exhibition of the mere wantonness of ordinary irreverence of boys for age or worthy character; we have rather a premeditated dishonor and a stinging insult to Elisha as the prophet and minister of the most high God. The scorn of these wicked youths was not so much against Elisha as a man, but upon his calling as a prophet. These defamers were despising Jehovah Himself. Elisha was simply the ambassador of God, and as such God rather than Elisha was the object of insult. His short-trimmed locks differed so widely from the shaggy hair of Elijah, which streamed down his shoulders, that the youths considered him and his claims to prophetship on that account, as well as because of their aversion to God and His worship, as a fit subject for denial and insult. We have thus dishonor cast upon God, and upon the office of prophet in the caustic language hurled at Elisha.

Elisha's "Curse."

This part of the narrative has been subjected to severe criticism. We must not suppose that Elisha in a petulant humor, and certainly not in the spirit of personal revenge, declared God's punishment of the sin committed. As God's prophet he was making his first appearance in Bethel. He could not allow this open mockery to pass in silence. Had he permitted these boys to go unrebuked he would have practically denied his holy calling, and would have dishonored his divine Master. Great Britain and the United States cannot allow any form of dishonor to be given to their ambassadors in any land; for these ambassadors represent the dignity, honor, and power of their respective governments. Elisha was the representative of the great God in the midst of the worshippers of calves, and the honor of God was involved in the honor of His prophet.

But what do we mean by Elisha's curse? What did Elisha do? Certainly he did nothing more and nothing other than to declare the divine judgment on the wicked spirit and language of these youths. He spoke in the name of the Lord, *beshem Jehovah*, by the name or authority of Jehovah. It is certain that Elisha had no power in or of himself to inflict the punishment which came upon these deriders of God; he could not cause bears to come out of the wood. All that Elisha could do was to declare the punishment upon these sinful youths; and certainly Elisha could do nothing less. It is to be said regarding this part, and all parts of the narrative, that possibly something is omitted in the record as we have it, or some expression has greatly changed its meaning since the record was made, and so difficulties in the narrative are multiplied. It is almost certain that if additional facts were given all apparent disproportion between the offence and the punishment, and regarding every other difficulty in the narrative, would entirely disappear.

The Punishment Inflicted.

What was the punishment thus inflicted on these derisive and irreverent youths? We are told that there "came forth two she-bears out of the wood and tare forty and two children of them." To this hour, as many travellers have observed, the road to Bethel winds up the defile, and under the hill there are ruins which are supposed to be those of Ai. There are still some trees found in this vicinity; but in Elisha's day the neighborhood was marked by a thick forest which was the home of wild beasts. We are now dealing, let it be carefully remembered, with the judgment of God which befell these depraved youths. God had distinctly said: "I will also send wild beasts among you, which shall rob you of your children and destroy your cattle, and your highways shall be desolate." When did these bears come forth in relation to the time of the committal of the offence by these young people? We are not told; the time may have been long afterward. Regarding this matter it is impossible to make an affirmation. But frankness compels us to say that the natural impression of the narrative is that this result happened soon after the mockery by the youths took place. Why are we distinctly told that the instruments of the punishment were "she-bears"? There must be a reason for this characterization, otherwise any bears might have served the divine purpose in the infliction of merited punishment. We know that she-bears are particularly fierce; especially when robbed of their whelps are they peculiarly ravenous. To this fact frequent reference is made in Scripture. It is not at all impossible that these forty-two youths who were thus injured, in a spirit of recklessness while employed in the wood may have robbed these bears of their young.

The bears having been robbed may have been in the track of these youths at the time they insulted the prophet. God's providence easily could have ordered this natural occurrence so as to give it the effect of a divine cause, as indeed it was. According to this conjecture, the bears were filled with wrath for the loss they had sustained, and the justice of God readily could guide them to the group of the insulting and blasphemous youths.

But what was the extent of the punishment inflicted? Much depends, in the correct interpretation of the narrative, upon a right answer to this question; and at this point careless readers and traditional interpreters have greatly erred. They assume that forty-two of these youths were killed. How do we know that they were killed? It ought to be constantly affirmed that it is not asserted in this narrative that these bears ate forty-two, or two, or even one of these reviling young people. The word means only that the bears rent, or tore, to a greater or less degree, forty-two of these insolent youths. The word is used with considerable breadth of meaning in different connections. Perhaps nothing more is asserted than that the flesh was torn, possibly only the clothing; and there is a bare possibility that simply the group was torn asunder, scattered pell-mell in every direction; although the special references to the forty-two would indicate that something happened to them which did not occur to others of the number. The natural impression is that an injury of some serious kind was inflicted, although its extent cannot be accurately learned from the word employed; but it is absolutely certain that it is not here affirmed that even one child was killed. This fact ought to be emphasized whenever the story is discussed. It is a thousand pities that meanings have been put into this word "tare" which it will not bear and which its connections nowhere suggest. The true explanation of the word tare relieves the narrative of the supposed disproportion between the crime committed and the punishment inflicted.

Lessons.

This story of the olden time is suggestive of lessons for modern life and daily duty. It is always a serious thing to reproach any person for infirmities or deformities. It is still more so to attribute physical or moral defects where they do not exist. Those who reproach a man because he is a servant of the most high God blaspheme God whose servant he is. There are times when righteous wrath is not only justifiable but its absence would be culpable. The nobler the soul and the purer the heart the more quickly will they flash out against injustice to God or man, and against moral wrong wherever found. God always has at hand the means of punishing the guilty. He has hidden resources in the soil to destroy the doomed cities of the plain. He has bears in the woods in leash waiting for the command to injure irreverent youths. He has in earth and air, in sea and sky, forces of nature which in harmony with natural law will inflict inevitable punishment upon all the violators of His law. No wicked words, no irreverent acts, no unholy thoughts escape the notice of the great God of heaven and earth. When the furious Saul persecuted the believers in Jesus he persecuted Jesus Himself. He who defames the prophets of God, or offends even the little ones who believe in Jesus, strikes a blow at the majesty of heaven and gives sorrow to the heart of the loving Saviour. God's feeblest saints are dear to Him as the apple of the eye; the names of His lowliest children are written in the palms of His hands, and every time the hands are opened He sees their names, and as often as the hands are closed all the forces of heaven and earth are employed for their protection.

XXIV.

THE DESTRUCTION OF THE CANAANITES.

XXIV.

THE DESTRUCTION OF THE CANAANITES.

WAS the destruction of the Canaanites justifiable? In the judgment of many earnest students, the moral difficulties in the Book of Joshua are greater than are the astronomical difficulties. The destruction of the Canaanites by the command of God, and through the instrumentality of Joshua, has been a subject of frequent attacks by infidels upon the morality of the Bible and upon the character of God. We all know that even the most earnest believers are often perplexed by the moral problems arising out of this subject and demanding solution. Why did God command, or even permit, this destruction? How could such massacres occur without utterly demoralizing the people responsible therefor? How could a book claiming to be divine even seem to indorse such terrible slaughters? These questions demand our careful consideration, and to them alleviative answers can be given.

Character of the Age.

The age was one in which might made right. God has revealed Himself to men in sundry parts as men were able to receive the revelation. That God commanded the extermination of the Canaanites is most certain. In Deuteronomy we read: "Thou shalt save alive nothing that breatheth; but thou shalt utterly destroy them," and the reason assigned for this command is, "That they teach you not to do after all their abominations." Is such a command in harmony with the divine attributes of justice and mercy? God has to do—it is said reverently—the best He can with the material in His hand. The age of Joshua was characterized by great ignorance of God. Thus there was a low ethical standard among men. Men were savage and brutal; acts were then permitted, and even commanded, which would have been utterly prohibited under the Gospel dispensation. Men had not then learned to say: "Our Father, who art in heaven"; and being ignorant of the Fatherhood of God, they were correspondingly ignorant of the brotherhood of man. The spirit of mercy inculcated by Christ was entirely unknown in that rude time. It is quite unfair, as we shall later fully see, to carry back from the New Testament the morality there taught, and apply it to the conduct and character of men who did not have the full and blessed light of this highest revelation of God. It was also a time when property belonged to communities rather than to individuals. Communities were, therefore, held responsible for the acts performed by their representatives. Punishment of nations was in harmony with the forms of justice then prevailing. Joshua believed himself to be the minister of God in the punishment of the Canaanites. He was what the courts and officers of the law are in our day. Have they right to pronounce judgment and to take life? Joshua had a higher right in both respects; he was God's direct instrument. The Israelites were in a sense responsible for the morality of the Canaanites; and frequent rebukes by God were administered to the Israelites for not having more fully obeyed His command in the punishment of His and their enemies.

It was also the practice in that day among all nations to put to death all prisoners taken in war. The humanity of our time is the development of thousands of years of Christian teaching. It must ever be borne in mind that the commands of God through Moses were greatly in advance of the moral education of the world at that time. Never was a leader of conquering armies less governed by selfish motives and unholy ambitions than was the brave and noble Joshua. Compared with Alexander the Great, Cæsar, Charles V., Philip II., or Napoleon, Josuha appears conspicuous for noble character, selfless motives, and religious consecration. Men must always be judged with reference to the standard of morality of the times in which they lived. Moses and Joshua were far in advance of the moral standard of their age; they were the unworldly and godly men of their time. The charge rightly made against Columbus is, that he lived below the highest standard of his time; a similar charge might be made against some of the practices of the Puritans, even after they came to the New World. All students of history must admit that the Jewish religion never introduced barbarism into the world; on the contrary, it greatly softened the spirit of cruelty wherever it was established. Such conquerors as the Assyrians, Babylonians, and Persians were far less merciful than was Joshua. The Greeks and Romans stained the progress of their armies by crimes from which Joshua was entirely free. These classic nations did not hesitate to dedicate captive women to the impure worship of Aphrodite or Mylitta. The violation of women was almost universal in the case of towns sacked by armies of the earlier heathen, and even of later Christian days. Goths, Vandals, Huns, Bulgarians, and Turks, frequently surpassed Joshua in their pitiless cruelties. The conduct of the Duke of Alva, Philip of Spain, and the Pope of Rome in relation to the Netherlands was vastly more abominable, in their various forms of atrocity, than was the conquest of Joshua over the Canaanites.

This a General Problem.

How could God, we may ask, permit the barbarities of pagan Rome against the early Christians? How could God permit the still more awful crimes of Papal Rome against those whom that church called heretics? How could God, in comparatively recent days, permit the satanic atrocities of the Spanish Inquisition? How could the nations of Europe and the republic of America permit the hadean slaughter of the Armenians by the Kurds and the Turks? How could the American republic long, without effective protest, permit the nameless cruelties of a Weyler in Cuba? We do not, indeed, answer one difficulty by suggesting other difficulties; but we show, at least, that the problem is not peculiar to Joshua or the Bible.

Let it be remembered that often apparent severity is the truest leniency in war. The storming of Drogheda in Ireland by Cromwell has been fiercely criticised, but his act received justification not only in his own day, but in our time as well. Carlyle affirms that, terrible as was Oliver's surgery, it prevented greater suffering by bringing the war to a speedy end; in this respect it was more merciful than would have been a gentler course. Cromwell was himself convinced that his severity "prevented the effusion of blood for the future." As a matter of fact, his sternness speedily ended the Irish war. The conduct of the British armies in suppressing the Sepoy atrocities in the Indian mutiny is a case in point. It was not in wanton cruelty that General Neill tied Sepoys to the mouths of cannons, and then fired the cannons, and shot the cruel wretches into fragments, thus inflicting apparently shocking forms of cruelty. He took advantage of a prevalent superstition among the Sepoys to the effect that the bodies thus mutilated would suffer additional humiliation and torture in the world to come. His act struck a degree of terror into the hearts of the rebels such as it is difficult for us to comprehend. It largely overthrew the rebellion. For every Sepoy thus put to death, it is safe to say that at least five hundred lives were saved. It is also certain that if the Israelites had followed up their first successes by similar crushing victories, they would have speedily become masters of Palestine, and would thus have saved many lives and averted many moral evils.

Guilt of the Canaanites.

We ought also to remember that the Canaanites were guilty of the most abominable crimes conceivable by the human mind. They sinned against the light of nature, against the example of the patriarchs, and against the warnings given by God in the punishment of Sodom and Gomorrah. In His commands against them God was but expressing His indignation against horrible forms of vice. We have only to turn to the Book of Leviticus to see the awful catalogue of abominations, which, we are distinctly told, were committed by the people of the land. Some forms of their crimes were long punishable by death in Great Britain and in her colonies. This writer once saw a young man on trial for his life under the forms of British law, charged with one of the crimes of which the Canaanites were guilty. No words are too strong to express the indignation which all true men must feel against the nameless crimes committed by these beastly Canaanites. Indeed, it is unfair to animals to put them in the same category with the inhabitants of the land which the Israelites came to conquer. When Israel refused to destroy these pamperers of vice, she lapsed into their idolatrous and lustful practices; she even sacrificed children on the altars of Moloch. Thus it was that their religion was degrading beyond description. When fifteen hundred years later some of their practices were introduced into Rome, the satirists of that day regarded the advent of these vices as an enormous calamity. These Canaanites knew of God's wonders in Egypt and of the victories over the kings of Gilead and Bashan. They knew that God had chastised the Hebrews for participating in the abominations of Baal-Peor. We know that Rahab informed the spies that she had known of God's mighty judgment; so, doubtless, did others. She repented and was saved, and perhaps a goodly number of others also repented and were saved. All might thus have been saved. God might indeed have punished the Canaanites by the operation of natural laws; He does punish in that way violators of moral laws in our day. No man can escape these laws; they follow him as does his shadow. But if God had punished the Canaanites by epidemics, by pestilence, or by some other display of His righteous wrath, His abhorrence of sin would not have been so clearly shown as when He used the Israelites as the instruments of His righteous anger. Nature inflicts its wrath now upon weak women and harmless children, and whatever charge may be made against the God of revelation must also be made against the God of nature.

A General Law.

Let it further be remarked that the nation that will not conform to the highest civilization of its time will by that civilization be destroyed. This statement is the formulation of a law universal as God and irresistible as gravitation. God was now about to introduce the fullest manifestation of His kingdom yet given to men; and He required a territory from which evil influences were absent for the display of His great purposes. Similar truths are illustrated in America. God had great purposes in the establishment of the American republic. But in order that Pilgrim and Puritan fathers might have an appropriate sphere for planting and developing the great principles of American civilization and Christianity, the Indian had to be driven back from his former hunting-ground. The process has continued until this day. The Indian's territory was demanded for a higher civilization, and for that purpose, by various providential combinations, it was taken. The Indian has been driven back and back almost to the other edge of the continent. The process will go on until he is either civilized or exterminated. Doubtless, great cruelties have been practised against the Indian on our own continent; doubtless, solemn treaties have been broken, and the white man has been guilty of much injustice toward his red brother. Nevertheless there is divine justice and an inevitable necessity in the operation of the law that nations that will not submit to the highest civilization of their time shall by that very civilization be destroyed. The greatest good to the greatest number necessitates the execution of this apparently severe but universal and eternal law. Dr. Arnold rightly teaches us that "The Israelites' sword, in its bloodiest executions, wrought a work of mercy for all the countries of the earth, to the very end of the world."

As a final consideration, it is to be remembered that there is an anger which is not sinful. Indeed, the tenderer men are the more righteously wrathful do they become against wrong wherever found. He is only a being of paste and putty whose anger does not flash out against certain crimes committed against God and man. Jesus was a terrible Preacher against the hypocrites of His day. There are times in which even the holiest souls find appropriate vehicles in the imprecatory Psalms for the expression of their highest thought. Dean Stanley calls attention to the fact that during the Sepoy rebellion the Book of Joshua was read in the churches with a great sense of appropriateness. There is need to-day of certain phases of the moral indignation against evil expressed in many of the Psalms and illustrated in the conduct of Joshua and the Israelites. Let us be modest in passing judgment upon those who had to deal with the abominable cruelties and indescribable impurities which the Moabites committed in honor of Chemosh, and the Philistines in honor of Dagon. Let us not be wiser than God. Only the man who is wiser, tenderer, purer, and holier than God may presume to criticise God. God had His purpose all through this bloody period. His people fought not simply against the enemies of Israel, but against the enemies of humanity. We to this hour are reaping good fruit from the seed which they sowed, though they often sowed it amid tears and blood.

XXV.

ARE THE IMPRECATORY PSALMS JUSTIFIABLE OR EVEN EXPLICABLE?

XXV.

ARE THE IMPRECATORY PSALMS JUSTIFIABLE OR EVEN EXPLICABLE?

By the Imprecatory Psalms we mean those psalms in which the author invokes curses upon his enemies, and does this in a real or apparent spirit of vindictiveness. In some of the psalms to which this title is applied the author seems to take positive delight in the suffering of his foes. Some psalms in their entirety are usually classed as imprecatory; and parts of other psalms bear this title. It is believed by competent critics that the psalms which are most intensely imprecatory bear strong marks of the authorship of David. The following are among the psalms or parts of psalms to which the title imprecatory is generally applied; these are not, indeed, all the psalms that could be selected of this class, but they are fair specimens of the spirit and style of all the psalms to which this title can properly be given: of the entire psalms usually classed as maledictory the following may be named: Pss. xxxv., lviii., lix., lxix., and cix. Parts of other psalms are usually placed in this category: Pss. iii. 7; v. 10; ix. 2–4; x. 15; xviii. 37–43; xxviii. 4; xxxi. 17; xxxv. 3–8; xxxvii. 12–15; xl. 14; lii. 5–7; lv. 9, 15, 23;

lviii. 6–10; lix. 12–15; lxiii. 9–11; lxiv. 7–9; lxviii. 2; lxix. 22–25; lxxix. 12; lxxxiii. 9–17; cix. 6–15; cxxxvii. 7–9. In some of these passages, especially cix. 6–11 and cxxxvii. 8, 9, the maledictory spirit is very marked.

No one can deny that these portions of Holy Scripture have seriously perplexed devout readers, and that they have also furnished plausible objections to those who deny the inspiration of these psalms. Some of these psalms breathe a spirit of revenge and malice apparently inconsistent with all our ideas of true religion; indeed, some of them shock sensitive readers, and startle those who are not sensitive. It has been gravely proposed by men not lacking in devoutness that an expurgated edition of the psalter should be prepared for general use, an edition which should omit all psalms possessing this maledictory spirit. Various theories have been propounded by scholars in different countries and centuries to explain the presence of these psalms, and portions of psalms, in a book claiming to be directly from God. No one will deny that the difficulty connected with their presence in such a volume is real and great. Perhaps it is impossible entirely to remove these difficulties. Difficulties, however, of many kinds are not peculiar to the Bible as a revelation from God; difficulties are found in natural science, in mental philosophy, and in practical morals which we cannot entirely remove. But although all difficulties connected with the imprecatory psalms cannot be removed, it is quite certain that some really alleviative suggestions can readily be made.

Alleviative Explanations.

It is quite certain that some critics have greatly exaggerated the spirit of vindictiveness recognized by all in some parts of the psalter; but it ought to be borne in mind that really very few of the psalms possess this characteristic. Dean Stanley in his lectures on the Jewish church, vol. ii., p. 170, calls attention to the fact that out of one hundred and fifty psalms in the psalter, only four are specially marked as possessing a vindictive spirit. In this connection we ought to emphasize the fact that much importance should be attached to the natural vehemence of expression among the Orientals, as compared with the habits of thought and language on the part of those living in cooler climates and possessing different characteristics. It is absolutely certain that much that is supposed in these psalms to be harsh and vindictive may be referred to the spirit of the age in which the psalms were written, and to the characteristics of the writers themselves. Critics of all kinds of literature ought to judge an author by the standards of his own age and place, and not by standards of our time and place. We constantly apply these principles to the Greek and Latin poets, to the records of knight-errantry in the Middle Ages, to the language of Covenanters and Puritans, and, indeed, to authors of all times and places. It is certain that Biblical authors are equally entitled to the application of this principle of literary criticism. It is quite certain that often uneducated men who use rough and seemingly harsh words mean to express no more harsh and cruel feeling than other men express in the smooth tones and courtly phrases of a more refined culture. He is an unfair critic, to judge the subject purely on literary grounds, who refuses in his study of the imprecatory psalms to give due weight to the genius of Hebrew poetry and the spirit of the age in which David lived. The true critic will always strive to distinguish between an author's real meaning and the color which his mental habit, national education, and immediate environment give to that expression. Except this principle be constantly borne in mind, we shall pass an utterly false judgment on the Covenanters of Scotland and the Puritans both of Old and New England. David certainly is entitled to a fair application of this conspicuously fair principle of literary criticism. We all know that the Oriental, even to this day, uses extremely strong language for the expression even of ordinary feeling and opinion. When Europeans would express the idea that God loves men, they use a simple statement to that effect; but when the Asiatic prophet expresses the same idea he says: "Thy maker is thy husband"; and he further expresses the idea by referring to the joy of the bridegroom over the bride as illustrative of God's joy in His people. These statements are almost objectionable because of the amatory element which the Occidental discovers; but the form of expression was most natural and proper to the Oriental. In like manner the Oriental expresses his sense of justice in language equally strong. The apparently terrific denunciations of the psalmist meant nothing more to him than language which we often use without offending the most sensitive readers. This principle of criticism ought carefully to be applied to the writings of all Oriental poets and prophets. Many opponents of the Bible have been guilty of great unfairness because of their failure to recognize this eminently appropriate principle in their interpretation of the psalter and other portions of the Old Testament.

Some have found an alleviative interpretation in the opinion that some of the imprecatory psalms are predictive rather than maledictive. This interpretation implies that the imprecations state what would be rather than what the writer desired should be. But this view must not be pressed unduly. The more careful study of the Hebrew original in these recent times does not warrant this view, except possibly in a very limited application. The scholarship of an earlier day made some of the passages to be rendered in the future rather than in the imperative; possibly in some cases the laws of the Hebrew language will permit this interpretation. So far as this explanation is permissible, the idea is that the punishment denounced is what sinners deserved rather than what the writer desired on their account. This language is predictive rather than imprecative. It expresses what, in the operation of natural laws with which we are all familiar, is sure to follow a course of evil conduct. Sin will be followed by sorrow; what a man sows that shall he assuredly reap. We cannot separate between sin and punishment; punishment will follow sin as the shadow follows substances in the sunshine. But even if this interpretation is applicable to a few passages the most serious difficulties still remain, as this explanation will not meet all the cases. It is quite certain that in some passages there is an expression of feeling, of desire, of pleasure in the invocation of terrible calamities upon the enemies of the writer. This is at best a timid way of dealing with real difficulties. Can this vindictive spirit be reconciled with the character of Christianity? Is it in harmony with any form of revealed religion? These are most serious questions, and they deserve the most careful consideration.

An alleviative interpretation has been suggested on the ground that the duty of forgiving enemies is not distinctly taught in the Old Testament. But this is not a tenable position. The Jewish Scriptures condemn a spirit of revenge. It would be easy to quote passages from Exodus,

Leviticus, Proverbs, and from still other portions of the Old Testament to show that even these Scriptures did enjoin the requiting of evil with good. It is also true that David recognized this obligation, and was himself frequently a noble illustration of the spirit of magnanimity toward his foes. It is to be said that in some cases the writer of these malefic passages merely records the feelings of others, and in those cases he is not to be held responsible for the language employed. This explanation covers a number of cases, and some of them those of the most serious character. The writer merely expresses the gratification which others would feel in seeing vengeance inflicted on their enemies, even though that vengeance should come in the most cruel forms. In these cases all that the writer, or the Spirit of inspiration, is responsible for is the correctness of the record. The writer is merely telling the story of the cruelty of others, and is not expressing any cruel feelings of his own. In Genesis xxxiv. 25–29, xlix. 6, 7, the inspired writer gives a record of the cruelty of the sons of Jacob; so in 2 Sam. xii. 31, we have simply a statement of the cruelty which had been inflicted and for which the writer had no responsibility whatever. One of the most startling of the imprecatory passages is the one in Psalm cxxxvii. 8, 9; this passage has shocked many devout students of the psalter; but it is simply a statement of the actual feelings of those who should wreak vengeance on Babylon. The pride and arrogance of Babylon had been so great that we can well suppose many who should see her terribly punished would have the utmost satisfaction, even though that punishment were savage and barbarous in the extreme. But there is nothing in this record necessarily to show that the author of the psalms rejoiced in the infliction of that punishment. This solution of the difficulty will certainly apply to some of the imprecatory passages. It is quite certain that Mr. Motley, in writing of the cruelties of Alva in the Netherlands, or of the Inquisition in Spain, or any recent writer speaking of the satanism of Weyler in Cuba, must not be supposed as sympathizing with the cruelty which he describes. This explanation will not apply to all the objectionable passages, but it certainly does to a number of them, and is an explanation to which due weight should be given.

Still Other Alleviations.

It has been proposed by some writers to explain these imprecations on the ground that they are the language natural to the human heart, language which naturally and actually occurred to the mind of the psalmist but which is not commended to us for imitation. Inspiration is not omniscience; inspiration is not perfection. The spirit of inspiration is not responsible for wicked thoughts on the part of the psalmist, any more than it is responsible for wicked acts on the part of Abraham, Jacob, David, or Peter. The biography of other men in the Bible clearly shows that they were guilty of acts which must be condemned even by their own standards of morality. If inspired men may do selfish and resentful acts, they may also speak passionate and unrighteous words. The Scripture is always honest in its statements even regarding eminent servants of God. It palliates nothing; it dares tell the whole truth. Without doubt this illustration of truthfulness on the part of the Bible is an element of its great power. It does not present to us the life of the most distinguished saint as free from struggles with sins and temptations. It does not give us the highest forms of religion conceivable, but it represents its noblest men as struggling with manifold temptations and so working out a noble character. The failings even of Moses, David, and Peter have given encouragement and inspiration to all subsequent ages, even as the heroic morality of Joseph and the unfaltering courage of Daniel have rebuked weakness and encouraged fidelity and loyalty. Thus the psalmist does not select simply his highest emotions and his noblest aspirations for exhibition in his writings; but he gives a true picture of his own heart in its various struggles against evil and toward good. The psalmist was only partially sanctified. No true view of inspiration requires us to deny that vindictive feelings might arise in the mind of an inspired poet and a partially sanctified king. The

Bible frankly admits David's great sins. The religious emotions of the best men are mingled with imperfections. The spirit of inspiration is not responsible for these feelings, any more than for the evil acts of those whose lives are recorded; it is responsible simply for a correct record of these feelings and acts. These portions of the writer's feelings are not given for our imitation. Inspiration is not sanctification. Balaam uttered true, glowing, and sublime prophecies, and yet Balaam was in many respects a bad man. No man will deny that such men as Augustine, Luther, Melanchthon, Calvin, Knox, and scores more in earlier and later days, were at times guilty of un-Christian feeling and unholy action. It should constantly be borne in mind that perfection is unknown even among the greatest saints of all ages and climes. A man may be a true historian and not be in the full sense a true man.

A very helpful alleviative interpretation is found in the fact that David identifies the enemies of God with his own enemies. The critics of these portions of the psalter have largely forgotten this fact, but it is a fact that ought never to be forgotten. David speaks not so much against the enemies of David as against the enemies of David's Lord. He well expresses his own spirit when he says: "Do I not hate them, O Lord, that hate thee?" "I hate them with perfect hatred; I count them mine enemies." The author of the article on the Psalms in Smith's

Dictionary of the Bible, in illustrating this point, calls attention to the fact that even Catiline had insight enough to say, "An identity of wishes and aversions, this alone is true friendship." Applying this test to David in his relations to God, we can see that the union between them was such that all God's enemies David regarded as his own personal foes. David was in a sublime sense God's representative; the honor of God's name and the glory of God's kingdom were in a marvellous way committed to the care of David. In requiting the wrongs of his Lord and King he forgot his own wrongs as committed against himself, and thought of them only as committed against his God. An American or British ambassador at a foreign court may entirely lose sight of an attack upon himself, and consider it simply as aimed at the government whose representative at that court he is. David's zeal for God made all God's enemies in some sense his own enemies. It has been well said, by the writer to which allusion has just been made, that it was when David felt God's honor to be insulted that he rose to so lofty a vengeance as to express himself thus:

"That thy foot may be dipped in the blood of thine enemies,
And the tongue of thy dogs in the same."

Many other similar examples of the manifestation of this spirit could readily be given. David rises to his noblest strains of righteous wrath when he is defending God's honor and is entirely forgetful of his own personal wrongs. It would be easy to quote passages from these psalms showing his kindness, gentleness, and forgiveness toward his own foes. There is a striking illustration of this spirit in Psalm xxxv. 12, 13: "They rewarded me evil for good to the spoiling of my soul. But as for me, when they were sick my clothing was sackcloth; I humbled my soul with fasting; and my prayer returned into mine own bosom."

Two Strong Alleviations.

We must recognize the fact that in the imprecatory psalms a righteous indignation is often expressed, a sense of outraged justice here finds voice. All true men must admit that there are times when the spirit of forbearance must give place to the spirit of righteous indignation. The holier the soul the hotter at times will be this spirit, and the stronger will be its expression. It has often been remarked that in the study of the satanic Inquisition in Spain, of the horrible St. Bartholomew massacre, and of the terrible Smithfield fires, even the gentlest spirit finds the imprecatory psalms an appropriate vehicle of expression. The humblest and most devout saints in India during the Sepoy rebellion found solid comfort in reading these portions of the psalter. Many of us during the fearful massacres in Armenia and still later in Cuba sympathized with the spirit of these Christians in India, and found corresponding comfort in these maledictory prayers. As one thinks of the devilish spirit of the liquor traffic he may without sin, in some modified sense, use these psalms as expressive of his feeling. There is an indignation which is righteous; there is an anger that is sinless. The holier the soul the greater will this indignant and righteous anger be. He is made of paste and putty whose spirit does not flame forth in indignant wrath against forms of sin unfortunately too common in every walk of life. It has been well said that David was the Milton and Cromwell of his time; he fought the earthly battles of his Lord and Master. We do not feel that Milton showed an un-Christian spirit when, catching the echo of David's lyre, he sang:

"Avenge, O Lord, thy slaughtered saints, whose bones
Lie scattered on the Alpine mountains cold."

We must also bear in mind that David was a magistrate, was a king, and was in a real sense the representative of God. It was a part of his function to discover and arraign the guilty and to dispense justice. We cannot deny that in certain conditions punishment is right. A law without a penalty is not law, but simply advice. Account for it as we may, there is something in our nature which approves of the infliction of penalty when crime has clearly been committed. The whole theory of government recognizes the necessity for arrangements for detecting and punishing crime.

We thus have an array of constables, jurymen, and judges. Is it not lawful for a detective, or a constable, or a keeper of a prison to pray that he may discover the guilty and inflict the appropriate punishment? Could not a detective officer in his private devotions or at his family altar offer a prayer that he should be successful in discovering and punishing fiendish criminals? Could not David appropriately offer a similar prayer? Is not his prayer in its essence simply that justice may be done and that righteous punishment may be inflicted? It cannot be proved that there is in the imprecatory psalms any more malice than might be found in the heart of an officer of the law even in our day when he is endeavoring to do his duty in capturing and punishing criminals. The nobler the student of Scripture the more readily will he see that even the imprecatory psalms have some place in human life, and so in divine revelation. It is not an evidence of a high spiritual conception that finds no place for the resistance to evil, and for the avengement of wrong, which is found in this portion of the psalter. All that is manliest in human nature and divinest in God will at times flame forth in denouncement of evil and in vindication of the right.

It ought to be borne further in mind that whatever difficulty exists regarding the imprecatory psalms is a difficulty created by the Bible itself. The sacred writers have given us this record. It is clearly seen in the Bible that all its parts have their own method of denouncing sin. In the historical books sin is denounced by simply showing its effects in harmony with natural law. Its results in national character are seen in the loss of vigor and nobility, and in the final enslavement of the people. The prophets denounce it with tremendous rhetorical vigor. If one will read the anathemas of Isaiah, Amos, and other prophets with this thought in mind he will see that David's imprecations are comparatively mild and gentle. No one uttered more fearful "woes" than fell from the lips of the loving Saviour. He spoke with a breadth of application and intensity of meaning which David could not understand. The purer and diviner the character of Christ the severer and fiercer the imprecations He uttered. Let it then never be forgotten that David spoke rather of God's enemies than of his own. The Bible with the utmost candor gives us the record. Its writers indulged in no feelings which they were unwilling to record. If we condemn these imprecations, we ought to remember that the spirit which leads to their condemnation has come from the Bible itself. The Bible is one book; all its parts are one revelation from God. We must judge its writings as a whole. Men and books must be criticised in their entirety. It is quite unfair to judge either by their beginning and not by their ending. Thus it will come to pass that the entire book, when rightly understood, is seen to be harmonious.

We have thus seen that there are many alleviations of these difficulties. The nobler the soul the more easy will he find it to interpret these imprecations. When right is on the cross and wrong is on the throne, when the wicked oppose and those who should be valiant for truth are silent, then noble souls in the fires of persecution catch the true spirit of the imprecatory psalms. In the day of peace and sunshine dilettante followers of Christ may seem shocked at the strong language and apparently vindictive spirit of these psalms; but in the day of terrific trial between right and wrong, good and evil, Christ and Satan, a holy resentment may become the divinest of emotions. Let us make due allowance for the Orientalism in the diction of these imprecations, for the heroic spirit of resistance to evil in the heart of the psalmist, and for the sublime identification of his enemies with God's foes, and many of these apparently insuperable difficulties will vanish. Let us not claim to be holier than was David, gentler than was Jesus, diviner than have been thousands of white-souled saints through the ages, who at times of righteous indignation have found these psalms in harmony with the tenderest love, the saintliest desire, and the holiest aspiration.

XXVI.

JONAH AND HIS BOOK.

XXVI.

JONAH AND HIS BOOK.

No book in the Bible has been so vigorously assailed by infidels as the book of Jonah, and thus many of the most beautiful lessons which the book teaches have been entirely forgotten in the criticism to which it has been subjected. This story, regarded simply as literature, is one of the most interesting short stories in any language. No book of the Old Testament so clearly teaches the lesson of universal brotherhood as does the book of Jonah. In portions of the book of Isaiah this lesson is taught, but with nothing like the emphasis given it in the book of Jonah. God rebukes the exclusiveness of the prophet and the narrowness of the Jews, and throws the mantle of His loving-kindness and forgiving mercy over the nation that cruelly hated the Jewish people. The lesson of human brotherhood taught in the book of Jonah anticipates the presentation of that great truth given by our Lord and by the Apostle Paul. In this respect the book of Jonah is unique among the books of the Old Testament. The great majority of critics almost entirely overlook this sublime truth in their carping criticisms and cavilling disputations. Jonah was really the first foreign missionary; he carried the message of mercy to a heathen people.

GROUNDLESS REASONING.

They are utterly at fault who affirm that if the historical character of the book of Jonah is disproved, then Christianity itself is destroyed. Those who so speak are guilty of unpardonable looseness of thinking. They practically affirm that if Jonah goes, the Bible goes and Jesus goes. No man is warranted in making so exaggerated and so reasonless a statement as that; indeed, it is difficult to understand how a man with a grain of common sense in relation to such matters can make such a statement. Those who so affirm make the historical interpretation of the book of Jonah of equal importance with the divine character and sacred mission of Jesus Christ. It used to be affirmed by men of this class that if it were shown that the world was not created in six literal days of twenty-four hours each, then Genesis was overthrown, the Bible was disproved, and religious faith was destroyed. It is rare to find any class of interpreters to-day who affirm that the world was made in six literal days. Perhaps each one of these creative days represented thousands, possibly millions, of years. But although we have changed our interpretation regarding the meaning of the word day, we have not lost our faith in spiritual realities or in the divine revelations given us in the Bible. There was a time when most interpreters of Scripture believed that the sun actually stood still in the heavens, at the command of Joshua; but many of the most devout and spiritual interpreters to-day believe, as is plainly stated in the narrative, that the description is a quotation taken from the book of Jasher, a book probably made up of national, historical, and triumphal songs of patriotic heroes; and that no such affirmation as that the sun stood still is made in the Bible narrative. We have unquestioning faith in God's miracles; but it is permissible to have but little regard for miracles which are the creations of extravagant commentators and unscholarly preachers. Several learned men have affirmed that merchants or Arabians, and not ravens, brought food to Elijah; by omitting, or slightly changing, the vowel points, which are admitted to have no great authority, the Hebrew letters may mean Arabians, or "merchants" or the "inhabitants of Oreb or Orbi." The word in the Hebrew is "Orebim." But should a man adopt any of these interpretations, we have no right to call him a disbeliever in the supernatural. Does a man who adopts this interpretation reject the New Testament and disbelieve in Christianity? John Jasper stands ready to charge with infidelity those who deny that "de sun do move." Augustine affirmed that the idea of an antipodes was unscriptural, for how could those who lived there see the Lord when He should return to the earth? Once many churchmen believed that the earth stood still, and that the sun revolved around it; and they thought a denial of that belief tended to disprove the Bible and to destroy Christianity. An "infallible" pope and the sacred congregation persecuted Galileo and were ready to torture all opposers of their crude beliefs. Luther condemned the Copernican system; he thought "the upstart astrologer" was a fool and was teaching contrary to Scripture. Calvin also believed that faith in Copernicus was infidelity to Scripture. The Roman and the Lutheran churches practically were the John Jaspers of an earlier day. Some evangelists and pastors of our day have fallen into false methods of interpretation. They have raised a false issue; they have manufactured a test of fidelity to Scripture which exists only in their excited imagination or in their untrained reasoning. It is extremely foolish for any man to say that if Jonah goes Jesus goes, and the Bible goes, and Christianity goes. I venture to affirm that our faith in Jesus Christ, and in a divine revelation, does not rest on the interpretation which we give to the book of Jonah, or to any other book of the Old Testament. As we shall see, there have been various theories of interpretation concerning this book; but whether we believe in the historical, the allegorical, or the parabolical interpretation, we do not thereby lose the symbolic and spiritual lessons which the book teaches; and we do not deny the authority of Jesus Christ in His interpretation of the book, and we certainly do not lose our faith in Christianity or revelation. It is quite certain that the chief value of this book in the time of our Lord was its symbolic significance rather than its historical reality. We may hold our belief that the book is truly historical, and yet guard ourselves against so unwise a proposition as that our faith in Jesus Christ depends upon the historicity, or upon any theory of interpretation, of the book of Jonah.

Theories of Interpretation.

There have been several well-defined theories of interpretation of this book. Some have affirmed that the entire narrative was a dream which Jonah had while asleep in the sides of the ship. This is certainly an easy method of disposing of all the difficulties which the narrative contains, but it probably suggests more difficulties of another kind that are found in the narrative as we now have it. Others have regarded the book purely as an allegory; they have considered it a parody upon, if not the original form of, various heathen fables, such as those of Arion and the Dolphin, or the wild adventures of Hercules. We know that Joppa and its vicinity were the home of many legends. The story of Andromeda and Perseus is located at this place, as are others of a somewhat similar character. Even if the book were a pure allegory, its spiritual lessons, as already suggested, would still remain, and our Lord's use of it as recorded in the twelfth chapter of Matthew would still be justified.

Many of the most orthodox interpreters have adopted the allegorical or dramatic interpretation of the Song of Solomon, but their orthodoxy in so doing has never been called in question. Singularly enough the allegorical interpretation of the Song of Solomon has been considered as conclusive evidence of orthodoxy; but the allegorical interpretation of the book of Jonah these same exegetes consider rank heresy. A third theory is that Jonah when thrown into the sea was picked up by a ship having a fish for a figurehead and bearing the name of a fish. We know that it was common then, and is now, to give ships the names of animals of various kinds and to ornament them with figureheads representing these animals. Dagon means a fish, and Dagon was the national idol of the Philistines, with temples at Gaza and Ashdod in this general vicinity. Dagon had the body of a fish and the head of a man. A German scholar has adopted this view and has argued at length in its favor. It is an interesting fact that Jonah's prayer, which, like Hannah's prayer, is rather a hymn of praise than a prayer, is uttered when he seems to have escaped from danger and not when he was in the midst of danger. This interpretation would make the prayer to have been offered after he was rescued from the sea and was safely aboard the ship. Akin to this interpretation is that which makes his rescue to have been due to a life preserver, or some similar means of escape. There are interpreters who affirm that the story has a historical basis, but with many fanciful and mythical additions; while still others believe that the story is purely moral and without any historical foundation. But quite recently another interpretation has been suggested. It is stated that the name Nineveh is no other than Ninua, or Nunu, which means "fish," and as the city was called the great city, its old Assyrian name was simply the Great Fish or the Fish City. To this day, it is said, the name on the monuments is represented by a fish in a basin or tank. This view would make Nineveh itself the "great fish" that swallowed Jonah, and in crying to the Lord for deliverance he gave the city its old Assyrian name, praying to be delivered from the "great fish." There is historical truth somewhere in these many interpretations. We can afford to be patient and to wait for fuller light. I am not disposed to give up the historicity of the narrative. Very weighty scholarship in Germany, and to a very considerable extent in Great Britain and the United States, is still in favor of the historical reality of the narrative. This view is held by such men as Hess, Hengstenberg, Baumgarten, Delitzsch, and by many in Britain and America of like broad learning and sound judgment. The fact is that the denial of the historical reality of the narrative involves difficulties as serious as its frank admission. There has been a vast deal of silly wit expended on this book as a "fish story" of the ancient time.

Confirmatory Evidence.

There is nothing whatever in the Old Testament or the New to show that this narrative is a myth or a parable; on the contrary, there is much to teach us that it is a record of an actual occurrence. The prophet Jonah is referred to in 2 Kings xiv. 25, and beyond question the prophet who gave his name to the book is the same to whom reference is there made. He was a prophet of God in the reign of Jeroboam II. The word Jonah means "dove," and his father's name, Amittai, means "the truth of God." It is almost certain that there could not have been two prophets bearing the same name and sons of fathers of the same name, especially of names so suggestive and rare as these. Jonah was of Gath-Hepher, a town in lower Galilee in Zebulon. It has been suggested that Jonah was a child when Homer sang his rhapsodies on the shores of the Mediterranean; that he was a contemporary of Lycurgus, the Spartan lawgiver, and that he was the senior of Romulus by one century and of Herodotus by four centuries. A criticism has been made on the book of Jonah because it is written in the third person.

but this is the very puerility of criticism. We know well that the commentaries of Cæsar and the Anabasis of Xenophon were also written in the third person. It has been charged that the style of the book threw doubt upon its reality, but a more careful scholarship shows that it is written in pure and simple Hebrew. Indeed, almost all the more genuinely critical examinations of these details are confirmatory of the historicity of the narrative.

This is especially true in its relations to Nineveh. The King of Nineveh at the time of Jonah's visit is supposed to have been Pul, and Layard places him at 750 B.C. Nineveh was the metropolis of ancient Assyria, and was called by the Greeks and Romans the Great Ninus or Ninua. It was probably situated on the east bank of the Tigris, opposite the modern Mosul. Recent excavations confirm statements made in the books of Jonah and Nahum regarding the immense size of Nineveh. These discoveries quite justify the statement that it contained more than one hundred and twenty thousand young children, thus indicating that it had a population of at least half a million. The people were wealthy and warlike Nineveh was long the mistress of the East. Within the last generation Layard, Botta, Smith, and others have been exploring its mounds and have made discoveries confirmatory of the Bible narrative. They have found sculptured memorials containing the actual Assyrian accounts of events recorded in the books of Kings and Chronicles. They make mention of the names of Jehu, Hezekiah, Omri, and also of various cities in Judea and Syria. They also give Sennacherib's own account of his invasion of Palestine. It is as surprising as gratifying that these long-buried tablets are confirmatory, even in minute details, of the statements contained in the Bible.

Additional Confirmation.

Even what is said in the book of Jonah regarding the gourd which so suddenly sprang up is fully corroborated by the rapid production of the plant known as the Palma Christi. This plant is found with broad leaves, giving a dense shade and supporting itself on its own stem. It is still almost a miracle in its wellnigh instantaneous growth. It is found in many parts of Arabia, Syria, and India. It is well known also that a species of the white shark, sometimes measuring sixty feet in length, has been found in the Mediterranean which easily swallows a man whole, and many statements have been made as to the discovery of men who had been thus swallowed. Infidels once objected to the narrative because of the use of the word whale, as it seldom enters the Mediterranean Sea, and because the throat of some species is too small to swallow a man; but the fact is that neither in the Hebrew of the Old Testament nor in the Greek of the New has the word that limited meaning, the species of marine animal or sea-monster not being defined. A knowledge of Eastern peoples to-day shows how readily a whole community may be startled into sudden repentance, or at least panic, by the solemn announcement of a man believed to be a prophet. Cases are on record in which a Christian priest startled a whole Mussulman town by declaring that he had received a divine commission to announce a coming plague. Plainly there was no permanent reformation, no revival, no genuine conversion in the case of Nineveh. We know, too, that there was a vigorous trade between Syria and Tarshish in that early day. Reference is made in the Bible to the "ships of Tarshish," as we long spoke of East Indiamen; as these in both cases were the greatest ships of their class. It thus comes to pass that in all these incidental ways confirmation of the ancient narrative is found.

It would not be at all surprising if natural law should yet show that the account of the swallowing of Jonah by a great fish is strictly scientific. Cases of catalepsy, hypnotism, ecstasy, and trance are almost equally mysterious. Cases of hibernation and æstivation are quite as difficult of explanation. There are well-attested cases in which breathing nearly or entirely ceases. There is a Rocky Mountain squirrel whose temperature is only three degrees above the freezing-point during its winter sleep. The woodchuck and the raccoon roll themselves into a ball and press their noses so tightly against their bodies that breathing is impossible. It is said also that the marmots pass into a state of such complete suspended animation that an electric shock will not arouse them, and the most deadly gases will not affect them in the least. Bats go to sleep in clusters, the central one often during the entire winter bearing a weight of ten pounds. Bats have been sealed in glass jars, and the most careful tests have been made to see if any of the oxygen had been used, but there was no perceptible change in the air. The common garden snail covers the opening of its shell with a silky membrane which becomes encrusted with carbonate of lime, hermetically sealing the creature, which is without food, air, heat, or circulation. Cases are known in which it has been artificially sealed for three years, and then brought to life. There may be truth in the stories told of toads embedded in solid rocks and then brought to life.

Human hibernation is equally mysterious. The fakirs in India may impose even on the most careful scientific men; but seemingly genuine cases of inexplicable hypnotism, or other unaccountable conditions, have occurred. Baird, in his treatise on the subject, published in 1850, tells of the case of a man in Lahore who was buried alive in 1837, in the presence of men determined to detect fraud, if any attempt to practise it were made, and who was long after dug up and restored to life. There are many things in heaven and earth not yet explicable by our philosophy.

The character of Jonah is also consistent throughout the entire book which bears his name. The story is simple, straightforward, and strikingly honest; it is almost painfully frank in its statement of the faults of its subject and writer. It bears every evidence of being a truthful statement. We must not suppose from Jonah's attempt to flee from the presence of the Lord that he thought he could ever escape from God's sight; he was too familiar with the truth as to God's presence to be guilty of such an error. We are rather to understand the language to mean that he was determined to go out from the presence of the Lord as His servant and minister; that is, that he determined to set aside his character and office as a prophet of the Lord. He gives evidence that he possessed a petulant, querulous disposition; indeed, he seems at times to have been afflicted almost with a species of insanity. This character of narrowness, petulance, querulousness, and hypochondria he maintains to the very last. We can easily see that he did not wish to be a prophet to the Ninevites, and his dislike of them and of his errand of mercy appears to the close of the narrative.

The Orientals have always had a high regard for Jonah. His tomb is shown with veneration near the ruins of Nineveh and also at Gath-Hepher, which was the place of his birth. The Mohammedans honor him greatly. It is a striking fact that an entire chapter in the Koran is inscribed with his name. The difficulties connected with the book, which have so strongly influenced the critics of the Occident, have never been influential in the minds of the people of the Orient. The book of Tobit recognized Jonah as an historacil character; and this fact is significant as indicating current Jewish opinion on the subject. The readers of Josephus know of the testimony of a similar purport which he bears to the historical character of Jonah.

The book should be studied afresh. The chief purpose of the author was to teach great moral and spiritual lessons; and such lessons our Lord taught us from the book. It shows God's forgiveness to a heathen city when its repentance became manifest. It shows that God cares not for the chosen nation alone, but for all men. Here are suggested large lessons of sympathy and love; here we see God's greatness and man's littleness, God's patience and man's petulance, God's charity and man's cruelty. Let us study the book for its beauty as literature, its charm as a souvenir of a remote time and civilization, and especially as a revelation of divine love and mercy. Whatever interpretation we may give to some of its parts, its great lessons will stand, honored by the approval of Jesus Christ and commended by our sense of God's justice, mercy, truth and grace.

www.ingramcontent.com/pod-product-compliance
Lightning Source LLC
Chambersburg PA
CBHW022142300426
44115CB00006B/313